AN ASKEW VIEW 2
THE FILMS OF
KEVIN SMITH

AN ASKEW VIEW 2
THE FILMS OF
KEVIN SMITH
A REVISED AND UPDATED EDITION

JOHN KENNETH MUIR

Published in 2012 by Applause Theatre & Cinema Books
An Imprint of Hal Leonard Corporation
7777 West Bluemound Road
Milwaukee, WI 53213

Trade Book Division Editorial Offices
33 Plymouth St., Montclair, NJ 07042

Unless otherwise noted, all photos are courtesy of Photofest

Printed in the United States of America

Book design by UB Communications

Library of Congress Cataloging-in-Publication Data

Muir, John Kenneth, 1969-
  An askew view 2 : the films of Kevin Smith / John Kenneth Muir. — Rev. and updated ed.
       p. cm.
  Includes bibliographical references and index.
  ISBN 978-1-55783-794-3 (pbk.)
1. Smith, Kevin, 1970—Criticism and interpretation. I. Title.
  PN1998.3.S5864M85 2012
  791.43'0233'092—dc22
  2012021296

www.applausebooks.com

CONTENTS

ACKNOWLEDGMENTS

This book—both editions—would not have been possible without the assistance and support of many friends, supporters, and colleagues. Special thanks to June Clark, who got the ball rolling back in 2001, and to Amy at View Askew Productions in 2002, who must have gotten tired of my daily calls when I conducted telephone interviews.

And special thanks to the efficient Gail Stanley, Kevin Smith's assistant, who was not only helpful and communicative when I prepared the first edition, but a constant source of information, support, and kindness.

Then there are the interviewees, whose recollections inform so much of this project. Much gratitude and respect to Jeff Anderson, Dwight Ewell, Walt Flanagan, Vincent Guastini, Bryan Johnson, Jason Mewes, Scott Mosier, Brian O'Halloran, Vincent Pereira, John Pierson, Jennifer Schwalbach, and Ethan Suplee, who spent hours recounting their experiences, perceptions, and memories of these interesting films. Thank you for being so candid, so funny, and so open.

And finally there's the man himself, Kevin Smith. Thanks, Mr. Smith, for creating a universe that has meant so much to so many.

An Askew View 2012

REINTRODUCING THE FILMS
OF KEVIN SMITH

I REMEMBER PRECISELY WHEN and where I got hooked on the films of Kevin Smith and View Askew Productions. It was May 13, 1997, at a 7:30 p.m. showing of *Chasing Amy* at the now defunct Matthews Festival in Charlotte, North Carolina. I was there with my wife, Kathryn, to celebrate our two-year wedding anniversary, but very soon after we were seated, the characters on the screen—*so passionate in expression, words, and deed*—demanded our full attention.

The film was Kevin Smith's third opus, concerning twentysomething comic book artist Holden McNeil (Ben Affleck) falling hard for Joey Lauren Adam's funny, experienced, and deeply affecting lesbian, Alyssa Jones. So raunchy and riotous one moment, so touching and raw the next, the movie was one of the most piercing and emotional viewing experiences of the 1990s—*Annie Hall* for the slacker set.

As *Chasing Amy* faded to melancholy black, my head spun. Here was a movie that joked about the nitty-gritty details of oral sex in one scene, and then turned around and broke your heart in another. The balance was so deft, so accomplished, that it felt authentically revelatory—the work of a major young talent.

I knew then that several books would be written about *Chasing Amy's* director. More to the point, I knew that I wanted to take a stab at one. Even then, as early as 1997, Smith's story boasted an irresistible hook. There was a self-financed, freshman home run (*Clerks*), a sophomore (or, as some reviewers insisted, sophomoric) fall from critical grace (*Mallrats*), and then *Chasing Amy's* glorious ascension to top form. That's more than enough plot for any film reference book. And that was very much the story I relayed to audiences in the successful first edition of this text, which was published in the year 2002, before *Jersey Girl's* release in 2004.

The Jersey born-and-bred filmmaker has seen some rough-and-tumble days in the public eye during the intervening decade, but this edition remains the tale of Kevin Smith as unlikely but dedicated torchbearer for the indie-film revolution of the 1990s... and now in the second decade of the twenty-first century.

An Irish-Catholic kid from the burbs who spent the early part of his twenties learning not about film grammar and *mise-en-scène*, but jockeying a cash register at a Quick Stop in Leonardo, this fledgling writer-director, along with a talented cadre of artists (most notably producer Scott Mosier), masterminded his own calling card to Hollywood.

And notably, Kevin Smith did so in the midst of a decade when interest in film—and accessibility to film technology—was at its greatest in history up to that point. Had Smith's initial effort, *Clerks*, not been so good, so funny, and so accomplished, he might easily have drowned in an indie tidal wave, sinking in a sea of promising, would-be "auteurs."

But Smith did not go quietly into that good night in the years following *Clerks*, a now classic film that has aptly been termed "shaggily revolutionary."[1]

Instead, in 2012, Smith remains, arguably, the most high profile writer-director of his generation. Smith's continued visibility is a result not only of his memorable appearances in his own films as stoner Silent Bob, but also his uncanny knack for effective self-promotion. He's been a frequent guest on *The Tonight Show*, appeared on late-night TV fare like *Loveline*, and hosted a slew of *Star Wars*-related specials such as *Exposure* and *The Official Star Wars Fan Film Awards* on the Syfy channel.

Smith has also appeared on the TV series *Veronica Mars*, in the sequel *Live Free or Die Hard*, on *Real Time with Bill Maher*, and—pretty dependably—makes a new movie every two years or thereabouts. His Twitter follower tally numbers two million, and his sold-out college lectures, road shows, and regular podcasts with Scott Mosier (called SModcasts) are always greeted with tremendous excitement by an ever-growing fan base.

But opportunity and visibility only carry one so far, even in Hollywood. As Kevin Smith himself noted:

> *I always felt lucky enough to get my foot in the door... Getting in is luck.*
> *Staying in is talent. I don't profess to be the most talented individual*
> *working in films today. But obviously I'm doing something right because*
> *I'm still here and we have a fan base.*[2]

So the question becomes this: What did Kevin Smith do right, to maintain a high-profile film career for a decade and a half after breaking through with the low-budget, homemade *Clerks?*

John Pierson, an executive producer of *Chasing Amy* and host of Independent Film Channel's *Split Screen*, offered a thought on the matter of Smith's continued success in 2002: "It's the quality of his humor, which is both hilariously down and dirty, but also unbelievably emotionally honest. That's the crux of the matter."

But where does that honesty, that understanding of the human condition, come from? Smith's wife, Jennifer Schwalbach, suggested a personal quirk that provides the curious some insight.

"*He digs.* Some of my friends can take it, and some can't. He'll have a conversation where he just wants to know. He doesn't want to talk about a new couch. He wants to talk about what someone's boyfriend said in bed when they broke up.

"He will dig, because he is genuinely interested in how other people live, how their emotions run, how they react, and the strange things that people do. Kevin doesn't go out to bars to drink. I've wasted years, just kind of living a twentysomething life. And instead, Kevin thought about things. He thought about his life; his relationships. And he's written about them. He doesn't write about fictional characters; he writes about himself and his friends. The movies he makes are a reflection of himself."

With one important caveat, as Mr. Pierson adds: "They're transcendent."

Pierson says: "He takes his own real-life experiences, but just like Janet Maslin wrote in that *Clerks* review from *New Directors*, he spins straw into gold. To me, the essence of him spinning straw into gold is taking actual experience that he knows oh so well, and somehow, both on the comedic side and on the emotional, heartfelt side, making it transcendent."

Just like *Chasing Amy.*

And that's one reason why, when searching for historical antecedents in cinema, it's a no-brainer to compare Kevin Smith to Woody Allen (hence the *Annie Hall* reference). As Pierson notes: "They're both writers first," movie directors second, and both use life experiences as a platform to reveal stories about human nature.

Sure, Smith's films routinely reference Superman, George Lucas, *Beverly Hills Cop*, and Steven Spielberg, rather than Fassbinder, Bergman, or Wagner, but that's merely a generational quirk. In common, Allen and Smith share a common "style of slightly exaggerated comedy"[3] and the propensity to resort to slapstick antics and crude humor amid their witty comedic word play.

But that's the universality of the human condition, too. As Smith has often remarked, "We all have sex, and we all take dumps."[4]

Smith is the Woody Allen for Generation X in the sense that he seems to be the only writer-director working today who asks the deeper questions about love, religion, and sex in a way that routinely makes audiences laugh. The countless *Scooby-Doo*, *Planet of the Apes*, *X-Files*, *Jaws*, *Dirty Dancing*, and *B.J. and the Bear* references in his films are merely touchstones for viewers to understand that, when all is said and done, Smith is one of us and speaks our language. Those TV programs and films represent a short hand not only to coolness, but also a shared heritage growing up in the 1970s. Smith is a director who, impressively, writes A-style personal material yet uses allusions to B-style productions as a hook to grab an audience weaned on network television of the disco decade.

That's my generation, and Smith undeniably remains a role model. Not coincidentally, his films have shadowed the progress of Gen Xers every step of the way during our rather mercurial and delayed maturation process: through our post-college career slump and ambivalence (*Clerks*), our professional blossoming and relationship blues (*Chasing Amy*), and even our skeptical but hopeful stance about religion (*Dogma*).

Smith countenanced another turning point for Gen Xers—*parenthood*—with his sixth feature, *Jersey Girl*, in 2004. And *Clerks II* in 2006 to a very large extent involves that bugaboo of the midlife crisis: the point at which career change and new life direction need be sought.

The ubiquitous potty mouth or the predilection for body-function humor feature prominently in his work, but Kevin Smith's films always spotlight a distinctive authorial voice, and his characters universally speak in dialogue of unique cadences, loaded with startling wit, irony, and intelligence. Smith's trademark dialogue has been termed a "form of wordplay so scrappy and alive that it could never have come out of some Hollywood hack's corporate screenwriting software."[5]

Indeed, the writer has frequently been compared to Shakespeare, both by reviewers and the actors who vet his dialogue. Who would have expected such brilliance (let alone such vocabulary) from the once derided *Brady Bunch* generation?

Accordingly, *Rolling Stone*'s Peter Travers has dubbed Smith "a fearless satirist"[6] and *Newsweek* has anointed him "cinema's funniest writer about sex...certainly its most candid."[7] He's even been termed "the William Faulkner of 90s cinema"[8] by some enthusiasts.

That Smith's films invariably stir the pot of cultural controversy (irking the M.P.A.A., the Catholic League, and the Gay and Lesbian Alliance Against Defamation in less than a ten-year period) is not only some kind of anti-PC record, it's also further evidence that Smith is doing something right.

After all, nobody (besides bored and bitter movie critics) goes after a stupid little comedy that misses the mark by a mile. People only attack that which is threatening, new, or daring.

Like *Dogma*. Like *Clerks*. Like *Chasing Amy*. And now, again, like *Red State*.

And best of all, Smith's very personal films—for all their sharp-words and invective—feel steeped in the filmmaker's Catholic upbringing and sensibilities.

"Here's the dark secret behind writer/director/geek icon Kevin Smith's oeuvre," wrote film critic Ethan Alter in 2008. "Beneath all the rampant swearing, graphic sex talk, and in-your-face scatological humor, his movies are—*gasp!*—deeply moral stories. No matter how askew things get in Smith's View Askewniverse...you can always count on seeing the good folks rewarded, the bad ones humiliated, and the power of friendship overcoming the toughest of obstacles."[9]

In particular, Smith's bailiwick seems to be characters straight from the drama of his own pre-Hollywood life in Jersey: "unambitious, easily offended young men preoccupied with the small but furiously important issues of manners, respect, and hoped for sex."[10] This insightful description, from film critic David Denby, fits Generation X to a tee.

In 2012, Smith—despite his many and widely publicized professional and personal ups and downs (including a brawl with Southwest Airlines over his weight)—has also become a filmmaker of tremendous influence, inspiring a new generation that consists of such widely admired talents as Judd Apatow and Seth Rogen.

And even now, Smith is *still* blazing new trails. As a result of some unhappy adventures in studio filmmaking, namely 2010's *Cop Out*, Kevin Smith has once again positioned himself at the vanguard of the independent cinema in 2011 by self-distributing his horror film *Red State*. In the process, he has delivered an electric shock to a complacent industry that demands things always remain absolutely the same and that filmmakers not rock the boat. This self-distribution initiative has made Smith—again—a lightning rod for controversy. Some folks view him as the angel of a new independent film movement, while others view the director as an existential threat to a stagnant industry that would rather destroy him personally and professionally than embrace the challenge of change.

Smith has stated his desire to retire after his next film (a two-part epic about hockey), yet it is entirely fitting that his film career should end on the same high note on which it began so auspiciously: blazing new trails; and refusing to accept the status quo as the only path to success. Bluntly put, if Smith had believed there was only one trajectory to reach success in the film industry, we wouldn't have *Clerks*.

I hope you'll consider this book a return trip to the View Askew universe, one that certainly finds Kevin Smith changed—a bit more cynical, perhaps— but still the same enthusiastic director audiences fell in love with during the 90s. The first portion of this tour is conducted by many of the individuals who conspired with Smith to make these films the stuff of legend. Scott Mosier (Smith's producer and partner in crime on every project), Jennifer Schwalbach (his outspoken and delightful lady love), and a host of other talents all contributed their behind-the-scenes remembrances to Part I of this text.

In addition, Jason Mewes, Jeff Anderson, Brian O'Halloran, View Askew historian Vincent Pereira, John Pierson, Vincent Guastini, Ethan Suplee, and Dwight Ewell all help us put Kevin Smith's early works into context, sharing how it was done, why it was funny, and what the experiences meant to each of them.

Part II of the text, "State of Red," gazes at the controversial developments in Smith's film career since the first book, and reveals Smith's uneasy fit with the Hollywood establishment.

The result is a kind of free-flowing history of one artist's not always easy, not always direct path to success in Hollywood, from independent filmmaker to blockbuster celebrity, and back to fiery rebel.

So let's take a stroll down the Jersey turnpike . . . again.

PART I

THE GOOD OLD DAYS (1970–2002)

1

Coming of Age in New Jersey

OF ALL THE COMIC BOOK STORIES ever printed, the origin story remains the most popular. It's an irresistible tale, as the longtime success of the superhero TV series *Smallville* (2001–2011) no doubt testifies. How did Superman come to arrive on Earth and grow into the Man of Steel? Or a Marvel corollary: How did Peter Parker acquire his spider powers? What were the events that led a brooding Bruce Wayne to take up the life of a crime fighter? These questions are so compelling because everybody wants to understand how heroes came to be extraordinary, how they grew to be who they are today.

Like any superhero—or film director for that matter—filmmaker Kevin Smith has his own beginnings too, his own origin story. These are the events that led him first to Vancouver Film School, and then, eventually, to the world of independent filmmaking. These are the influences that made him so keen an observer of human behavior and this is where you'll meet the Lois Lanes and the Jimmy Olsens of his life. Or in this case, Walt Flanagan, Bryan Johnson, Jason Mewes, and the other friends who helped spark Kevin Smith's creative impulse.

And, like the best of the origin stories, Kevin Smith's adventure commences in a strange and wondrous land. Not far away Krypton, but New Jersey... the 'burbs.

The son of a postal clerk, Donald, and his wife, Grace, Kevin Patrick Smith was born in the little town of Red Bank shortly after the commencement of the disco decade, on August 2, 1970. He arrived into a lower-middle class family with two older siblings, Virginia and Donald, Jr., and was raised in the Borough of Highlands in Monmouth County, just outside of Leonardo (population: 5,500), some twelve miles from the larger city of Long Branch.

Just a hop, skip, and a jump from New York City by land or sea (under thirty miles, actually), the Borough of Highlands is very nearly located on top of Sandy Hook and the Atlantic Ocean. Its most notable construction is the Twin Lights, two lighthouses constructed in 1862.

Bryan Johnson, the director of *Vulgar* (2000) and the actor who portrays comic book snob Steve-Dave in the View Askew universe was born in Highlands and later attended Highlands Elementary and Henry Hudson Regional High School (the latter named after the sea captain who first explored the region in 1609). He describes the borough as a "really small town, kind of blue collar," where expectations for children and teens were "fairly limited."

Years after his success in films, Smith would affectionately describe Highlands in another manner:

It was the asshole end of the movie universe.[1]

It was in this environment that young Kevin Smith, like virtually all children of the 1970s, began gathering his inspirations and influences, predominantly from TV series and movies. Because he was not particularly athletic, and self-conscious about his weight[2] Smith escaped to the worlds of *Gilligan's Island*, *The Brady Bunch*, *Batman*, and other rerun staples of the era.

Though it is difficult to imagine in today's universe of entertainment plenty, the early to mid-1970s represented a world without cable television and without streaming video, where syndicated series (reruns) once broadcast on the big three networks (ABC, CBS, NBC), dominated the programming schedules of local affiliates. *All in the Family, M*A*S*H, Star Trek, The Twilight Zone,* and *Green Acres* formed the intellectual and entertainment gestalt of the decade's youth. This tends not to happen anymore with the CW, Fox, AMC and basic and premium cable channels offering more programming choices. But for Kevin Smith's generation, these TV series are something akin to the Greek myths: a tradition, a bond, a short hand ... even ice-breakers at bars. Many people who grew up in the 1970s watched *Happy Days*, loved the Fonz, and remember "sit on it" as the ultimate insult.

Donald Smith, Kevin's father, often took Kevin out on Wednesday afternoons, following half days at school (another wonderful tradition of the 1970s and N.J. school systems), to see matinees at the local theater. When Kevin was five, his father brought him to see Steven Spielberg's 1975 horror blockbuster, *Jaws*.[3] When Smith was seven, he saw another movie that would impact his life and work, the George Lucas space opera, *Star Wars* (1977).

Depicting an exciting universe of space battles, daring rescues, and colorful alien creatures, *Star Wars* offered Smith the ultimate escape from humdrum life in the Highlands.[4]

Growing up in a predominantly Irish-Catholic community, Smith attended parochial school, Our Lady of Perpetual Help, on Navesink Avenue. During his adulthood, Smith remembered one particular instructor, Sister Theresa, who had a great impact on him. A fan of Thomas More, she exposed her class, including Smith, to one of his now-favorite films, and one he reportedly watched some fifty times: *A Man for All Seasons*.[5]

Released in 1966, *A Man for All Seasons* was directed by Fred Zinnemann and based on the play of the same name by Robert Bolt. Telling the story of Thomas More's conflict with King Henry VIII (who wanted to reject Catholic doctrine so he could acquire a divorce and a new wife), the Academy Award-winning film starred Paul Scofield as More, Robert Shaw as King Henry, Leo McKern, Orson Welles, John Hurt, Susannah York, and Nigel Davenport.

But the quality that impressed Kevin Smith most was the rich dialogue; the language of the film. So in many ways, *A Man for All Seasons*, like Richard Linklater's *Slacker*, forms the foundation of Kevin's Smith cinema: it is wordy, witty, and unremittingly smart. Like Smith's own *Dogma*, it debates the law of man and God in a barrage of delicious dialogue, all of it delivered with tremendous flair.

By the time Smith attended Henry Hudson Regional High School in the mid-1980s, he had turned his affection for film and television into something more than a hobby. Jeff Anderson, a Connecticut native who moved to Jersey when he was nine years old and grew up to be *Clerks'* slacker philosopher, Randal, sets the scene:

"Henry Hudson was such a small school [it encompassed grades seven through twelve], and that's where I first met Kevin. Our graduating class had about seventy-two kids in it. Everybody knew everybody, and there were six hundred kids in the whole school."

Those six hundred students formed the basis of Kevin Smith's first audience. "He would always do these skits in the talent show, like *Saturday Night Live*-type things." Anderson remembers. "That was always the big thing for the talent show. There was the kid at school who could play guitar really kick-ass, and then there were Kevin's sketch comedy acts. That was why you went to the talent show."

And sometimes, as Anderson recalls, the skits were...avant-garde. "I remember going to the talent show one year, and we are all curious to see what Kevin was going to do, because it was always something crazy."

Anderson didn't go home disappointed. "Kevin and Ernie O'Donnell [*Clerks'* Rick Derris] did this skit where Kevin was playing Ronald McDonald and Ernie was the Hamburgler. I don't quite remember why, because I was hyped up on a pint of peppermint schnapps in the audience; I just recall Kevin coming out on stage as Ronald McDonald. I can still picture it: Ronald tying up the Hamburgler and Kevin shoving a hamburger in Ernie's mouth. Somewhere, photographs of this still exist."

But if the subject matter of the skit was odd, it nonetheless forecasted Kevin Smith's later efforts. Some of the McDonald's Land characters (Mayor McCheese and Police Chief Big Mac, specifically) figure prominently in the third episode of the *Clerks* animated series—as Leonardo's city officials, no less.

If the Henry Hudson talent shows proved anything, it was, as Anderson reports dramatically, that "early on, yes, we can say Kevin knew what he wanted to do."

In 1989, Kevin Smith graduated from high school, and his desire to break into comedy writing took him from New Jersey to Eugene Lang College, a division of the New School for Social Research in Manhattan, where he studied creative writing. While he was there for one semester, Smith frequently spent time "hanging out" at Rockefeller Center, hoping to be discovered by the talents managing *Saturday Night Live*.

When that dream didn't materialize, a disillusioned Smith retreated to New Jersey and began working a series of low-paying counter jobs at convenience stores. But it was a job at the Highlands Community Center, a recreation center for high school students with nowhere to stay after school, where Smith first began to assemble a special group of friends, the troop that would later become the inspiration for many of his movie adventures.

Walt Flanagan is one of those friends. A dark-haired, shy type with an open and friendly face, this future "Fanboy" of the View Askewniverse was born in Perth Amboy, New Jersey, a town north of Highlands and south of Metuchen. Two years older than Smith, Flanagan attended high school with Smith at Henry Hudson for a time.

"I knew him, but I wasn't friends with him," Flanagan reports.

Instead, that friendship would blossom at the community center. Though they didn't really talk to each other for the better part of the year, one day the subject of comic books came up.

"I think Kevin saw I had on a shirt with Batman on it," Flanagan recollects, "and he made a comment that he used to watch the *Batman* TV show. I mentioned there was a really good *Batman* book, *The Dark Knight Returns*, the Frank Miller book, and he'd never heard of it. So the next day, I let him borrow my copy. And he loved it. He said, 'There's more stuff like this out there?' And I said 'Yeah,' and he wanted to go right out to the stores and have me show him what was good. We became friends through comics."

It probably isn't an exaggeration, then, to report that fans the world over who have enjoyed Smith's superhero chronicles in *Green Arrow*, *Daredevil*, and other books may have Flanagan to thank for fanning the artist's interest in the medium.

"I only *re*-introduced him to comics," Flanagan points out with modesty. "He had purchased comics growing up, but had fallen out of it, and didn't really follow them closely."

Smith also made another friend at the community center, a fellow by the name of Bryan Johnson. Like Flanagan, Johnson also knew Kevin from Henry Hudson, but never really talked to him until their tenure together at the recreation center.

"The first time I ever spoke to Kevin was the day I broke up with my girl-friend, a girl I'd been going out with for two years," Johnson details. "It was one of those high school romances where you just know you're going to get married. But we broke up. I was really down that day, and I was talking to a friend of mine about it, and Kevin was sitting there and said, 'Oh, you broke up with your girlfriend?' That was the first thing this guy had ever said to me, and I just said, 'Yeah.' So he said, 'Really? Can I have her?'

"I thought, 'This impudent dog! This insolent prick!' But actually, Kevin made me laugh and feel a little bit better."

Before long, Kevin, Walt, and Bryan were the best of friends and hanging out together, attending comic book shows in the city. And, then, on one fateful day, someone else walked into their lives, a rambunctious teenage kid who—one day—would star in several of Kevin Smith's movies as the motor-mouthed stoner, Jay.

"Jason Mewes started coming down to the rec as a kid," Bryan Johnson remembers. "I think he was fourteen at the time. He was a participant in the after-school program, and Kevin, Walter, and I were sort of overseeing him."

And what was the irrepressible Jason Mewes like at age fourteen?

"He was pretty energetic, to say the least," Johnson remembers. "He had the skinniest mohawk I've ever seen on a person. He was very wild, just all over the place, like a pinball, bouncing from here to there. But he was also a lot of fun. He was the kind of kid you could just tease, and he'd give it back."

Years later, Smith described Mewes as "the kid that everybody knows in town; the kid that belongs to that town; the kid of urban legend."[6]

Jason Mewes also recalls those early days, when he first met Kevin Smith: "I used to go [to the community center] after school and during the summer there was a program too. Walter and Bryan and Kevin used to collect comics, and I remember the first time we all hung out. They were going to a comic book show in New York, and Bryan asked me if I wanted to go. I wasn't there, but this is how Kevin tells it. They told Kevin I was going, and he was like, 'I don't want that kid going!' In his eyes, he saw me as one of those kids in town who everybody knew. 'Oh, that kid Jason Mewes, he busted a window. Or, he got caught making out with a girl behind the church.' All these silly things he heard about me; that I was a foul mouthed kid and stuff.

"So he told Walter and Bryan that I was underage and he didn't want to take me. And he wouldn't drive me to New York in his car, so Bryan offered to drive.

"We all went to New York, and it was a good time, but Kevin said that I was being obnoxious making my jokes the whole time. Walter and Bryan thought I was funny, but Kevin didn't. They were laughing, and Kevin told me later that he was always the funny guy in the group, and now someone else was coming in and being funny, stepping on his territory."

Then, one fine day, Jason Mewes arrived at the community center and finally did something Kevin Smith found amusing. Allegedly, he mock-fellated every phallic-shaped object in the room: flag-poles, doorknobs, you name it. "He didn't care who was there, who was watching. He had an agenda,"[7] Smith later recalled.

"He said that the day he found me funny I ran into the rec and started sucking everything off," Mewes reports with bemusement and a hint of skepticism. "I don't really remember that ... "

It was the beginning of a beautiful friendship between the men who would be Jay and Silent Bob. When Johnson went away to school at the University of Massachusetts and Flanagan got married, the friendship between Smith and Mewes deepened. On days when Mewes didn't have anything to do, he visited Smith's house after work to watch movies and read comics with him.

Then, in the late spring of 1990, Kevin Smith took a job working at two adjacent shops in nearby Leonardo: the R.S.T. Video store and Quick Stop

COMING OF AGE IN NEW JERSEY 15

Groceries. "That's when we really started getting to know each other," Mewes confides. "We used to sit at the convenience store every Sunday, and I helped him make the [news] papers and stuff."

It was also at the Quick Stop in Leonardo where Kevin made the acquaintance of one more important friend, this one a few years younger than the future director: Vincent Pereira, often termed the official historian of the View Askew universe.

"I got a job working at the Quick Stop a few months before Kevin got his job there," details Pereira, a well-spoken native of Monmouth County, whose photographic memory regarding the details of the scripts, production, and marketing of Kevin Smith's movies is nothing less than remarkable.

"It was funny, because for the first couple of weeks we didn't really talk much. Then one night I was hanging out and I asked him if he was a *Twin Peaks* fan. He said yes, and that kind of sparked the whole thing, because I was a total *Peaks* fan. So we started to talk about *Twin Peaks*, and I started to talk to him about filmmaking."

It was a subject that the knowledgeable and intense Pereira was well-versed in, having been a movie buff all his life. A voracious reader and student of film, it was Pereira, with his excellent memory and encyclopedic knowledge of the medium, who really turned Smith on to the nuts and bolts of the filmmaking process (as well as the glories of the now-defunct laserdisc home viewing format).

Smith's friendship with Pereira eventually resulted in late night pilgrimages to New York City, where the duo would go see offbeat, non-commercial films. Smith would often note the strange titles in the ads of *The Village Voice*, read reviews by Amy Taubin, and suggest to Vinnie that they give a movie a try.

"After we closed up on Friday nights," Pereira remembers, "we would go out to the night shows at the Angelika in New York. The first movie we ever saw there was *The Dark Backward*, this bizarre movie with Bill Paxton as a guy with a third arm [written/directed by Adam Rifkin]."

And then, of course, there was the trip that changed the course of Smith's adulthood. On his twenty-first birthday, he and Pereira went to the Angelika Film Center to see Richard Linklater's low-budget independent film, *Slacker*.

Produced for under $25,000 by the Texan Richard Linklater (future director of *Dazed and Confused* [1993], *Before Sunrise* [1995], *The Newton Boys* [1998], and *Waking Life* [2001]), *Slacker* was a strange, almost stream-of-consciousness odyssey through the daytime and nightlife of a quirky college town, Austin.

A film about everything from parallel realities, chaos theory, and the patriarchal aspects of the *Smurfs* cartoon, to new conspiracy theories about the J.F.K. assassination, *Slacker* followed young, twenty-something characters seemingly at random. In the process, the movie exposed a well-educated but ultimately aimless and disaffected generation.

Making it even more noteworthy, *Slacker* had no protagonist, no climax, and no big name actors to provide the audience a lifeline to the always-transforming material.

In an interview conducted in 1994, Kevin Smith told journalist Kenneth Chanko and *The New York Times* how *Slacker* both stunned and empowered him:

> *I was a* Star Wars *generation kid. But here was a movie,* Slacker, *that had no plot, no car chases, no villain, and no three acts, and yet it was really engaging because of the dialogue. And dialogue is the thing I did best.*[8]

John Pierson, author of the Hyperion/Miramax best seller, *Spike, Mike, Slackers & Dykes: A Guided Tour Across a Decade of American Independent Cinema*, also represented Spike Lee's first film *She's Gotta Have It*, Michael Moore's first documentary *Roger & Me*, and *Slacker*. He puts into context for us the reasons why *Slacker* was a revelation to Kevin Smith.

"Here's a guy from some part of New Jersey that is within easy-striking range of Manhattan, the art film capital of North America," Pierson begins. "It's right there; within an hour of where he lives. But it's not like he's ever going there to see movies. Instead, he's seeing things that are playing in the malls. So, when he does go to the Angelika Film Center in big, old Manhattan—legendarily on his twenty-first birthday—he sees a film called *Slacker*, urged on by his friend Vinnie. And he sees this quasi-non-narrative film."

"He sees something unlike any experience he's had before. Essentially, the *Slacker* viewing experience is one of taking great joy, and sometimes laughing out loud at the stuff that is funny. Because Kevin is watching a film like that, which is playing with an audience, he thinks, 'This is funny, and it doesn't really have anything resembling the three-act story line a studio movie would have.' So he thinks, 'Shoot, I can write something funnier than this, something that has a little more story, and a little more structure.' I think Kevin knew he could do a movie like that and make people laugh."

And, unbeknownst to Smith during the drive home from New York City that night, he had selected the absolute best time to emulate the *Slacker* formula, right down to the low, low budget.

"Several films came out around the same time as *Slacker*," Pierson reports. "*The Living End* was one, and *El Mariachi* was another movie in that under-$30,000 budget range which made its mark in the world with critics and, to a certain degree, with audiences.

"And, to give Peter Broderick his due, he wrote that story in *Filmmaker Magazine* where he broke down the budgets for those films. I guess *Laws of Gravity* fits into the under- $50,000-type movie too. So there was an available illustration of how it is that you can shoot a 16mm film for this little. I think people were inspired by the aesthetic [of *Slacker*], but were also given practical information that became a blueprint or a guidebook to how this was done."

"We went to see *Slacker* in 1991, in the late summer," Pereira explains, "and I guess I could see it in Kevin's eyes driving home. 'Wow, I can make something like that.' You could just see it in his face."

Smith's interest "made sense," according to Pereira, "because Kevin is such a good writer." In fact, Smith was so inspired by *Slacker* that on the drive back from the showing, he had already begun contemplating the preliminaries of his first feature.

"We actually discussed ideas for films on the way home," reveals Pereira, "and talked about this bizarre David Lynch-ian thing he thought about doing for a time."

It wasn't long after his screening of *Slacker* that twenty-one-year-old Kevin Smith made another decision. It was time to gain access to the knowledge and technical tools that would get him closer to his dream of making a movie.

"Kevin started looking around to see where he could go learn filmmaking real quick," notes Pereira, "and I think there were ads for Vancouver Film School in the back of *The Village Voice*."

That private trade school, which had opened its doors in 1987 to a class of only a dozen students, promised superior technical training. Located on the western coast of Canada, with mountains to the east and the Pacific Ocean to the west, the film school is located in a city often voted one of the most desirable places to live. But the cost of admission for the program was considerable: $9,000 for an eight-month curriculum.

British Columbia was a long way from Jersey, and some of Smith's friends were troubled when they first learned that their good friend would be moving away from the Garden State for nearly a year.

"Kevin, Walter, and I went to this pizza place, and Kevin told us he was going to film school to become a filmmaker," Bryan Johnson recalls. "We all thought it was a little weird, and there was a part of me that was upset he would be moving to Canada. We were good friends, and I thought: 'Don't go! We have so much hanging out to do. So many comic book shows to go to. So many beers to drink.' I suppose it didn't really dawn on me at the time that he was going to be a real filmmaker. To me, it was just like he was going away to school."

ÜBER PRODUCER

With the first half of his tuition ($4,000) paid, Kevin Smith attended Vancouver Film School in British Columbia in early 1992. One of his classmates was Scott Mosier, the man who would partner with Kevin Smith as producer and editor on his first films, and a driving force behind View Askew Productions throughout the 1990s and 2000s.

Born in Vancouver, Washington, Scott Mosier spent the early part of his life moving with his family up and down the west coast, from Washington State to Los Angeles, and finally to Vancouver, Canada, when he was ten. From an early age, Mosier, like Smith, fostered a love of film.

"I always liked movies, but probably when I was in high school, I started to formulate an idea that I'd like to try it as a career," Mosier recounts. "When I went to college, I exposed myself to a lot of different kinds of movies. Once I started to watch some Fellini films and *Brazil*, I started thinking I wanted to make movies."

To make that leap, Mosier knew he needed to understand more about the medium, and immersed himself in the details of film study while enrolled in the Orange County College film program, which he describes as "pretty dinky."

"I took a course in the history of film that started with the silent era and I read books. Once I left the classroom, I continued reading and watching as much as I could. Even if you don't like certain movies, if you watch them from an historical standpoint you can see the development of an art form. To understand Scorsese, you have to see that he didn't come out of nowhere, that he was influenced by someone else before him."

Mosier still remembers his first attempt to shoot a movie of his own. "As opposed to achieving anything on a scholastic level, I just kept reading, and made this short video with this girl. It was just terrible, because we were neophytes. When I watch it now, I go, 'Oh my god! It's so scattered!' There's no concept of eye lines, or what have you.

"Then, after two years, I transferred up to UCLA extension and went to night school. I couldn't transfer in because my grades were terrible and I didn't have enough credits. So I took the extension classes and all of these screenwriting classes. One was a lecture series where you go in a room and see Joe Eszterhas and Steven De Souza. One of my teachers co-wrote *Rock 'n' Roll High School*, which was pretty killer for me; I think I was twenty at the time. And the other teacher wrote *Death Race 2000*."

Even with his interest in film, Mosier felt his attention lagging. "I've always been underwhelmed by school, and I got bored and stopped going at a certain point. I didn't like living in L.A. anymore, and it was becoming obvious I wasn't going to get a degree. I wanted to go home to Vancouver [British Columbia], where my parents had moved, live at home and go to this tech school, and they'd help me pay for it."

So Mosier set about enrolling in the Vancouver Film School. "I called the school and they had two slots left. I said, 'Yeah, I'll take it.' The program was full-time for eight months and I was like, 'I can handle this ...' which I barely did."

And it was there, at film school, that Kevin Smith and Scott Mosier met. But contrary to expectations, it wasn't exactly love at first sight.

"Initially we weren't crazy about each other," Mosier acknowledges. "I think I looked like I'd been in L.A. at that point. And he looked strange to me. I wasn't impressed—it wasn't magic. There was no instant connection."

A friendship formed nonetheless. "Once we started taking classes and were split into groups, we started talking about things we had in common, being Americans. He'd read a lot, and I read a lot of *Film Threat* and *Variety*, so we'd read the periodicals. And that was sort of the beginning, where we separated ourselves from everyone else by having seen certain independent films. After that, we were hanging out all the time."

In fact, Kevin Smith and Scott Mosier teamed-up for a class project—their first official co-production. The students planned to shoot a ten-minute documentary together, but things didn't quite turn out as planned.

"Everybody in the class splits into groups of two," relates Mosier "and Kevin's idea was to make a movie about a pre-op transsexual. But we weren't being very serious about it. I think he'd gone out somewhere and talked to some girl. He was in the city all the time, and I lived out in the suburbs with my folks, so sometimes he had nothing to do, and he met this transsexual before I did."

"So he said, 'Let's do it,' and we did a proposal. Before we pitched, we met with Mae [the subject], and she invited us to this thing called The Seven Deadly Sins, this sort of Transvestite Ball. So we borrowed a camera, and Kevin and I went to the Transvestite Ball in downtown Vancouver. We hung out backstage with her and got some footage we thought we could use later on. We watched the show and it was pretty fun."

But then the two fledgling filmmakers had to sell their instructors and classmates on their notion. "We had to pitch it to all of the students and the teachers, and they would pick four out of twelve groups that would get to make their movies," Mosier describes. "We sat outside before the pitch and created something very sincere. It was a good pitch, but underneath it all, I don't know how much we really wanted to do it. It was more like preparing for a competition; we both just wanted to win.

"When the teachers said we could do it Kevin and I were a little bit disappointed. Like, 'Oh, really?' So we had to pick our crew, and I guess you could say that our person [the transsexual] wasn't really nailed down. We weren't really prepared to do it, and basically, the crew didn't like us. And, at the last minute, when things were going badly, we couldn't get in touch with this girl.

"We just didn't really have a plan," Mosier concedes. "We finally got together and shot one night with our subject, Imelda Mae, and then she blew [out of] town. She flaked on us. And we were like, 'Oh shit!' So Kevin and I came up with the idea of doing a documentary about how everything fell apart. We went in and proposed it to the teachers, and they told us we'd fucked up, but we were fairly defiant and our attitude was we should be able to do what we wanted. This wasn't fucking high school; we'd paid our money, we should get to do it.

"Then Kevin wrote this spine for it, these scenes with us backlit. That was all scripted by us. Then we shot it and compiled it, and it became easy. It became fun at that point, because it was all about amusing ourselves. Once we did that, we were totally interested. How could we make ourselves laugh? Then we went forward full-bore."

The resulting project, *Mae Day: The Crumbling of a Documentary* has become something of a legend at Vancouver Film School. "I've heard a lot of things,"

Mosier notes. "I know they show it a lot. I can't remember if they show it as an example of what to do, or as a cautionary tale of what can happen. I guess the cautionary tale would be: don't let the two most sincere guys do something, because they're full of shit. That's the lesson to be learned on that."

After the *Mae Day* documentary, the film program at Vancouver was just about half over. "That was the four month mark," Mosier explains. "It was a period where you worked on two separate short films, and that's when Kevin left. He was going to save the rest of his tuition. If he went another day, he'd have to forfeit his money, so he sort of bailed and put that money to use in *Clerks*."

Smith returned home to New Jersey, resumed work at the convenience store and R.S.T. Video, and began writing the screenplay for his first film. While he wrote, he also did what Quentin Tarantino would later report doing: he became the undisputed master of the video rental.

"I used to stop at the video store and rent movies from Kevin," Jeff Anderson remembers. "It was great, because nobody ever went to this video store. I would get all the latest releases and Kevin would never charge me. He was sort of my Roger Ebert. He'd point to a movie, and I'd get it and go, no charge. He'd tell me to bring it back when he was working.

"When I was returning movies, I'd always hide the movies under my shirt to see if he was there. It's not an overly big store, so if I saw somebody else, they'd say, 'Hey, do you have movies there?' I'd say, 'No, no,' and come back when Kevin was back."

In Canada, life went on like normal, for a while.

"I was working at a stock room in The Gap, and working on some short films as an editor," Mosier remembers of that period. "And right when school was over, Kevin sent me the script for *Clerks*."

The rest, as they say, is history.

2

Clerks (1994)

I'M NOT EVEN SUPPOSED TO BE HERE TODAY!

Just because they serve you, doesn't mean they like you.

Cast and Crew

VIEW ASKEW PRODUCTIONS PRESENTS *CLERKS*

Written and directed by: Kevin Smith
Produced by: Scott Mosier and Kevin Smith
Cinematography by: David Klein
Camera Operator: David Klein
Assistant Cameraman and Cat Wrangler: Vincent Pereira
Edited by: Scott Mosier and Kevin Smith
Sound Editors: Scott Mosier and James Van Buelow
Sound Mixers: Scott Mosier and James Van Buelow
Synchronization: Joia Speciale
Music Supervisor: Benji Gordon
Post-Production Supervisor: Charlie McClellan
M.P.A.A. Rating: R
Running Time: 92 minutes

Starring

Brian O'Halloran | *Dante Hicks*
Jeff Anderson | *Randal Graves*

Marilyn Ghigliotti | *Veronica*

Lisa Spoonauer | *Caitlin Bree*

Jason Mewes | *Jay*

Kevin Smith | *Silent Bob*

Scott Mosier | *Willam Black, the Idiot-Man-Child; Angry Hockey Playing Customer; Angry Mourner*

Walt Flanagan | *Woolen Cap Smoker, Egg Man, Offended Customer, Cat Admiring Bitter Customer*

Scott Schiaffo | *Chewlies Gum Rep*

Al Berkowitz | *Old Man*

Ed Hapstak | *Sanford; Angry Mourner*

Lee Bendick | *#812 Wynarski*

David Klein | *Hunting Cap Smoking Boy; Low IQ Video Customer; Hubcap Searching Customer*

Pattijean Csik | *Coroner*

Ken Clark | *Administer of Fine; Orderly*

Donna Jeanne | *Indecisive Video Customer*

Virginia Smith | *Caged Animal Masturbator*

Betsy Broussard | *Dental School Video Customer*

Ernest O'Donnell | *Trainer [Rick Derris]*

Kimberly Loughran | *Heather Jones*

Gary Stern | *Tabloid Reading Customer*

Joe Bagnole | *Cat Shit Watching Customer*

John Henry Westhead | *Olaf Oleeson*

Chuck Bickel | *Stuck in Chips Can*

Leslie Hope | *Jay's Lady Friend; Angry Crowd at Door*

Connie O'Conner | *'Happy Scrappy' Mom*

Vincent Pereira | *Hockey Goalie; Engagement Savvy Customer*

Ashley Pereira | *'Happy Scrappy' Kid*

Erix Infante | *Bed Wetting Dad, Cold Coffee Lover*

Melissa Crawford | *Video Confusion Customer; Candy Confusion Customer; Angry Crowd at Door*

Thomas Burke | *Blue Collar Man*

Dan Hapstak | *Door Tugging Customer*

Mitch Cohen | *Leaning Against Wall; Angry Crowd at Door*

Matthew Banta | *Burner Looking for Weed*

Rajiv Thapar | *Cut-Off Customer*

Mike Belicose | *Customer with Diapers*
Jane Kuritz | *Customer with Vaseline and Rubber Gloves*
Grace Smith | *Milk-Maid*
Frances Cresci | *Little Smoking Girl*
Matt Crawford | *Angry Crowd at Door*
Sarla Thapar | *Angry Crowd at Door*
Brian Drinkwater | *Hockey Player*
Bob Fisler | *Hockey Player*
Derek Jaccodine | *Hockey Player*
Matthew Pereira | *Angry Smoking Crowd*
Frank Pereira | *Angry Smoking Crowd*
Carl Roth | *Angry Smoking Crowd*
Paul Finn | *Angry Smoking Crowd*

THE STORY SO FAR . . .

IN LEONARDO, NEW JERSEY, Dante Hicks, a directionless twenty-some-thing is called into work at the Quick Stop Grocery Store on his day off. Dante reluctantly reports to duty, only to be confronted by the worst day of his life.

To start with, someone has jammed gum in the locks of the store's metal shutters. Worse, one of his first customers is a Chewlie's Gum representative who calls him a death merchant for peddling cigarettes. Adding insult to injury, Dante learns that his current girlfriend, Veronica, has performed oral sex on some thirty-seven boyfriends.

Then there are the problems with R.S.T. Video, next door. Randal, the slacker who works there is late as usual and customers are angry. When Randal finally does arrive, he pisses off the customers and debates with Dante about a variety of minutiae. Dante pays little attention, as he learns that his old girlfriend, with whom he would like to reconcile, has just announced her engagement to an Asian Design Major in the newspaper.

Outside Quick Stop Groceries, two stoners, the hyperactive Jay and the taciturn Silent Bob, ply their trade and are visited by Bob's cousin Olaf from Russia. Olaf wants to be a metal singer and has written a ballad called "Berserker." The lyrics, however, lose something in the translation.

The day wears on and Dante and Randal continue to debate trivia (such as the ending of *Return of the Jedi*), and serve a variety of colorful customers.

The Idiot-Man-Child, Willam Black, the Egg Man—a deranged guidance counselor searching for the perfect dozen eggs—and a woman who manually masturbates caged animals for artificial insemination, all come and go.

Before the day is over, Randal and Dante have closed the store to play a hockey game on the roof, inadvertently sold cigarettes to a minor, and disrupted the wake of Julie Dwyer, an old girlfriend of Dante's who died of an embolism. Even worse, Dante's relationships with former love Caitlin Bree and current girl Veronica are shaken by a series of bizarre events and Randal's endless meddling.

At the end of a trying day, Dante and Randal reflect on their choices, and ask important questions about their lives. A little wiser, Dante and Randal part ways for the evening and Dante closes the convenience store.

SILENT BOB'S WORDS OF WISDOM

"There's a million fine looking women in the world, but they don't all bring you lasagna. Most of them just cheat on you."

THE STORY BEHIND THE MOVIE

In this world, there are thousands if not millions of dreamers who believe they can make a movie, but few actually get beyond the fantasy. Even fewer deliver a professional, feature-length film to a festival, let alone Sundance, and walk away from the party sporting a deal from a prestigious operation such as the Weinsteins' Miramax Films. Yet that's precisely what Kevin Smith, producer Scott Mosier and fledgling View Askew Productions accomplished in 1993 with Smith's celebrated first film, *Clerks*.

There's an old adage that authors ought to write "what they know" and perhaps that proverb is the best entrée into the world of Kevin Smith's films. With *Clerks*, Smith successfully transformed a minimum wage job jockeying the counter at Quick Stop Groceries in Leonardo, New Jersey into cinematic gold. Using tales of the convenience store (and its partner operation, R.S.T. Video) as fodder for his comedy, Smith drafted a 164-page screenplay for *Clerks* in thirty days, in early 1993.

The resulting script, concerning a day in the life of two disenfranchised young adults of Generation X in dead-end customer service jobs came replete with elements that would soon become Smith's hallmark, namely witty and ribald dialogue. It might be stretching the truth to say that *Clerks* was auto-biographical, but there was no doubt that Smith's work experience played a role in its creation.

"I think movies are usually one step behind the story teller," Producer Scott Mosier suggests. "You can't project into the future, so Kevin was making a film about his own previous experience, and maybe Dante's fear of being trapped in that time and place was something that Kevin, by writing this script, had already conquered."

Only the script's conceived ending, a tragic and fatal turn of events for Dante Hicks, hinted at a deep nihilism bubbling beneath the slacker angst. Smith later reported to John Pierson in *Spike, Mike, Slackers & Dykes* that the film's fateful climax was inspired at least in part by Spike Lee's *Do The Right Thing*, one of Smith's five favorite films.

> The tone of that movie was humorous and then it turned. And I thought
> I'd like to do that in a movie. Humorous, then turn it.[1]

But even before *Clerks*' surprisingly dark ending had been crafted by Smith, the *Clerks* script had gone through a great many developments, as View Askew historian Vincent Pereira explains: "We were driving home from seeing *Slacker* and right on the spot Kevin thought of something based on *Slacker*'s opening scene, where Linklater is talking about the Schroedinger's Cat."

As aficionados of Linklater (and quantum mechanics) may recall, the Schroedinger Cat paradox was an idea first put forward in 1935 by Erwin Schroedinger. Briefly summarized: if a cat is deposited in a box and thus no longer observed, can it rightly be said to exist? Or—until observed again—is it actually nonexistent?

The Schroedinger's Cat idea was also brought up in another film of the same vintage, John Carpenter's 1987 horror picture, *Prince of Darkness*. The concept isn't mentioned by name in *Slacker*, but the film opens with a character portrayed by Linklater contemplating parallel realities and the vicissitudes of perceptions and dreams.

"It was a very Lynch-ian sci-fi type of film," Pereira confirms of Smith's first idea. "Kevin then wrote a one-page synopsis of what he wanted to do with *Clerks*, which at the time was titled *In Convenience*. That plot line had to do with a guy working the midnight to 6:00 a.m. shift in a convenience store, and all the bizarre people who came in. It was very Lynch-ian and Kevin didn't write it in a linear fashion; really just scenes. And at one point he handed me fifty pages of scenes that were sort of in order, and that was the first time I knew he was writing a straight comedy. It was very funny."

Forecasting the first dark ending of *Clerks*, Smith also included an action-chase subplot that landed protagonist Dante in great danger. "In one of the pre-drafts there was something that never made it to the first draft," Pereira remembers. "There was a character who in Kevin's words was loosely based on me. I was kind of a hot-tempered guy at the time, and this character was going to be the mob boy at the convenience store who gets fired and is scoping out the bank with a rifle because he knows Dante is going there to deposit the money. So he's going to kill Dante and steal the cash. There was this whole subplot where Randal is watching events unfold on the TV at the convenience store, with Dante being chased all over town."

Pereira liked the interlude, but recognizing money would be tight, voiced his reservations about the set piece. "Kevin asked me what should be cut and, first and foremost, I thought that subplot should go because it would have been really expensive to shoot, even though it was very funny."

Once the *Clerks* script was written and then pared down to a manageable 135 pages, Smith and his cohort from film school, Scott Mosier, set out to produce the film. Making *Clerks* was not an easy task for two young students with little cash and less experience, but they both dove in, head first, to make the film a reality.

"I didn't really know how to start the process of making this movie at all. Based on going to school, I wasn't prepared to do it," Scott Mosier remembers of the producer's job. "I understood the broadest of strokes, and I sort of broke it down in a practical way. I knew I needed to rent equipment and so forth. In *Filmmaker Magazine*, Peter Broderick used to do these articles about low budget films, like *Laws of Gravity* and *Slacker*, and print their budgets. So I used those articles as a sort of template of what the categories were. We needed cameras and lights, and this and that."

And, at that point, another important decision was made. Shooting the film would be David Klein, a native of Idaho and classmate whom Mosier had befriended at Vancouver following Smith's return to New Jersey.

"When Kevin left, I started hanging out with David a lot," Mosier explains. "He became the 'next' person. I had talked to him throughout the class and we'd gotten along, but once Kevin left we finished the class together."

According to Mosier, it was important to him that Klein shoot the film. "I talked to Kevin about Dave and said, in a selfish way, that I wanted to work with someone of our age and experience level so we'd all feel comfortable. I didn't really want to hire somebody from New York who had shot a bunch of short films because I felt we'd be better off being in our little bubble and doing things the way we wanted. The whole movie might have been a disaster because we were so isolated, because we were just dealing with the basic knowledge each of us had. I knew how to record sound, not to say well, but I took the foundations of what I knew and did it. Dave did the same thing. Kevin did the same thing."

In the pre-production phase of *Clerks*, Mosier's most important job became determining the production equipment needs. "I'd get up in the morning on the West Coast at about five a.m., because long distance was cheaper, and I'd call all of these New York facilities to get cameras and make a plan of how much we would have to spend. And Dave came up with a list of the things he thought he would need. It was a little unnerving because we were afraid we would get to the set and realize we'd forgotten something. It seems so simple: get three cameras, a Nagra, a boom, a mike, and a light. You think it can't be that simple, but in truth, it really was that simple."

The budget for *Clerks* was an issue, of course, but nobody set out with a defined ceiling on the project. "*Slacker* cost $24,000" Mosier compares, "but making *Clerks* was simply about spending as little as possible. Kevin really carried the financial risk of the project."

Smith not only sold his comic book collection to finance the picture, but according to Mosier, he "took a loan of $3,000 from his parents at the outset, and put the rest on his credit cards. And at the end, my parents loaned us $3,500 for the final print. But it was Kevin who took the brunt of the financial risk. If it didn't work, he was in for it."

Smith's credit card approach, already modeled successfully by Robert Townsend and the film *Hollywood Shuffle*, allowed the film's final budget to reach $26,685.

On Smith's end, permission was secured to film the movie in the video and convenience stores after closing time from the owners, Tralochan and Sarala Thapar. It was at that point that casting began in earnest for the picture.

Interestingly, not everybody who hoped to be involved was certain that Smith's intention to make a movie was for real. "I remember the first time Kevin told me he wanted to make a movie," Jason Mewes remembers. "He said, 'I wrote this script, I want to shoot this movie, and I wrote a character for you.' My other friend, Kevin Horvath, and I had gotten those little Fisher Price video cameras that had little black and white cassettes for Christmas. We used to make these funny little movies, so when Kevin said he'd written a script, I just thought it would be the bunch of us messing around with those cameras."

Jeff Anderson, who eventually came to play the wisecracking Randal, remembers how he first learned of *Clerks*. "I hung out with Ernie O'Donnell's roommate, and Ernie told me that Kevin was making a movie. When I visited him at the video store, Kevin was always at his word processor working on the script and we talked about it some. But then Ernie showed me the script, and told me Kevin had written it, and I thought this was totally unheard of. A movie? This was out in the woods! *Moving pictures?*

"Ernie told me that Kevin was holding auditions at the local playhouse [The First Avenue Playhouse]. He said I should go because there would be a lot of attractive girls there. So I went along with Ernie's roommate to watch Ernie audition for *Clerks*."

From there, Jeff Anderson watched actors come and go, and remembers being particularly impressed by Marilyn Ghigliotti, who eventually played Veronica. "I mean, we were at a playhouse in Atlantic Highlands, and the actors weren't terribly impressive, but Marilyn did this crazy audition where she was crying and doing all kinds of emotional things and I thought, 'My god, this chick can act.' After she was done, it was just quiet. Even I was impressed, and I was only there to mock Ernie. We were all thinking, 'Wow, that was really some acting…'"

By a strange twist of fate, Jeff himself ended up on the stage that day.

"We were at the playhouse looking at all the girls and Ernie was on stage reading with some of them," Anderson describes. "We thought Ernie's reading had gone badly so we really started mocking him after he finished. 'How long have you had that script? I don't think you've ever looked at it!' And he said that he didn't see us reading any parts, so I grabbed the script, went up on stage and read for the part of Jay, which was pretty funny.

"Kevin told me I could audition for Jay, but I'd have to wait until the owner of the playhouse left the premises. I asked why, and he told me to look at what Jay was saying [lots of cussing]. Kevin was getting this playhouse for free and didn't want the owner to think he was doing a piece of trash. So as soon as the owner walked out, they stopped whoever was auditioning and told me to go on. So I ran up on stage and spouted all these expletives. Then the owner walked back in and they stopped me. That was my big audition."

In the end, Anderson didn't get the role of Jay—he was destined for something else. Instead, the role went to Smith's young friend and sometimes housemate, Jason Mewes. A talent with raw energy to spare and a screen presence that *Entertainment Weekly*'s Owen Gleiberman later described as "Dana Carvey's Garth stoked with Eminem's street rage and the raunch of Al Goldstein... the cinema's original suburban hip-hop id."[2]

"Kevin wrote the character of Jay because he, Walter, and Bryan thought I was funny," Jason Mewes reveals. "They liked the way I acted, and Kevin was always curious if other people would find it funny, or if it would just be our circle of friends. So he wrote the character based on me."

Contemplating the character, Mewes reflects on how much of Jay is actually him. "That's how I was when I was younger, when I met Kevin, when I was thirteen. I'm still like Jay, maybe about sixty percent, but in about eleventh grade I realized I had to straighten up, and that there are boundaries. The difference is that now I understand boundaries. I feel people out, and I know who can take a joke. And I don't pull my pants down anymore. I used to pull my pants down a lot."

Also attending the auditions for Clerks was an accomplished young actor named Brian O'Halloran, born in the Bronx, who had appeared in stage productions of *Dracula* (as Renfield), *Charlotte's Web*, and *Wait Until Dark*.

"I went down to the playhouse," O'Halloran explains, "and I saw Vincent Pereira with a video camera, and Kevin was there, and maybe Walter too. I filled out a questionnaire form that Kevin had printed up for the auditions, and then asked how many principals there were. They said six, but the roles had already been taken, so I was really auditioning to play an extra. But I went up and did this monologue from *Wait Until Dark*. I was the villain in that show and was really intense, and a couple of days later I got a call from Kevin inviting me for a callback.

"So I came back, he handed me two or three script pages, and I read the scene. Then I came back for another callback, and he asked what I thought about Dante. I said 'Dante's funny, but his friend is funnier.' Then Kevin told me I had the part and I didn't believe him, because I thought all the principals were taken. He told me not to worry about it, and gave me the script to read. He asked me if I wanted to do it, and I said yes."

The key to playing Dante, according to O'Halloran, was sympathy. "I could relate completely to what Dante was going through. I'd been working in the service industry [at a grocery store] for the last four years, so I knew about dealing with customers. I think I just brought sympathy to the character. If you could make him sympathetic, he wouldn't be whiny, and he just became a very loveable character."

As the fidelity-challenged girlfriend to Brian O'Halloran's long suffering protagonist, Kevin Smith cast Lisa Spoonauer after seeing her in a performance during a class at Brookdale Community College.

The fledgling filmmaker wasn't above a bit of nepotism either, recruiting his sister Virginia to portray a woman who stimulates caged animals for artificial insemination. His mother Grace was also brought in to portray a "milk maid," though she later complained that the finished sequence made her hips look "too big."[3] In one scene Smith's girlfriend, Heather Loughran, played opposite Ernie O'Donnell's chick-magnet, Rick Derris.

As for Jeff Anderson, he didn't score with his audition of Jay. "From my first audition, I got a smaller role," he reveals. "It was actually the role that Kevin's sister ended up playing in the movie, only at the time the character was killing chickens for the railroad. That character had several occupations over time, and that one [animal masturbator] was just the one that got left in. Anyway, I read for that smaller part, and the next day Kevin called me and asked what I was doing. He wanted to come over and have me look at another part.

"So he came over to my house, and that night we sat on my couch and he said, 'Listen, let's read through the script just you and me, and I want you to read for this Randal guy.' And then we just sat there and read the script and when it was over, Kevin said, 'You're my Randal.'"

Except it wasn't that simple . . .

"I said to him, 'I am *not* your Randal! I don't have that good a memory! I can't spout all this out!'" Anderson laughs. "But Kevin thought I could do it and told me we'd do it a little at a time. He asked me to come to rehearsals and said we'd read the script just the way we did there, on the couch."

Ironically, it was during the rehearsal process that Kevin Smith nearly "lost his Randal," according to Anderson. That first night, Brian O'Halloran, Marilyn Ghigliotti, Jeff Anderson, and Kevin began rehearsals in the convenience store after hours.

"We sat on the coolers where the Salsa Shark scene takes place. I met Marilyn and Brian and they asked me what I'd been in. I thought, 'Oh dear Lord, I've never done anything.' And they were a little shocked by that. When they read me their resumes, I knew I was in trouble.

"So we did a read-through and it went okay. Then we did a rehearsal. And the next night, we did another rehearsal and Lisa [Spoonauer] came in and I thought, 'Oh my, this is looking up, she's really hot!' So we did a read-through with Marilyn, Brian, Lisa, myself, and Kevin. At the end of it, Kevin closed the script and told us it was pretty good, and that we'd just keep plugging away at it.

"But then Marilyn piped up and asked to say something. Kevin was like, 'Sure.' And Marilyn says, 'Uh Kevin, I don't think he's going to be able to do this,' and she pointed right to me. I was mortified. She said, 'He's never acted before, and he doesn't sound good.' She said this in front of everybody! It wasn't in a private conversation, and I just turned twenty shades of red. Kevin assured her I would be okay by the time we got to shoot."

But the damage was done, and Anderson's confidence was shot. "I went to work the next day, and now I was dreading going to rehearsal. I finally decided not to do the movie. So on the way home from work, I stopped at the convenience store and gave my script back to Kevin, saying, basically, 'Thanks, but no thanks.' I told him I meant no offense, but I wasn't being paid for this. I was just doing it as a kick, and now it wasn't very much fun.

"Kevin was very definite, telling me not to quit. He said he would rehearse Marilyn and me on different days. But I didn't want to do that either, because I didn't want to be some problem where now Kevin had to schedule us apart. I just wasn't comfortable. As it was, I was uncertain about acting, but to have her eyes on me—I was just afraid I'd mess up."

Though Kevin Smith convinced Anderson to stay aboard the project, Jeff remembers how his experience with Ghigliotti reinforced his feelings about actors. "Acting people always struck me as so serious. She was sure I couldn't do it, and there was no tact in the way she said it. It was in front of everybody and I thought, 'Man, this girl is brutal.'"

So, Anderson admits it was sweet when time came to film Randal's one scene with Veronica. "The first scene we actually shot on *Clerks* was the one with me and Marilyn. We never rehearsed it, but Kevin told me to do the scene with her, and I'd never have to see her again. I remember the first take of that scene: she messed up her line. I was so happy, I thought, 'Thank God!' And from there it got better. I harbor her no ill will."

Pereira also recalls the lengthy rehearsal process leading up to production, which stretched throughout February of 1993. "Kevin would get the actors together and go through the script until the actors were as off the book as possible. Kevin worked in the store till about 10:30 p.m., and the actors would start showing up at 10:00 p.m. I have this image of driving back from a showing of Peter Jackson's *Dead Alive* in Toms River one night, and seeing Kevin at the store rehearsing. These people were just sitting on the freezers, going over the lines."

But if rehearsals lasted well into the night, shooting the film itself became an ongoing marathon of all-nighters. "We were young," Mosier comments, deadpan. "I was twenty or twenty-one at the time, and the thought of sleeping on the floor for two hours a night didn't seem that bad. I lost weight because we just smoked and drank coffee and shot all night long for three weeks. Sometimes we'd sleep two hours a day, and we shot seven days a week, except for Easter. Kevin was just working insane hours. He'd work at the convenience store and sleep sometimes while we were setting up. Then Dave and I would sleep a few hours in the video store in the morning. If somebody proposed to me to do it now, at my age, there'd be certain things I'd need. Like a bed and a certain amount of sleep to function. Today, I wouldn't last more than a few days."

Playing against type, Jeff Anderson was anything but a directionless slacker at the time *Clerks* was made, a fact that complicated his schedule. "At the time, I worked for AT&T. I was supervisor of a mailroom in charge of three different locations of 50 people. I'd work from 7:30 in the morning to 4:30 in the afternoon. Then go to school to study architecture and design from 5:00 p.m. to 7:00 p.m., and then be down at the store by 11:00 p.m. and shoot until 6:00 a.m. in the morning. Randal was pretty different from me: I was working in a professional environment, and I could only wish to lash into people the way he did."

The aggressive shooting schedule of *Clerks* in March of 1993 also took its toll on the hard-working Smith, who continued to toil at the Quick Stop to augment the film's budget. He gained thirty pounds in twenty-one days and smoked one-and-a-half packs of cigarettes a day.[4] Some of the stress he must have felt at the time may have resulted from the fact that some of his performers were not completely dependable. Many simply forgot to show up.

"For *Clerks*, every single character I did was a last minute thing," Walt Flanagan, who played Egg Man and other bizarre Quick Stop patrons, recalls. "We were waiting for actors to show, and the whole movie was shot after hours so we'd be scheduling a scene at 2:00 in the morning for an actor to come in and buy cigarettes. So we'd wait and we'd wait and then realize this guy just wasn't going to show up. So Kevin would turn to me and ask if I wanted to do the part. I would say, 'Kevin, I just did a character.' But he'd make me look different each time and I'd be all right."

Wearing hoods, suits and ties, glasses, caps, and wigs, Walt Flanagan was quickly dubbed the "Lon Chaney of the 90s" by Kevin Smith for his versatility and dependability.

While shooting *Clerks*, everybody in the Quick Stop had to learn to chip in, just like Walt, because there were few hands available, as Pereira remembers. "Originally, I was going to be the camera assistant, but David didn't have enough time to teach me how to change magazines and all that. When you were there in the store, you just did whatever needed to be done. So usually I helped, because there were maybe five or six people there. I left early some nights, but I was there for most of the shooting."

The old axiom "never work with animals" also proved true for the crew of *Clerks* during production when the black cat appearing in the film bolted between shots. "That was a stray cat from the area who started coming to the store," Pereira notes. "Kevin put him in the script. Basically, we were shooting a take and somebody opened the door, and the cat was getting agitated by the lights, and the people in the store, so he just bolted. We went out after him and called for him, but he wouldn't come back. He eventually came back, but we were all outside at around four in the morning trying to find this black cat—which was hard to see in the dark!"

Another hurdle in shooting *Clerks* involved Jason Mewes's confidence level. Simply put, the young man felt uncomfortable being in front of the camera and performing Jay's outrageous stunts. "I was so nervous," he confides. "Every day before shooting, they had to go buy me a bottle of blackberry brandy. I had to get really drunk to do the part, and then I'd make everybody go inside that didn't need to be out there. Usually, it was just Kevin, Scott, and Dave. Kevin would stand next to me, Dave was the DP, and Scott was doing the sound. But if I could avoid having anyone there at all, besides those three, I would do it."

For Jeff Anderson, the filming went fine, though he was still anxious about his first performance. He feels that to some extent the situation affected his work with Brian O'Halloran. "I like Brian," he stresses. "But after the Marilyn thing, I put my guard up against Brian because I knew he and Marilyn were friends and had done theater together, and I guess I found them intimidating. I shouldn't have done it, because Brian had nothing to do with it. But at the time, I thought he was one of them! So when we shot *Clerks*, it was just like, let's get through this, and Brian and I didn't pal around a lot."

On the technical side of the process, only a few shots had to be re-staged when it was learned that some footage of Mosier as Willam the Snowballer was ruined by film burns. That turned out to be nothing, however, compared with Mosier's worry that things could have been a lot worse.

"We didn't have enough money for dailies, and when we got done shooting and it was time to synch everything up I had a pit in my stomach," Mosier recollects. "I thought, 'Holy fuck, am I going to be able to synch this?' Through the whole shoot I wondered about that. It was one of those things that I knew other people would worry about too if I told them, so I just kept it to myself and bore the brunt of it. That was the only thing that stressed me out."

What Pereira remembers about the shooting of *Clerks* is that even at that protean stage of his directing experience Kevin Smith had already found his chops. "His main focus was on the actors," Pereira recalls. "In comedies like *Clerks*, Kevin is big on line readings. The screenplay reads a certain way, he hears it in his head, and then listens to the actor's delivery. Then he brings the two readings closer together. He likes David Mamet, who does that kind of stylized dialogue, and he loves fast-talking 1930s comedies, like *His Girl Friday*. Howard Hawks stuff."

For O'Halloran, he and Smith spoke the same language, which made their working relationship a comfortable one. "I could really relate to Dante and to Kevin in general. We had similar upbringings. He had older siblings, I have older siblings. He comes from an Irish-Catholic background, and so do I. He was an altar boy, and I was an altar boy. I understood his humor immediately. It has the whole twang of Jersey-ness to it.

"I could really relate to Kevin, so when we talked about a scene we understood each other. Direction-wise, we talked mostly about intonation. He writes with so many words, and when I had big chunks of dialogue, he would give me my pauses, and tell me what marks to hit. His writing has a great flow to it. He uses all those words we got in English class and hoped we'd never have to see again. But man, the guy has a large vocabulary and isn't afraid to use it."

After *Clerks* finished shooting in March of 1993, it was finally time to put the pieces together and edit the film. "So much of it was just picking the takes, because the film is basically a series of two shots and static shots," recalls Scott Mosier. "It wasn't like we were cutting so much as choosing takes. One shot in there is seven minutes long. You could put twenty minutes together and do only four cuts.

"I had more experience on the flatbed, so I synched all the dailies and started the process of cutting. Then I got exhausted and brought Kevin in. I would work all day, he'd watch what I was doing [and] then I'd work in the store while he cut. But a lot of it was just Kevin watching the takes and telling me which ones he wanted to use."

In the case of *Clerks*, there wasn't a whole of lot of excess footage to litter the cutting room, or rather video store floor. "It was just a matter of cutting things down," Pereira observes. "The draft Kevin shot was about 135 pages, and even that cut together to 105 minutes for the first cut. It was interesting, because you always read that one page equals one minute of screen time, but being a comedy, the dialogue was so fast-paced that it ran much quicker. The first cut of the film was 105 minutes and contained about 99 percent of the shooting script."

O'Halloran remembers checking in on the editing process and being pleasantly surprised. "They were editing in the video store on a Steenback editor, where you literally take the negative, cut it, put it together, tape it, and run it. So I asked how it was going and Kevin and Scott showed me some scenes and it was really funny. It looked good."

Perhaps one of the most controversial aspects of *Clerks* first cut was the original ending. Dante was shot dead from the gun of a mysterious customer in a beautifully executed final sequence. Filmed as a tracking P.O.V. shot, a la John Carpenter's *Halloween*, the ending gave the film one powerful jolt of a climax, and re-cast the meaningless events of Dante's day in a whole new—and rather disturbing—light.

"I thought the script was funny, but I hated that ending," O'Halloran admits. "I never thought it worked. I just thought it was too quick of a twist. I remember going to Kevin, and I believe I told him I didn't like the ending. But we did it anyway, and in the end, it got taken out."

"It was a massive change of tone from the rest of the film," Pereira acknowledges, "but Kevin shot that scene so well. On the DVD they messed it up. If you watch it on DVD or laserdisc, as Dante is laying there on the floor, the sound of the convenience store fades and the picture goes to black, but that's not how it was originally mixed. If you saw the original tapes, what Kevin and Scott did was to bring up all the background noise of the store to be really loud. The sound ramps up and up, and then it cuts to black and silence. It was very powerful."

By the same token, Pereira admits that the grave initial denouement, cut before the film's showing at Sundance, would have changed the tone of the Kevin Smith film series rather substantially. "If *Clerks* was just going to be *Clerks*, then the ending might have worked, having Dante die. But it became this whole series of movies, and it would have been strange to have the specter of Dante's death hanging over the sequels. Could you imagine *Jay and Silent Bob Strike Back* with Randal alone in the convenience store?"

With their film cut together, many of those involved with *Clerks* thought that would be the end of the project. "I didn't even think anything about it," Mewes admits. "I continued to go to work; I was roofing at the time. We ate some chips and watched the movie in the video store one night, me, Kevin, Scott, and Dave. Then Kevin told me he was going to try to get it distributed."

On that front, Kevin Smith and Scott Mosier paid $500 to enter *Clerks* in the Independent Feature Film Festival held on October 3, 1993, at the Angelika Film Center in Manhattan. The *Clerks* showing was programmed at Sunday morning at 11:00 a.m., and was, euphemistically stated, sparsely attended.

"There were about twelve people in the audience, and about eight of them were us," Mosier remembers. "There were four others, and a few who wandered into the back to watch a little then leave. That happens a lot in these things. But we had spent all week trying to get people to go, and it was pretty hard because we didn't know what else we could do. But Bob Hawk was in the audience and told us he worked for Sundance."

The View Askew team's response?

"We didn't quite believe him," Mosier admits. "He didn't have any credentials, and I was just depressed. I wanted to leave. But then he started telling a bunch of people about the movie, pushing this little snowball down the hill, and it started getting bigger and bigger."

Robert Hawk, who attended the screening that day, was indeed a highly influential independent film consultant and member of the nominating committee on the Sundance Film Festival. He loved *Clerks* and began making calls to influential critics and film people on its behalf.

Before long, further interest in *Clerks* came from *The Village Voice*'s Amy Taubin (an early champion of Linklater's *Slacker*). Eventually word got back to film representative and marketing genius John Pierson, the undisputed guru of indie films, that he should take a look at *Clerks*. There was only one problem: Pierson wanted out of the business.

"I didn't really want to rep films anymore," Pierson acknowledges. And for good reason. He'd just come from an especially unpleasant experience working with the colorful Rob Weiss, director of the independent film *Amongst Friends*, and had no desire to get back in the game. It was his wife and long-time business partner, Janet Pierson, who finally swayed him.

"I was away speaking in Louisville, Kentucky, and Janet saw the film first. And it was just like seeing *She's Gotta Have It* and saying 'I have seen the future of cinema and his name is Spike Lee.' She told me flat out on the phone, 'If you don't want to rep films anymore, you shouldn't watch this.' And I came back and watched *Clerks* and fell off the chair laughing."

"I watched the film three times," Pierson continues "and I'm laughing harder and harder each time. Sometimes, if you watch a movie repeatedly, you see nothing but the dead spots. But with *Clerks* I had exactly the opposite experience. It was effortless to let the dead spots just fly by."

Still, Pierson was reluctant to jump back into the repping game unless *Clerks* and its makers met three very important criteria. The first was that Pierson had to like the film; the second was that he had to believe it was marketable; and third, he had to feel as though he could work with the team who made the film.

On the first criterion, there was no problem; Pierson loved *Clerks*. On the second, he had reason to hope. "I've been involved with people since the get-go who are fantastic self-promoters, and I think Spike is the first example of this. He was a fantastic salesman for his work, with a really good back-story, even before his first feature."

Rob Weiss, another of Pierson's clients, was also a brilliant self-promoter. However, unlike Spike Lee or Kevin Smith, his film work was hardly exemplary, and his relationship with Pierson was a rocky one. After his one and only film as a director, *Amongst Friends*, ballooned from a $250,000 to a $600,000 budget, Weiss faded quickly, despite media reports that, like the gangsters of his flick, he may or may not have been involved in criminal activity.

"Weiss tried hard," Pierson offers another example. "He was already post-modern about that sort of thing. He was just desperate to make a name for himself and be a tough guy...and maybe he killed somebody and maybe he didn't. Instead of making a movie like *Mean Streets*, it's like he *was* a character from *Mean Streets*. But that was so self-conscious and so annoying and so counterproductive in the end that it made me re-consider how essential it was for people to have a great, self-promoting back-story."

And Kevin Smith, the talent who had earned his keep in convenience stores before writing his ode to them?

"His story was great," Pierson affirms. "He did have this great self-promotion, and a couldn't-be-better-if-you-made-it-up-in-thin-air back-story."

Even better, Pierson liked him. "He's a fantastic person, one of my favorite people I ever met in my life. You couldn't find a more upstanding citizen, or just a great human being."

He felt the same way about Mosier. "Kevin doesn't really need a stabilizing force, because he's a very stable person on his own, but everything is that much more solid and rooted because Scott doesn't get worked up in a tizzy about things. He's just extremely confident."

But, just because its behind-the-scenes talents had admirable character traits, that didn't mean selling *Clerks*, a low-budget, black-and-white film with no recognizable actors, was going to be an easy proposition.

"Pierson told Kevin he wasn't sure what he could do with *Clerks*," Mosier remembers. "He liked it, but wasn't sure how to sell it. But he got us a lawyer, John Sloss."

Even more dramatically, John Pierson hooked Kevin Smith up with C.A.A. (Creative Artists Agency)[5] and agent Tory Metzger. Almost immediately, even before *Clerks* had gone to the Sundance Film Festival, Kevin Smith was attending pitch meetings in Hollywood for his next writing assignment. He was offered the opportunity to script a number of bizarre projects, including a comedy called *Beer Money* and a Michael Jackson "vehicle" entitled *Hot Rod*, which saw the gloved one blessed with the ability to transform into a super car and befriend children in need.

There was also talk of a second project related to *Clerks*, to be called *Busing*. Basically, it was *Clerks* in a restaurant.[6]

"I rolled out to L.A. with Kevin to these strange meetings where people were pitching him weird scripts," Mosier describes. "I just sat there thinking that it was all intensely stupid. But we were able to go to all the studio lots, like 20th Century Fox, and even if nothing happened, it was fun."

The View Askew brain trust: Director Kevin Smith
and producer Scott Mosier, circa *Clerks* (1994).

An askew view: A publicity still of the *Clerks*
"dramatis personae." From left to right: Brian
O'Halloran, Kevin Smith, Marilyn Ghigliotti, Lisa
Spoonauer, and Jeff Anderson.

"I'm not even supposed to be here today!" A close look at *Clerks*'s put-upon protagonists, Dane Hicks (O'Halloran) and Randal Graves (Anderson).

The sting of friendship (and F.D.S.): Dante (O'Halloran) and Randal (Anderson) reconcile a messy food (and feminine product) fight in the denouement of *Clerks*.

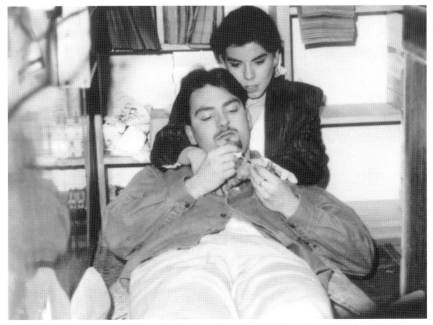

"A generalization about broads…" Dante (O'Halloran) paints Veronica's (Ghigliotti) fingernails as the couple debates their sexual histories.

Stoners Jay (Jason Mewes) and Silent Bob (Kevin Smith) enjoy their regular digs in front of the Quick Stop.

No more worlds to conquer... Brodie (Jason Lee) and Quint (Jeremy London) survey the breadth of their shopping domain in *Mallrats* (1995).

Shannen Doherty strikes a pose (and attitude...).

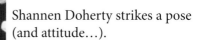

Breaking up is hard to do: Renee (Doherty) and Brodie (Lee) discuss the division of their mutual assets.

Silent Bob (Smith) peruses John Pierson's best selling *Spike, Mike, Slackers and Dykes* while his hetero life mate, Jay (Mewes), selects less intellectual reading material.

Feel the force flow from within. Kevin Smith directs stars Doherty and Lee on the set of *Mallrats*.

Gerbils! Gerbils! Gerbils! Quint (London) and Brodie (Lee) catch up with Jay (Mewes) and Silent Bob (Smith) in front of the pet store.

"There is no Easter Bunny!!!!" Willem (Ethan Suplee) rages against shopping children.

Just cross your eyes. Mallrats Quint (London), Willem (Suplee), and Brodie (Lee) search for the secret image in a kiosk poster.

Girl talk: Gwen (Joey Lauren Adams) advises Brandi (Claire Forlani) on matters of the heart in *Mallrats*.

"Where's the strangest place you've ever made whoopie?" Quint (London) and Brodie (Lee) plot their final answers in the conclusion of *Mallrats*.

Mr. Svenning (Michael Rooker; far left) watches as the troubled couples (far right) reconcile their differences.

A Mid-mall's fantasy. Foursome Brodie (Lee) and Renee (Doherty), Quint (London) and Brandi (Forlani) celebrate a quasi-Shakespearean happy ending in *Mallrats*.

Back east, John Pierson was working harder than ever to make things happen for *Clerks*. He felt strongly that Miramax would be the perfect outfit to distribute the film and had worked with them before.

Miramax Films, a company that had formed in 1979 after brothers and co-chairmen Bob and Harvey Weinstein acquired a film called *The Secret Policeman's Ball* from the Cannes Film Festival, had become known in the intervening dozen years as a house where quality films were distributed. Named after the Weinstein brothers' parents, Miriam and Max, Miramax distributed the controversial documentary *The Thin Blue Line*, as well as Steven Soderbergh's first film, *Sex, Lies, and Videotape*. More recently, it had distributed the scandalous Madonna documentary *Truth or Dare*, and the nearly X-rated *The Cook, The Thief, His Wife and Her Lover*, directed by Peter Greenaway.

In 1993, Miramax was purchased by Disney, but the Weinsteins' dedication to the distribution of high quality films continued. In its many years in business, Miramax movies such as *Good Will Hunting*, *Pulp Fiction*, *The Crying Game*, *Wings of the Dove*, *Shakespeare in Love*, and *Life is Beautiful* earned more than three dozen Academy Awards, and more than 130 nominations. Its chairmen, Bob and Harvey Weinstein, have long been reputed to be among the most powerful and influential men in Hollywood.

"Miramax and I had been through the sale of *Working Girls*, *The Thin Blue Line*, and the attempted purchase of *Anna*," Pierson reports. "They were really pissed that Vestron got that one [*Anna*]. If I hadn't gone to a studio, they would have had *Roger & Me* too, which was like a week's worth of negotiating."

So it was with some confidence that Pierson helped to orchestrate a showing of *Clerks* at Miramax in mid-December of 1993 with the full support of executive Mark Tusk, an admirer of the film from Miramax. "That was the only nerve-wracking time on *Clerks* with Miramax. It didn't play out exactly like we planned."

As Pierson describes the problem, chain-smoker Harvey Weinstein didn't appreciate the anti-cigarette tone of the Chewlies Gum Rep scene and bailed out of *Clerks* after just-under-a-quarter hour.[7] "That was like, 'Oh shit,' because I thought it was a good orchestration," Pierson considers.

Miramax's failure to purchase *Clerks* near Christmas of 1993 meant one thing: the fate of Kevin Smith's first film would be decided at the Sundance Film Festival.

When *Clerks* and its filmmakers arrived in Park City, Utah for Redford's 1994 film festival, word-of-mouth about the film began to grow. The film not only won the Filmmaker's Trophy for the year, but instant popularity.

"We had four screenings at Sundance and I heard it was the first film to sell out there," O'Halloran comments. "I took a trip out to Sundance and saw people scalping tickets for it. That's when things really started to get weird for me. We had sell-out audiences, and we went to these screenings and people were just dying. Hearing an entire theater filled with laughter was great and, afterwards, people would run up and ask us for autographs."

John Pierson had just one more opportunity for Harvey Weinstein to see the picture and purchase it for Miramax. There was one last *Clerks* showing during the festival.

"That was one of those things where you set something up with your fingers crossed, and then just hope it works," Pierson explains. "You could feel the momentum for that film building throughout the week. And though Kevin isn't a big fan of [producer] Cary Woods, Cary and Mark Tusk were instrumental in making sure that Harvey was there and well-positioned in the middle of the theater for that screening, where he was both absorbing all the laughter and increasing the laughter on his own. But the pump had really been primed. Had he seen the first show, the first weekend, on the first Saturday, it would have been a really different experience."

"There was fantastic momentum in having that deal happen," Pierson further elaborates. "It led up to critic's week selection for Cannes, New Directors, and having all this focus in the international news and media, Connie Chung going to the Quick Stop, and all that stuff. It was the perfect moment for that to culminate."

But that didn't necessarily mean that things were going to work out.

"We weren't the hot property of the festival," Mosier notes with modesty. "There weren't a dozen people bidding on us. A lot of people didn't know what to do with a foul-mouthed, black-and-white grungy movie."

But at a restaurant called the Eating Establishment, over an after-dinner plate of potato skins, Harvey Weinstein [brother Bob did not attend Sundance that year], Miramax executive David Linde, and Mark Tusk sat down at a table with John Pierson, Kevin Smith, and Scott Mosier. In short order, a deal was cut to buy *Clerks* and then distribute it.

"Harvey had those potato skins, and wanted to buy the movie," Pierson reports. "We agreed on the outline, and he left, and David and I wrote it up."

Miramax paid $227,000 to purchase *Clerks* outright. The deal included a theatrical release of the film, and the distribution agreement began a long-standing relationship between View Askew and Miramax.

Pierson thinks the deal was a matter of serendipitous timing. "It was probably the last time in their [Miramax] corporate history that they ever would have gotten involved with that kind of film. So there does seem to be something resembling fate involved in things coming together at that moment."

"It was pretty amazing," Mosier acknowledges. "That was the beginning of this whole ride that started in 1994."

At Cannes 1994, the ride accelerated. *Clerks* garnered an International Critics Week Prize. It was also nominated for three Independent Spirit Awards, including Best First Picture, Best Debut Performance (for Jeff Anderson), and First Screenplay (Kevin Smith).

But with a major release slated for fall of 1994, there was still much work to be completed on *Clerks*. Fifteen minutes were cut from the film between its Sundance showing and its theatrical run. Gone for good was that pesky ending that saw Dante killed in the line of counter duty.

"It was a key moment for me after watching the film three times, when I realized it didn't have to end in a blood bath," reports Pierson. "Crossing that bridge was just a complete light bulb going off."

When Pierson suggested trimming the ending, removing Dante's death, Smith was receptive. "He was immediately prepared to do it," Pierson remembers. "As he's said, that was his reach for greater meaning. That was his *Do the Right Thing* ending."

"And frankly, there's still about ten percent of his audience—the smarter, educated, intellectual, existential crowd—who think that *Clerks* should have had that original ending. But they're dead fucking wrong," Pierson asserts. "I appreciate the fact there is always going to be a certain number of people who go for purity. But I thought that the ending was tagged on. It wasn't like the last gasp of existential horror. I think Kevin knew that, and I think that's why it was easy to give away. I just happened to say it first, but I know Larry Kardish at the Museum of Modern Art, who is the main proponent of New Directors, New Films, felt a huge relief when he knew the end was going. You can't fall in love with these characters and then kill them."

So, to Brian O'Halloran's relief, Dante lived, and *Clerks* rolled on. Clever trailers of the film were run before screenings of Quentin Tarantino's *Pulp*

Fiction, and Kevin Smith shot a music video for *Clerks* for $15,000. He walked the band Soul Asylum through a rooftop hockey game, mirroring the film's events. The resulting video, "You Can't Even Tell," was the first opportunity for fans to see the Quick Stop, Randal, Dante, Jay, and Silent Bob in color.

Other tunes were added to the film including the very funny "Chewbacca" by Supernova (played, appropriately, during Randal and Dante's debate about *Return of the Jedi*) and "Got Me Wrong" by Alice in Chains.

It was during this period of hard work that Smith and the View Askew people realized that their $227,000 check from Miramax would not necessarily make the filmmakers rich men. "Once the movie got bought at Sundance, Kevin came back and laid out all his credit card bills and saw what it was, had things not worked out," Mosier remembers. "The price of the film had grown from interest to over $30,000."

And there were bills yet to be settled. "A hundred thousand went to finish the movie," Mosier tabulates, "and around $34,000 went to paying off the credit card debt. So essentially you were talking about $93,000 back, but then Kevin immediately paid all the actors and crew, and I got a paycheck out of that. By the time I was done living without a job for over a year, I just basically broke even. I had enough money to pay down my debt, but I still had to get a job at the Banana Republic as a stock room guy. I had to make money, because there really wasn't much left after it all got divided up."

Sometimes Pierson will occasionally second-guess the Miramax deal. "The issue I have, years later, is that they've been slow to pay the overages on that film, and it's made a ton of money over time. And I'm sitting here thinking, 'It's great that we got $227,000 then, but maybe we should have gotten $527,000.' It's one of those things that you turn over in your head."

Yet, as Mosier is quick to point out, *Clerks* was a worthy investment. "It was scary, but to put it in context, how much is NYU a year? *Clerks* was a kind of school for all of us, and at the end of the day we made a product that gave us careers."

With the theatrical release of *Clerks* approaching, Kevin Smith and his friends must have believed the gods were favoring their freshman effort, but a controversy soon occurred that would, in some ways, set the tone for Smith's career.

Before *Clerks* was released, it was submitted to the Motion Picture Association of America for a rating. Though the film featured neither violence nor sex, the M.P.A.A. slapped it with an NC-17 rating, the kiss of death from a marketing standpoint. Few theaters are willing to play an NC-17 feature, and even fewer newspapers are willing to advertise them.

The chairman of the Motion Picture Association of America, Jack Valenti, went so far to declare, in relation to *Clerks*:

> *There are millions of Americans who become hysterical about the kind of bad language that may be* de rigueur *around dinner tables in the East Side of Manhattan. But in the cities and villages and towns across this free and loving land, it's not that way at all.*[8]

In response to the unexpected broadside, Miramax tapped famed defense attorney Alan Dershowitz to appeal the M.P.A.A.'s decision, though the O.J. lawyer didn't actually end up arguing the case in court. But the decision was eventually reversed, and *Clerks* was awarded an R rating in time for its October 19, 1994 opening in the Big Apple. In late 2001, a similar battle with the M.P.A.A. was waged over the content of *Jay and Silent Bob Strike Back*, Smith's fifth film.

Ironically, the colorfully worded script of *Clerks* was also something of a concern for some of the film's stars. "My initial perception was, 'My God the language!'" O'Halloran relates. "But it was so funny!"

In particular, Jeff Anderson remembers shooting the scene wherein Randal orders a gaggle of pornographic videotapes (such as *Men Alone: The KY Connection*) from a distributor as one instance of the film's racy nature. "We were filming *Clerks*, and it's a foul-mouthed little movie. I didn't think anybody was going to see it beyond a videotape that I would throw in at parties. But I did know that at some point my parents would want to see it. And I think, 'My mother can't hear all this!'"

"So we're doing the scene where I order the videotapes on the phone. I had read it in the script, and was just dreading it. And when we got to it, there were these titles written down on a piece of paper. We ran a rehearsal and I asked Kevin if it was really necessary to read all those titles. I thought you'd get the picture after three or four, and asked if we could tone it down a little, since my mother was going to watch this.

"Kevin said, 'Absolutely, I understand.' So I handed him the piece of paper, and people were fixing the lighting and we got ready to shoot. Kevin called action and as he handed the paper back to me, I saw he had added four titles to it. So I'm reading this list and I think: 'Kevin, you bastard!'"

"When we went to the premiere," Anderson continues, "my parents were with me. *Entertainment Tonight* was following me around for the day and I thought this would be the perfect opportunity to let my parents see the movie because they were all wrapped up in what was going on and I didn't even think they'd notice the film. I sat next to my mom until that scene, and when it started, I got up and left the theater. But she never called me on it. She said I was acting, and I hadn't written it, so it was okay.

"Well, cut to Vulgarthon [a View Askew convention] a few years later and my mom comes to see a showing of my movie, *Now You Know*. There's an interesting scene of a transvestite with a bottle up his ass—and I *did* write that movie!"

After *Clerks* premiered, the reviews rolled in and nobody seemed much bothered by the language that had so vexed Jack Valenti. In fact, the movie garnered raves from every media outlet in the States. Carrie Rickey noted that the film was "extremely raw and extremely funny."[9] *Newsweek*'s David Ansen enthused that Smith's "chatty, affectionate salute to brainy guys in brainless jobs exhibits a deadpan mastery of verbal timing any veteran director might envy,"[10] and *The New York Times*' Janet Maslin called *Clerks* an "exuberant display of film-student ingenuity.[11]

Some critics even went so far as to indicate the film's profanity was a real plus. Jeff Gordinier for *Entertainment Weekly* noted that "the strategic use of a raunchy rant gives an artist a kind of literary panache" and compared Smith to Henry Miller.[12]

After *Clerks'* successful release, it was time to take it around the world. "We toured with *Clerks* forever," Mosier remembers. "Miramax just sent us all over the place. The Sundance Institute took five award winners over to Tokyo and all the filmmakers had screenings. It was us and David O'Russell from *Spanking the Monkey*. Victor Nunez [director of *Ruby in Paradise* and *Ulee's Gold*] was there. Laura San Giacomo [of *Nina Takes a Lover*] was there. David [Siegel] and Scott [McGhee] from *Suture* and *The Deep End* came along.

"We had a great time and the Japanese people sort of thought we were a sensation. We were a cool film, I think. We represented youthful America, and there's such a large youth culture in Japan that embraced us. We were on TV, and it was a blast. Then we went to France and Munich and toured the States forever."

It was a great time for the cast and crew of *Clerks*, basking in critical praise and pop culture popularity. But the canny Smith understood it would not always be so. In a bit of prophetic self-examination, he noted that expectations were so low on his first film that "I don't think any movie I'll ever make will be as well-reviewed as *Clerks*."[13]

Still, Kevin Smith, Scott Mosier, and a team of dedicated filmmakers had beaten the system. They created a brilliant first movie on a shoestring budget, saw it distributed by prestigious Miramax, and then won the hearts of audiences across America. And, in another ironic bit of good news, *Clerks*, by grossing some $2.5 million by January of 1995, became the highest-grossing movie of 1994 on a pure percentage basis.[14]

"Having said all that," Pierson contemplates, "you can easily ask the question, and Kevin and I often talk about this, if Miramax hadn't bought the film immediately after that screening, what would have happened? I can tell you, of all the serious, major players, nobody was going to buy the film right then. That doesn't mean Kevin Smith doesn't happen or that *Clerks* goes away, because it was already headed to New Directors, and it was already going to be reviewed in *The New York Times*. Assuming that Janet Maslin reviewed the film the way she reviewed the film, I don't think there was any doubt that one of the holdback companies from earlier, or even Miramax, would have come back knocking."

Summing up the *Clerks* experience, Scott Mosier reports that "it was the most fun ever. There were some testy moments [shooting] when people were tired or when someone was hanging out while the rest of us were working, but overall it was the best experience ever. All we could do is ask ourselves if the movie was making us laugh, and it was. We were just in the clouds, having fun, and didn't know enough to be scared."

THE GRUNGE GODOT?

Kevin Smith is usually the first person to tell interviewers that his films are nothing but "dick and fart jokes," but anybody who watches his films with an observant eye understands that his work speaks to much more than body function humor. Smith is a self-deprecating and unpretentious fellow, so you're not likely to find him uttering whispered truths about *mise-en-scène*, post-modernism, Pirandello, Biblical interpretations, or other heavy subjects. Nonetheless, his films concern many weighty human and existential dilemmas. What makes Smith so unusual and worthwhile a voice is that he tackles these subjects in a non-academic, clever way instead of a remote, didactic one.

Without too much difficulty, it is possible to view *Clerks* as a work of art more sophisticated than a foul-mouthed paean to the travails of minimum wage workers. For instance, Margot Hornblower dubbed Kevin Smith's film The Grunge Godot" in *Time*.[15]

Those among us who survived drama classes in college remember Godot, *Waiting for Godot* actually, a play by Samuel Beckett about the utter meaningless of life. The play was set in a strange locale (a long stretch of barren road) and it involved two fellows named Vladimir and Estragon. These odd folk were waiting for the arrival of the enigmatic "Godot," who many scholars believe represented God.

The following review does a good job of expressing the feelings the play evoked in many audiences:

> *Many spectators complained that the play made no sense. It lacked physical action, and the plot didn't seem to tie the events together. The mixture of philosophy, Biblical references, broad comedy and nonsense dialogue confused many people.*[16]

Interestingly, the above-noted clip might also adequately serve as a review of *Clerks*. There's virtually no physical action dramatized in the film (but for a food fight and a hockey game) and most of Dante and Randal's adventures are merely discussed, not dramatized (such as Randal's casket tipping incident at Julie Dwyer's funeral).

Does the plot tie the events of the film together? Perhaps, but it also ends with many questions left unanswered. What will become of Dante's traumatized lady-love, Caitlin Bree? Or Veronica? Will Dante learn to "shit or get off the pot?" Will he return to school, or stay in a dead-end job because he is afraid of change? None of these issues are resolved, as they would be, for example in a comedy by Shakespeare.

Additionally, *Clerks* mixes philosophy (including Randal's theory of a ruling class, his debate with Dante about free will versus personal responsibility, and whether title dictates behavior, or vice versa), broad comedy (the Egg Man, the food fight) and, yes, even nonsense dialogue ("Did he say 'making fuck'?").

And then there's Vladimir and Estragon, the two tramps living out their meaningless existence. In *Chasing Amy*'s opening moments, Smith compares Jay and Silent Bob's iconic alter egos Bluntman and Chronic to these literary characters. Yet for the purpose of *Clerks*, the Godot duo is more likely represented by Dante and Randal, two characters who don't really know or understand what they are waiting for. Both young men are smart, thoughtful, and teeming with potential, yet both choose to stay put on their intellectually barren stretch of road, the Quick Stop and R.S.T. Video store. They could attend college, seek better employment, or even embrace traditional cultural and romantic ideals like a committed relationship. Yet they don't. Instead, they dwell in a world of absurd minutiae, re-hashing and over-thinking simplistic movies like *Return of the Jedi*.

On a much less literary level, *Clerks* also reflects the time in which it was created, the early 1990s. America had just come out of a deep recession in 1992, and Generation X was graduating from school to discover there were not so many great job opportunities out there. After the yuppie prosperity of the 1980s, this new generation learned the hard way in the era of down-sizing that it might be America's first to make less money and be less successful than its predecessors.

This realization led to a kind of disenfranchisement among an overeducated group of youngsters who, thanks to the benefits of a liberal arts education, had enough perspective to understand their dilemma. Their English degrees provided them the knowledge to quote Shakespeare, but their job opportunities were often limited to the question, "Do you want fries with that?" In essence, Gen Xers were educated enough to bemoan their situation. That equation is clearly the zeitgeist of *Clerks*.

"I hate this fucking place," Dante notes helplessly, early in *Clerks*, and Veronica replies that he should be going to school because he has "so much potential that's going to waste in this pit."

But Dante does nothing.

Smith escaped that minimum wage trap by sheer ingenuity and determination, but *Clerks* is a cautionary tale about bright people who aren't so lucky and aren't so self-motivated. It would probably be over-the-top to call *Clerks* "the wake-up call" for a generation, but it remains the film that best exemplifies the "deflated" feeling of this specific generation as it left school in the early 90s and became embittered by the lack of opportunity. And in his examination of this time and feeling, Smith is surprisingly even-handed. He doesn't let the generation off the hook. He sees these young adults, at least to a certain extent, as their own worst enemies.

"Go ahead, keep cracking wise," a customer (#812, Wynarski) warns Dante. "That's why you're jockeying a register in some fucking local convenience store instead of working on a steady job."

That line better exemplifies Gen Xers than just about any dialogue in the film. These young people are smart and witty, but they turn that intelligence to whining and sarcasm rather than improving their lot. That many Gen Xers are depicted smoking in the film is another curiosity that speaks to the contradictions of these characters. They are better educated than any previous generation about the hazards of cigarettes, and yet they continue to smoke. What's that about? Why is there such a self-destructive impulse among this generation?

David Fincher's 1999 *Fight Club* is one of the few films other than *Clerks* that looks at this phenomenon and it draws much the same conclusion. Gen Xers are reluctant to assimilate into the American mainstream society because it seems to have failed them—repeatedly. Politics are corrupt, science is fucked, and nobody is taking care of the environment. A generation that grew up after Watergate and Vietnam, that witnessed the accident at Chernobyl and the destruction of the space shuttle Challenger, would rather comment sarcastically about society's failings than embrace that society. *Fight Club* expressed this idea in terms of violence, *Clerks* does so in terms of ennui and cynicism.

"When it comes down to it, I think *Clerks* represents a moment in this generation when we didn't know what we wanted to do," O'Halloran says shedding light on the meaning behind the film. "We just wanted to live and get by, without really having any direction, yet we still had to deal with regular, every day jobs, which didn't necessarily sit well. Dante is definitely afraid to take a chance, to go beyond what makes him comfortable. That whole monologue that Jeff has after the fight scene says it so perfectly. That's the whole point of the film, right there."

The black-and-white, documentary look of *Clerks* strongly enhances the film's sense of crushing authenticity. As more than one critic noted, audiences might as well be watching these events unfold on a convenience store security camera. It seems real, not like some product from the dream factory.

Perhaps more to the point, Kevin Smith stages *Clerks* almost like a theatrical play. Klein's camera often shoots from a "head on" perspective in scenes at the counter, and even at the exterior of the Quick Stop and R.S.T. Video Store. Rarely does the audience see this scenery from an "askew" angle and this dedication to a "straight" theatrical dimension makes the settings appear almost like the sets of a play.

Ultimately, this approach works well for the film, since it is the dialogue and characterization, not necessarily the sets that are important. It's surprising that no one has yet adapted *Clerks* to the Broadway stage. It's a natural, with so few central characters and limited settings.

But what makes *Clerks* so damned funny? In the final analysis, it isn't merely the rapid-fire, brilliantly crafted dialogue; it is Kevin Smith's adherence to a long-standing comedic film tradition. Specifically, he often holds the camera back, limiting it frequently to long shots, medium shots, and two shots. There are few outright close-ups in the film, and that decision makes abundant sense in a comedy. The old rule about comedy is that audience identification must be limited. If a fellow slips on a banana peel, the audience doesn't want to see it in close-up, because that angle will foster identification with the character's pain when he hits the pavement.

But pull the camera back a bit, and the same tumble is considered funny, because the audience has sufficient distance from the pain. The camera in *Clerks* is distinctly removed from much of the action, so the audience can laugh at Dante and Randal, Jay and Silent Bob, and the rest of the *dramatis personae* without necessarily feeling sorry for them. Imagine how disturbing it might have been to see Caitlin Bree, reacting in horrified close-up, to the fact that she had just copulated with a corpse. It wouldn't be funny; it would be sickening and disturbing. By contrast, imagine how David Lynch or Wes Craven might stage such a sequence.

But in *Clerks*, the scene is shot from far enough back that it becomes intensely humorous, despite the character's obvious dismay. Bracketed inside the frame by a disturbed Dante on the left and an unaffected Randal on the right, Caitlin's plight is represented by three perspectives, not just the victim's, and identification is lessened.

People might complain the movie appears cheap, or lacks visual panache, but it seems that Smith and Klein hit on a style that is both efficient and artful. For instance, the lack of many cuts and the inclusion of long dialogue sequences also enhance the theatrical aspects of *Clerks* and generate a real sense of camaraderie among the characters, a factor that would have been sacrificed if there had been more use of coverage. As these scenes play now, they boast a distinctive rhythm and pacing, and cutting into that "space" would have only sacrificed those qualities.

In the end, it is always up to the individual viewer to judge a film. One can look at *Clerks* as a "grunge Godot," a reflection of its unique historical context, as a well-shot, almost theatrical comedy, or merely a very funny film that serves as a time capsule of the early 1990s.

"Bob Hawk can write that it's a wail of ennui, and I'm glad that was in the catalog, and maybe it helped give *Clerks* a greater weight," Pierson notes. "It's great there's subtext there, but to me, the reason it's successful is that it's funny."

For Scott Mosier, the appeal of *Clerks* is also simpler than any film theory: "My perception of that movie is that it's about friends. It was always about friends. A lot of it is sketch comedy, but in the end it does become a meditation about friendship, about these two guys who were both in that place and time where they didn't know what would happen, if they would commit to something bigger, to growing up. In that moment when Dante and Randal are sweeping up together, nobody's doing any talking for the first time, and that's a sign of friendship. They can just hang out and be friends."

ASKEW VIEWS

BERSERKER!: The character of Olaf, a Russian "metal head" who sings "Berserker" for the band Fucking Yankee Blue Jeans (and who is immortalized on Jay's T-shirt in *Jay and Silent Bob Strike Back*), is based on a character improvised by Walt Flanagan.

"Kevin, Bryan Johnson, Ed Hapstak and I were at the mall in Jersey and there was this mannequin in J.C. Penny that had this really strange wig on it," Flanagan explains. "So I snagged it and put it on, but it looked so odd because I was wearing it backwards, and the bangs were like halfway above my head.

"So we walked into this store and ran into these two seventeen or eighteen year-old girls, and the guys were saying that I was Russian and couldn't speak English, but wanted to be a rock star. The girls bought it hook, line, and sinker. I was just trying to keep a straight face because I didn't even know what a Russian accent should sound like. I'd just grunt and groan, and they bought every minute of it."

Still, that didn't mean Flanagan was ready to play Olaf in the movie. "My initial response was that I didn't want to do it. I was uncomfortable singing in front of people even though Kevin wanted me to play Olaf. I said no because I was just too self-conscious."

INFIRMITY: Brian O'Halloran fell ill during the shooting of *Clerks*, as he recalls. "I think it was the last five days of shooting, so we'd done the majority of the principal shooting, and I had this bad head cold. I think it was only apparent in one scene. After Caitlin leaves, Dante is leaning against the counter with Randal next him, and I think you can hear me sniffling and talking at the same time. I was miserable, but you can't say 'Hey, stop,' because they're renting this camera, and time is literally money."

WHERE'S STEVE-DAVE?: A familiar face missing from *Clerks* is *Vulgar* director Bryan Johnson, the actor who plays Steve-Dave in *Mallrats*, *Chasing Amy*, *Dogma*, and *Jay and Silent Bob Strike Back*.

"When Kevin came back from film school, we had a falling out," Bryan Johnson recalls. "Many different circumstances led to it, and we were both being hard-headed. That's why I wasn't in *Clerks*."

But out of the blue, things changed. "Kevin went off and made *Clerks*, and then went to this self-help seminar called The Forum that encourages you to expand your horizons and see things that maybe you hadn't seen before; to build yourself up as a person. One of his tasks was to call someone who he hadn't spoken with in a long time, and didn't really want to talk to. I guess I fit the bill.

"So I was at home watching TV, the phone rang and I answered it. He said, 'Bryan Johnson?' I said, 'Kevin Smith?' And my initial thought was that Kevin must really be in a lot of trouble if I'm the only person he can turn to. But then he explained to me what he was doing, the idea of The Forum. Fences were mended and we shot the Soul Asylum video [for *Clerks*] some time that fall." Ironically, the character in that video was not Steve-Dave, according to Johnson. "I think he was just hockey player #3."

YOU CAN SMELL IT: The sickly respiratory organ a Chewlies Gum representative throws on the Quick Stop counter isn't actually a lung at all. "I think we used a calf's brain or tripe," O'Halloran recollects. "It was horrible. They ground in cigarette butts and all sorts of stuff to make it look nasty. It was there on the counter for probably a good hour-and-a-half by the time we got the coverage we needed. It smelled really bad."

SYNTAX: Kevin Smith often calls his movies a collection of dick and fart jokes, but John Pierson, for one, doesn't like the descriptor.

"I hate that he sums it up that way. I know it works as shorthand, but you'll never hear me use it. One of the reasons I hate it is that there aren't that many fart jokes. I know it's a category of humor. There's a huge number of dick jokes but not that many fart jokes. Even the stink-palm isn't a really a fart joke. It's a hand in your ass joke. There are more anal sex jokes than fart jokes.

"I've been in rooms where he's said that so many times, and people laugh. Kevin is a modest person, but on the other hand, he knows he has talent. So it isn't false modesty, but it's not like he's naive. The shorthand really works for him when he's trying to be humble."

CONTINUITY: Rick Derris (portrayed by Ernie O'Donnell in *Clerks*) is a character referred to in *Chasing Amy*. The girl who dies in the pool, Julie Dwyer, motivates much of the action in *Mallrats*, and if one listens closely, even Alyssa Jones, the character portrayed by Joey Lauren Adams in *Chasing Amy*, is mentioned by name in the scene with Rick Derris.

THE ULTIMATE NUMBER: The number 37 is one that recurs in the films of Kevin Smith. In *Clerks*, it is the number of men on whom Veronica has performed oral sex. The number re-surfaces twice in *Jay and Silent Bob Strike Back* and twice in *Chasing Amy*.

HOSANNAS: *Clerks* is dedicated to three giants in the history of independent films: John Cassavetes, Jim Jarmusch, and Spike Lee.

KEVIN SMITH ON *CLERKS*

"*Clerks* was born out of working for three years in that fucking store... Things like the Milk-Maid and the Egg-Man came directly from register-jockeying experience, as does the spirit of most of the discussions Dante and Randal share. When you're bored...you begin talking about some inane and merit-less shit, just to get you through the day."[17]

3

Mallrats (1995)

A LAUNDRY LIST OF COMPLAINTS

They're not there to shop.
They're not there to work.
They're just there.

Cast and Crew

UNIVERSAL STUDIOS AND GRAMERCY PICTURES PRESENT AN ALPHAVILLE PRODUCTION, IN ASSOCIATION WITH VIEW ASKEW PRODUCTIONS

Written and directed by: Kevin Smith
Produced by: Sean Daniel, James Jacks, and Scott Mosier
Cinematography by: David Klein
Edited by: Paul Dixon
Music: Ira Newborn
Line Producer: Laura Greenlee
Production Designer: Dina Lipton
Casting: Don Phillips
Costume Designer: Dana Allyson
M.P.A.A. Rating: R
Running Time: 94 minutes

Starring

Jeremy London | *T.S. Quint*
Jason Lee | *Brodie*

Shannon Doherty | *Renee Mosier*
Claire Forlani | *Brandi Svenning*
Ben Affleck | *Shannon Hamilton*
Joey Lauren Adams | *Gwen Taylor*
Renée Humphrey| *Tricia Jones*
Jason Mewes | *Jay*
Kevin Smith | *Silent Bob*
Ethan Suplee | *Willam Black*
Stan Lee | *Himself*
Priscilla Barnes | *Ivana*
Michael Rooker | *Mr. Jared Svenning*
Brian O'Halloran | *Gil Hicks*
Bryan Johnson | *Steve-Dave*
Walt Flanagan | *Fanboy*

THE STORY SO FAR...

DUMPED BY THEIR RESPECTIVE GIRLFRIENDS, the stolid T.S. Quint and his buddy, Brodie drown their sorrows by visiting the local mall. There, they run into a variety of colorful patrons, including rage-aholic Willam Black, a fifteen year-old sex-researcher "Trish the Dish," obnoxious comic book fans Steve-Dave and Fanboy, and stoner duo, Jay and Silent Bob.

When T.S. learns that his girlfriend, Brandi Svenning, is appearing on a game show called Truth or Date at the mall that very night, because her Dad is the producer, he vows to stop the program. But Brodie has problems of his own. His girlfriend, Renee, is courting Shannon Hamilton, the "date-rapist" manager of a store called Fashionable Male.

Evading mall security with the help of Jay and Silent Bob, Brodie, and Quint set out to reclaim their girlfriends and bring down Mr. Svenning's game show. They use every weapon at their disposal including a malodorous weapon Brodie calls "the stink-palm."

Before the night is over, romantic relationships are restored, Gil Hicks (Dante's cousin and a game show contestant) is humiliated on stage, Svenning's show is in shambles, Brodie has met his hero, comic book legend Stan Lee, and Mr. Svenning continues to suffer the debilitating effects of Brodie's nefarious stink-palm.

SILENT BOB'S WORDS OF WISDOM

"Adventure? Excitement? A Jedi craves not these things!"

THE STORY BEHIND THE MOVIE

In 1995, mere months after *Clerks* was released to critical raves and financial success, director Kevin Smith and his View Askew team resurrected slacker anti-heroes Jay and Silent Bob for a bigger budgeted ($6.1 million), Universal Studio-financed sequel. *Mallrats*, the second movement in what Smith soon announced would become the "New Jersey Trilogy," was a more colorful, more mainstream, action-packed romp than its black-and-white predecessor.

Although the end credits of *Clerk*—in James Bond style—announced that Jay and Silent Bob would return in a movie called *Dogma*, the two Jersey slackers were to take a trip to the mall first. And director Kevin Smith was to take a detour into the morass of studio politics and critical expectations. The result was a film that made little money, satisfied few critics, and even prompted a public apology (actually a joke) from Smith but then went on to become an unqualified, monster hit on the DVD and home video markets.

The idea to write and direct *Mallrats* actually came to Smith following the showing of *Clerks* at the Sundance film festival in Utah. There, he and Scott Mosier were introduced to producer James Jacks (late of another cult hit, *Tremors*, and eventually producer of *The Mummy* and *The Mummy Returns*).

Jacks liked *Clerks* and thought there was an opportunity to repeat the same material, essentially as a big "A-list" picture that dramatized all (or most of) the wacky adventures which Randal and Dante only talked about in the low budget film.

"We met Jim Jacks at the closing ceremonies of Sundance," reports Scott Mosier, "and he entertained the idea of remaking *Clerks* in color. He asked us what we wanted to do next, and Kevin came up with the idea for *Mallrats*. Then we went to Los Angeles in April [1994] to pitch it. So before *Clerks* ever came out, based on our meeting with Jim Jacks, we generated our second project. By the time *Clerks* was playing in October, we were already in development on *Mallrats*."

With *Mallrats* on the boards, much of the View Askew team reunited. Mosier was producing, Klein was behind the camera, Smith was writing and directing, O'Halloran was playing a supporting role as a different Hicks and

Smith's friends Vincent Pereira, Walt Flanagan, and Bryan Johnson planned to go to Minnesota (where the film was to be lensed) to work as production assistants.

With his team ready and a new script he'd fashioned in sixty days, Smith set out to create a mainstream comedy that paid homage to the teen films of the 1970s and 80s. Those were films Smith had admired growing up; from John Landis's *Animal House* to the works of John Hughes, such as *Sixteen Candles*.

As for Jacks and Universal Studios, there was a slightly different model that was considered worthy of emulation, and *Mallrats* quickly became dubbed a "smart *Porky's*." Still, everyone agreed on one thing: the film would be an R-rated youth comedy.

But developing a studio film with a budget of $6.1 million was a drastically different ball game for View Askew, much different from shooting *Clerks* for roughly $27,000.

As Scott Mosier succinctly puts it: "Producing *Clerks* meant nothing. A lot of the stuff I did on *Clerks* I no longer had to do. On *Mallrats*, I had to learn the job all over again, and that meant being more of an overseer. On *Clerks*, I made the calls and rented the equipment, and suddenly I didn't do that anymore. My role was to be a real producer and I had to learn how to do that. I was a little overwhelmed."

Though Smith and Mosier both believed they could make *Mallrats* for an amount significantly cheaper than their allotted budget, they quickly learned that cheap was not necessarily the name of the game in Hollywood.

"Once you enter the process of making a movie at a certain level, there's a whole world of things that are dictated to you because you have six million to spend," Mosier explains. "You have to make a union deal. You have to hire a certain amount of drivers. You need to have a certain number of trucks. Then technical people come in and tell you that they need this, that and the other thing. You have to attack it all from a different place.

"On *Clerks*, all we could afford were three lights. On *Mallrats*, if you wanted to light an entire mall, you couldn't fucking use three lights. And you couldn't call up these vendors and complain that you have no money and need a break. They'd very quickly remind you that you're a Universal film and that Universal has money, $6 million, in fact."

Thrown into a new world of higher budgets, Mosier knew the best thing he could do was simply soak up the landscape. "My attitude was to shut up and learn as much as I possibly could. I was Kevin's partner, the guy who was always in his corner, no matter what anyone else thought. He never had to feel like he was alone. That's really all I could do. On *Chasing Amy*, all that changed. By the end of *Mallrats* I knew things, but for the time, the biggest role I could play was to support Kevin and remind him that I was as much a neophyte as he was, and tell him that I'd back him up, no matter what.

"The line producer on *Mallrats*, Laura Greenlee, also did *Dogma* and *Jay and Silent Bob Strike Back*," relates Mosier. "I sat down with her and told her I didn't know what possible use I could be, because I didn't even know how to read a budget. I didn't even know what a fringe was [things that get added into departments, like union dues and Medicare]—I just thought it was something that hangs off a jacket. Even though I was her boss, I told her I'd do whatever she wanted me to. We got along and I learned."

While Mosier developed the skills that transformed him into what Smith has often called "an über producer," the studio had concerns about the script for *Mallrats*. Namely, Universal complained that some sequences were too raunchy, and that there was too much swearing.

"It was originally a lot more vulgar, a lot rougher," Vincent Pereira says of Smith's now-legendary first draft (which featured the oral sex scar scene that was later to be such a hit in *Chasing Amy*). "The studio reined it back and wanted more plot, more action."

"My opinion of the first draft was that it seemed more like *Clerks*," Mosier considers. "It just had that meandering quality to it, and injecting all of this plot wasn't really necessary. Our thought was that the movie should just be as funny as possible."

There was also one scene that never made it to the shooting stage, in which a body fluid (later popularized in 1998's *There's Something About Mary*) was splashed around the mall by none other than Silent Bob.

But if Smith and Mosier came out of the script meetings for *Mallrats* feeling bruised, the battles over casting must have been scarring. Of all things, the big problem was the break out star of *Clerks*, Jason Mewes. In portraying the strutting stoner named Jay, Mewes had delivered big-time laughs in *Clerks* and a high-degree of authenticity too, and that apparently scared the studio higher-ups.

Mewes was excited about the prospect of resurrecting the character. "I was so psyched about *Mallrats*. I thought, 'Ooh, another movie!' And I was going to get paid this time, because I didn't get paid for *Clerks*."

But then Mewes learned that executives at Universal had reservations about him, and his excitement quickly turned to anxiety. "I was nervous," he says, "because it would have sucked if I didn't get the part. And in a way, I knew they were right. I didn't have any training or anything. I mean, I was nervous about acting in front of a bunch of my friends for *Clerks*, and these guys were saying that this time it would be no joke. There would be forty people around me on the cast and crew."

Despite Universal's misgivings, Smith stood behind his decision to re-enlist Mewes as Jay. The studio, like the Galactic Empire of *Star Wars*, struck back. It temporarily approved Mewes as Jay, but then imposed a plethora of conditions and restraints.

First off, the studio refused to pay for Mewes's air flights, his hotel room, or even his participation during the rehearsal period of the film. Then, the studio demanded that Smith and Mosier audition other actors for the role, including Seth Green (of *Austin Powers*, *Buffy the Vampire Slayer*, and *Greg the Bunny*).

On Mewes's first day of shooting, studio suits were ready on the set to fire the young actor should they assess his performance as not passing muster.

Aware of the pressure, Kevin Smith took Mewes aside and talked to him. "He told me I had to do it," Mewes remembers. "And I decided I wasn't going to give up the chance, and told Kevin I'd get over my fear quickly. I'd gotten through the auditions, but I was still on trial. My first day, the two producers were there and they were sitting watching me. Kevin said, 'Yo, there they are; they're watching! You've got to do this. You can't be nervous. Just go with it and do your best.'"

Mewes took the advice to heart and went all out. "We did one scene, then another right after it, and when we were done, Kevin pulled me over and said the producers had left, and that they'd said I was perfect. They laughed. It felt so great."

In fact, the studio execs made an abrupt about face. They didn't just like Jason Mewes, they loved him. "They sent the dailies to the producers and everyone at Universal would sit there, watch my scenes and crack up," Mewes reports. As a result of his efforts, the film's eventual advertising campaign was built largely around the character of Jay and his new catchphrase: "snootchie bootchies."

Universal also reportedly interfered in the remainder of the casting. It wanted Ethan Hawke, Mike Myers, Chris Farley, or Adam Sandler to headline in *Mallrats*,[1] all choices that Smith and Mosier deemed inappropriate because of their age.

"At the time, I wondered if they could really be suggesting Mike Myers, but now, with perspective I realize these lists are generated without thought," Mosier explains. "The top five names might have some thought; the rest don't. You realize the studio doesn't necessarily want you to cast Mike Myers, they're just looking at anyone of a certain age group and a little popularity. At the time, we wondered what the fuck was wrong with these people. Couldn't they look at Mike Myers and see that he was too old? But distance changes your perception. Now I understand that they were just throwing an idea out, and even they probably knew it was absurd."

"Your first experience reading notes is the same way," Mosier goes on. "Some of the stuff seems ridiculous, but you learn along the way how to deal with it. The ideas the studios actually want are the ones they bring up a second time. The ones that come up just once are probably filler."

One actor who was cast in *Mallrats* was Ethan Suplee, who had worked recently on the TV series *Boy Meets World* and later went on to acclaimed performances in *American History X* and *Blow*. Suplee came into the acting profession honestly: his parents had met while performing *A Streetcar Named Desire* at Carnegie Mellon. His dad was Stanley; his mom was Stella. In later years, Suplee was further encouraged to pursue acting by a friend one grade up, actor Giovanni Ribisi. *Mallrats* was the first movie he auditioned for.

"I had an agent and he picked up a script for *Mallrats*," Suplee explains. "A friend of mine, Danny Masterson, who's on *That '70s Show*, was there while I was reading it, and told me that this guy, Kevin Smith, had a movie playing and that I had to see it.

"He took me to the art-house theater on Sunset, and the movie [*Clerks*] was hysterical. You could tell immediately it wasn't a studio film at all, yet at the same it had so much more going for it than a lot of studio films. So I went in and met the casting director. Then I had a meeting with Kevin and Scott, and I remember it was pretty cool because after I read for him, Kevin applauded. He clapped for me and I thought, 'Wow...that has to be a good sign.'"

Suplee was auditioning for the role of Willam Black, the "snowballer" of *Clerks* fame (essayed by Mosier), but the character underwent a radical re-think for *Mallrats*, becoming angrier and far less mellow. Smith has thus postulated the "Willam of Two Worlds Theory" to explain the differences. Fans of *Star Trek*'s mirror universe, or *Superman*'s nemesis and opposite, Bizarro, will grasp the reference: Willam of *Clerks* and Willam of *Mallrats* inhabit alternate realities.

But all that mattered to Suplee was that he deemed the script terrific. "I loved the shit-palming. And I loved the joke about fucking the girl in an uncomfortable place. Everything Jay did in that script was awesome."

After his audition went so well, Suplee was invited to a casting party that later become notorious.

"There was this thing called the Don Phillips Pizza Party where he [the casting director; Phillips] got together three or four choices for each part in *Mallrats*, and they had a day, like a whole Saturday, with all of these actors," Suplee sets the scene. "The casting area was just overflowing with young actors—probably thirty people—and they were all reading for the same parts, so it was crazy."

"Everybody got in at about 10:00 a.m. and it was announced that only one part was taken: the role of Willam. So I was sitting there in front of all these actors, knowing I had the part, wondering if I should go home. But they still had me read with people. It was funny, because throughout the day I would meet people and think how nice it would be to work with them, and then they wouldn't get the part."

One of the actors who made the cut that day was a pre-stardom Ben Affleck, who went on to achieve Oscar glory with his screenplay (co-authored with Matt Damon) for *Good Will Hunting*, as well as superstar status with *Armageddon*, *Pearl Harbor*, and *Changing Lanes*. Affleck would be playing the role of the nefarious Shannon Hamilton, Brodie's most powerful nemesis, and rival for girlfriend Renee's affections.

Actress Joey Lauren Adams, a native of Little Rock, Arkansas, had been promised the role of Renee in *Mallrats*, but in the end settled for the supporting role of Gwen Turner before appearing in such films as *Michael*, *Chasing Amy*, *Big Daddy*, and others.

British actress Claire Forlani (who starred with Brad Pitt and Anthony Hopkins in *Meet Joe Black* in 1998) and Shannen Doherty (late of *Beverly Hills 90210* and *Charmed*) represented female leads Brandi and Renee, respectively. Of Doherty, Smith reported that the reputed bad girl "was a dream" and that her "reputation may be unmatched . . . but people grow and change."[2]

Michael Rooker, the star of the chilling *Henry: Portrait of a Serial Killer* and *Cliffhanger*, would appear as the film's menacing adult antagonist, Mr. Svenning, after William Atherton passed on the role (to appear in *Bio-Dome*).

The two male leads, ironically, were among the hardest roles to cast. For a time, Brian O'Halloran, the star of *Clerks*, had his eye on one lead. "I did audition for *Mallrats* because I wanted to play T.S. They were holding auditions in New York with Kevin and Scott, and when I went in, Kevin pretty much told me he wanted me to play somebody else instead. I think the studio really wanted at least one "name" person in one of the lead male roles, so they brought in Jeremy."

The Jeremy that O'Halloran speaks of was Jeremy London, of the Fox network TV series, *Party of Five*. O'Halloran instead got to "once again play the straight man," Gil Hicks, a character related to the Quick Stop's Dante. But to essay that role, O'Halloran decided it was time for a makeover. "I needed a departure from Dante, because he was such a memorable character to so many people, so I went into *Mallrats* with a different look. I grew my hair long and cut off the van-dyke."

In the end, O'Halloran ended up shooting in Minnesota for the better part of eleven days, and thoroughly enjoyed his stint. "It was fun working with Jeremy and Jason [Lee] during the game show scene. We had a lot of laughs filming that, and it was just so strange and amazing going from *Clerks* for $27,000 to *Mallrats* for $6.1 million. It was a huge leap."

Casting the critical role of Brodie (a character based in part on Kevin Smith's friend, Walt Flanagan) was also a difficult task. Kevin Smith and Scott Mosier had their eye on a young skateboarder, Jason Lee, who had never worked in film before, but there was initially some resistance.

Suplee remembers the situation. "I was already friends with Jason Lee. After they told me I could go home from the casting party, I stuck around, and it was down to the wire with Jason. Everybody else was gone and we didn't think Jason was going to make the cut, but they finally pulled the trigger and announced that Jason had the part."

It was a good decision, for Jason Lee not only inhabited the role of Brodie, he became a regular and beloved contributor to View Askew films, appearing in *Drawing Flies, A Better Place, Chasing Amy, Dogma, Jay and Silent Bob Strike Back, Clerks II,* and *Cop Out.*

O'Halloran recalls that even on the set of *Mallrats*, the neophyte Lee was able to nail his scenes. "He was an absolute pleasure to work with. I understood it was his first film, and that he came from a skateboarding background, but he had it. He had such a natural, innate talent for delivering Kevin's dialogue, as well as great timing."

Not surprisingly, it wasn't long before Lee became a full-fledged star, headlining in films such as *Mumford*, *Almost Famous*, and *Big Trouble*, among others.

Making a cameo appearance in *Mallrats* was perhaps the biggest star of the bunch, comic book icon Stan Lee, the creator of *The X-Men*, *Spider-Man*, *The Incredible Hulk*, and *The Fantastic Four*. Smith is an unabashed fan of Lee's creations, and has gone on record noting that Lee is "right up there" with George Lucas and Steven Spielberg; that he is a "modern myth maker."[3]

Walt Flanagan, who runs the comic book store *Jay and Silent Bob's Secret Stash* in Red Bank, New Jersey, loved meeting the soft-spoken, beloved creator of so many Marvel classic heroes in the flesh. "He was an extremely nice guy to every single person. It didn't matter if you were a star or anybody else. He was friendly and willing to share whatever he could remember."

Though its screenplay was set in New Jersey, it was in Eden Prairie, Minnesota where principal photography on *Mallrats* commenced. The mall in Eden Prairie was largely vacant and the proprietors were open to the idea of a movie company taking advantage of the empty space. Thus production designers went to work building special, fictional shop-fronts.

Among these so-called "low rent" mall store sets were Rug Munchers (a carpet outlet store run by two very successful businesswomen) and Burning Flesh Tanning Salon (a former Arthur Treacher's Restaurant, Brodie's birthplace). Then there was Fashionable Male (where Ben Affleck's evil character, Shannon Hamilton works as a manager) and Popular Girl (where starlet Adams repeatedly disrobes, much to the delight of Silent Bob).

Replete with a food court, a cookie bakery ideal for "mid-mall snacking," a pet shop advertising "Gerbils! Gerbils! Gerbils!" and a prominent elevator where Brodie and Renee catch a passionate quickie, the mall proved to be a perfect microcosm by which Smith could satirize the aimless existence of a new group of Generation Xers.

But behind the scenes of *Mallrats*, unbeknownst to some, an interesting phenomenon was occurring. Vincent Pereira, Walt Flanagan, and Bryan Johnson had trucked out from New Jersey to work on the film as production assistants. Unfortunately, they met with some intense jealousy from other members of the crew, who quickly dubbed this trio of Jerseyites "The F.O.K.s"—Friends of Kevin.

"We had no idea what being a production assistant on a film would be like," Johnson acknowledges. "We thought it was going to be fun, that we would hang out, drink soda, and get paid. Mosier told us we'd get to carry walkie-talkies, and for me that was practically like being a movie cop! But once we got to Minnesota the job was the most hellish experience you can ever imagine. It's like you're nothing, the lowest person on the ladder. You eat after everybody else eats. You pretty much get stepped on, shut up, and spit on. For easy-going people like Walter and me it just wasn't for us.

"The first day was fifteen hours of running around being man servants to the whole crew. At the end of the day, I remember Walter just collapsing on his bed and ordering this $17 piece of chocolate cake from room service. Vincent was the only one who lasted the whole time. I lasted five days. But then I heard people refer to us as the F.O.K.s—the Friends of Kevin, and I just thought, whatever."

"I lasted a day," Flanagan admits. "I hated it. It sucked so bad. People were just yelling and screaming all the time. 'Bring coffee! Do this! Bring that!' So I decided to quit, hang out, and just do my scene. I had no idea what I was getting into."

Still, Johnson remembers that the *Mallrats* experience had some funny moments despite the fraternal rivalry. "On Walter's day as a production assistant, he was assigned to help Craft Services, the lady who provides the snacks. She constantly complained about everything, even to the point where she walked up to Kevin and said, 'See this?' and pointed to a cold sore on her mouth. She told him it was from the stress of production, but she'd only been on the set maybe a day or two.

"Anyway, Walter was her assistant, and she had an eight-foot table with tons of food on it and this coffee urn that must have held five gallons. She had to move it around a lot to accommodate the shooting, and so she takes this wagon and puts one end of the table on it, and then tries to pull it from the other end. I'm watching from about ten feet away, and almost in slow motion I see the table twist and start to fall. And there's shit everywhere! Five gallons of coffee went on the floor, mixed with potato chips and candy. I thought it was hysterical. Then maintenance came out and gave her this mop that looked like a Playskool mop, like My First Mop. It had the smallest head, and here's the Craft lady trying to clean up five gallons of coffee with it. It took her forever."

Ethan Suplee, for one, enjoyed getting into his comedic character. In particular, he found that his first scene on *Mallrats* dictated the direction that the "new" Willam would take. "If you watch *Clerks*, Willam is not an angry guy. He's kind of the opposite; he didn't really do any yelling," Suplee notes.

"But the first thing I shot on *Mallrats* was the scene with Willam exploding at the little kids."

The scene grew organically out of the shooting situation, according to Suplee. "I've got to tell you, these children were the most annoying kids you've ever met. You know; little stage kids who are always projecting and emoting and enunciating every word. And they had the biggest, phoniest smiles. It's kind of creepy, like those Little Miss Pageants they have out west somewhere. And their parents were following them around constantly fixing their hair and stuff. And I guess I got a little irritated with the kids and their sparkling white teeth, and felt like instilling the fear of God in them. So I let 'em have it once, and Kevin liked it. Then we kicked it up even more. It just kind of stuck."

For Jason Mewes, *Mallrats* was the opportunity to play more broad physical comedy than he had in *Clerks*, and even perform his own stunts. "We got stunt bumps!" he enthuses. "We got extra money for performing our own stunts. I would ask them to let me do all the stunts, because I wanted more money, but studios won't let you do everything, because you can get hurt."

In particular, Mewes remembers hanging in mid-air with Kevin Smith for the scene in which Jay and Silent Bob use Bob's "bat grapple" to evade mall security and the villainous La Fours. "We weren't up in the air that long. They'd pull us up and shoot it, then bring us down really fast. We did it twice, and I remember the first time Kevin got a little nervous because we were strapped together up in the air and he saw his harness was kind of slipping slowly through the clip. It was just adjusting, they told him when we got down, but up there he was pretty scared. It wasn't too scary for me, because there were pads beneath us, plus I had Kevin to break my fall."

Replete with action and comedy and some brief nudity, *Mallrats* promised to be a fun film, and the feedback coming from Universal on the production's progress was encouraging, as Mosier explains. "They were enthusiastic all the way to the end. They liked the dailies; they liked the cuts. [Exec] Tom Pollock said to Kevin when he saw the Stan Lee/Brodie material that it reminded him of Wolfman Jack and Richard Dreyfuss in *American Graffiti*. We heard that on the set, and it was amazing. The previews went well too, but then it all blew up."

One bone of contention between Universal and the filmmakers involved the opening act of the film. In the original script, Smith had written an effective and economical opening act on a local game show, one that was filled with verbal comedy (regarding geography, of all things) and would bookend nicely with the game show sequence at the film's climax. But the studio wanted the opening of *Mallrats* to be bigger and more elaborate than what Smith had engineered.

Pereira remembers the change. "Kevin followed the studio instructions, and wrote and shot all of this new material."

The new opening of *Mallrats* occurred at a fancy Governor's Ball, and saw the clumsy T.S. accidentally shooting a blank (from a Revolutionary War musket) at the New Jersey Governor (a Christine Todd Whitman figure). In the process, he embarrassed Mr. Svenning, who was seeking to acquire state funds so as to continue his game show.

"It was quite elaborate and long," Pereira notes of the re-vamped opening, "but I liked the scene—not just because I was in it. It looked really good. There was this opening crane shot, which was beautifully executed, and Michael Rooker's character certainly would have benefited from the scene, because his dislike of T.S. makes more sense with that opening."

When preview audiences saw the new, almost half-hour-long opening of *Mallrats*, they weren't nearly as impressed. "Kevin and I had done a two hour and seventeen minute cut," Mosier confides. "It was a disaster. That's when we cut off the new opening. The studio never even got to see it in there, but we said, 'Trust us, it doesn't work.'"

"It's funny," Pereira remarks. "The preview audience said the movie was called *Mallrats*. Why don't they get to the mall in the first half-hour? So Kevin had to cut the opening and make it much more like his original, low-key opening."

This created some problems since the events at the Governor's Ball were referred to frequently in the remainder of the film (notably in Jay and Silent Bob's introductory sequence in front of the pet store, and a short scene late in the film in the mall's parking lot). When the opening was deleted, the actors had to loop new lines that reflected the changes, but which ended up sounding flat-out weird.

"There was some crazy A.D.R. because of that," Pereira reports of the deletions. "In the first scene with Jay and Silent Bob, Brodie says the word 'excellent' for no reason. In the original script, he'd been correcting T.S., noting that Brandi was his 'ex-girlfriend.' It made no sense."

When *Mallrats* completed principal photography, the film premiered at the 1995 Comic-Con International in San Francisco, and the reviews were universally positive, though that crowd was probably geared to appreciate Smith's comic-book vision of twentysomething life.

But Vincent Pereira, for one, was afraid that the studio was not really marketing the film effectively. "It seemed like a weak sell. I remember seeing the trailer for the first time and thinking it was weak. If I knew nothing about the film, I probably wouldn't go to see it based on the trailer. And the tagline was: 'What else would you expect from the director of *Clerks?*' Well, *Clerks* made about $3 million in theaters, and I just don't think you can sell a big studio film to an audience solely on the basis of *Clerks*." Furthermore, Pereira notes that the early posters for the film were "terrible."

When *Mallrats* opened in general release near Halloween of 1995, it became clear that Kevin Smith's sophomore effort was not being received like another *Animal House*, or even a *Porky's*. On its first weekend, *Mallrats* played on 650 screens nationwide, and the one-night money tally signaled the overriding disinterest to come. Grosses were dismal: less than half-a-million dollars ($400,000) on Friday night, traditionally the strongest night of the weekend, at least for teens.

Adding insult to injury, critics were unkind. Kenneth Turan called the film a "numbing and dispiriting experience."[4] Michael Medved wrote that the film was "so cheerfully mindless, so proudly puerile, that it defeats all attempts at reasonable criticism."[5] J. R. Taylor of *Entertainment Weekly* categorized *Mallrats* as "hopelessly stupid."

Despite the brickbats, *Mallrats* did receive some nice notices. Writing for *Time* magazine, Richard Corliss noted that *Mallrats* was a "50s teen flick for the 90s" and that Smith was "flouting the sophomore slump."[6] Gary Dauphin noted in *The Village Voice* that Jason Lee was "a perfect slacker hero," and Janet Maslin of *The New York Times* similarly commented that Lee "has the grunge and surliness to give him credibility . . . but also a sweet, funny indignation over life's little outrages."[7]

"Kevin has all the clipping of the reviews for *Mallrats* and they aren't as devastating as some would have you believe," Pereira reports. "Obviously, Roger Ebert hated it. But it's not like the film was universally reviled, just on the whole it was not received nearly as well as *Clerks*. The real failure of that film was at the box office. Kevin wasn't expecting great reviews for *Mallrats*; he was making a very broad comedy that he hoped would connect with a large audience."

"I think *Mallrats* was designed to be a commercial hit," John Pierson considers. "To me, Kevin's talent is way beyond that. That's just one side of him. I think there's some pretty lousy stuff in *Mallrats*, and some really funny stuff in

Mallrats. I just think when a film is designed to be a money making machine, there's something really deflating about it not working out that way."

Reflecting on the *Mallrats* experience, and the differences from the *Clerks* experience, Scott Mosier is thoughtful. "Now, producing was a career and there are all of these people standing around, and there's a studio watching the dailies, and that changes the face of things. Your enjoyment is no longer the only thing to consider; it gets spread out over all these people. And suddenly there are all these other opinions and, whether you give a shit or not, they're important.

"The guy at the studio can make life hard on you. Sometimes you don't respect his input, but the fact is that if he likes what you've done, your life is easier. Sometimes you become anxious wondering what people will object to; whether there's too much cursing or whatever. Now, because I'm getting paid to produce, I have certain obligations. I have to answer to people, even though I don't want to. It's the name of the game, and it does taint the process. You have to use precedents from other movies to defend your case for doing things a certain way."

Smith was also thoughtful about the lessons learned on *Mallrats*: "I tried to do something different, and I didn't have anything to say at that point, so I just made a John Hughes movie.[8]

John Pierson, Smith's friend, confidante and booster from the days of *Clerks*, may have parsed the experience best:

> *You cannot get from* Clerks *to* Chasing Amy *without something like* Mallrats *in between. Where do you think the cast for* Chasing Amy *came from?*[9]

Elaborating, Pierson asks: "Would he have had any access to those actors immediately after *Clerks*? I don't think so. Maybe in 2002, he might. But not in 1995, 1996. No way."

Scott Mosier is quick to reiterate that statement. "As much as *Chasing Amy* was a transitional film to *Dogma*, kind of instilling new confidence in us, *Mallrats* was a transitional film to *Chasing Amy*. The learning process started with *Mallrats*. It was a film where we were dealing with a new environment. *Chasing Amy*—the budget level and money spent on it—was a much more realistic step to take than going from $27,000 to $6 million."

Many of the key participants in *Mallrats* were shocked when the film failed to find an audience, and the test of time has borne out their perspective.

"Everyone I know who sees it, likes it," Jason Mewes stated on the collector's edition DVD release of the film.

Indeed, the home video and DVD market gave *Mallrats* a huge reprieve. Smith's second film quickly became a popular cult hit and consistently ranked high on Amazon.com's best-seller list (often in the top one hundred). It is now an acknowledged classic of the teen comedy genre. The stink palm, no doubt, is immortal.

A MID-MALL'S DREAM

Looking at *Mallrats* today, over a decade-and-a-half after its theatrical release, one might easily determine the reasons why, among many critics, *Mallrats* is not the most favored of Kevin Smith's first five films. It is not the blunt-faced, sharp-witted revelation that *Clerks* was. Nor is it the human, authentic love story that *Chasing Amy* is. It lacks the overtly provocative, social and intellectual stirrings of the ambitious *Dogma*, as well as the celebratory, satirical style of that lunatic rant, *Jay and Silent Bob Strike Back*. Yet, in its own way, *Mallrats* is a solidly crafted work, and a really good time at the movies.

Mallrats passes the most important test of any comedy: it is relentlessly funny. And then there's Jason Lee's brilliant performance holding it together. He makes Brodie a sarcastic, humorous B.S. artist with the heart and humor to go side by side with his more caustic qualities.

And, even if critics found the scripted material low brow, Brodie's "stink-palm" schtick is still one of the funniest (and most disgusting) sequences in any teen comedy of the 1990s. Watching Michael Rooker's pompous Mr. Svenning lick that melted chocolate pretzel off his hand, and knowing what else he is ingesting is, well, a stomach-churning riot.

Though reviewers will no doubt barbecue me for saying so, *Mallrats* is also a film that was truly ahead of its time. The "gross out" comedy sub-genre was not really popular with American audiences again until the Farrelly brothers struck gold with the megahit *There's Something About Mary* in 1998. Then came *American Pie* in 1999, followed shortly by *Scary Movie*, *Road Trip*, and the inevitable (and unfortunate) *American Pie 2*. All of those films championed lowbrow, gross out body humor, often to surprisingly good reviews and big money. Are any of those films as good, or better, than *Mallrats*?

Mallrats' perceived critical failure might simply be a result of nothing more significant than timing. Today it would most likely be viewed as a rather funny and valuable companion piece to *American Pie* or *There's Something About Mary*, being similarly loaded to the gills with outrageous dick and tit jokes. If *Mallrats* had been released, say, in the summer of 1999 or 2000, would the reviews have been so persistently negative? One has to wonder.

It is true that Jay and Silent Bob come off as a bit more toothless and inoffensive in *Mallrats* than in other View Askew outings, but to its credit, *Mallrats* nicely opens up the parameters of their world. It makes the case for the stoner duo not just as verbal comedians, but as physical ones to boot. Bob's imitations of the Dark Knight, or rather the *Dork Knight*, are not only funny, they jibe nicely with Smith's on-going inclusion of comic book and superhero references in his films. Approve of these slapstick hijinks or not, they're consistent with Smith's oeuvre.

A few years ago, a friend of my wife complained that Martin Scorsese was always making gangster movies; that *Casino* wasn't really much different from *Good Fellas*. I reminded her that one sign of a true artist is consistency. A fine filmmaker will return to similar ideas, worlds, and themes, because it is often enlightening to compare different perspectives on like material. The same argument is true of *Mallrats*. It is filled with pop culture references (like *Clerks*, *Chasing Amy*, and *Jay and Silent Bob Strike Back*), and features two buddies of a certain "maturing" generation (like *Clerks* and *Chasing Amy*). So *Mallrats* isn't some freakish anomaly in the View Askew canon. It's like *Clerks*, only more mainstream.

Mallrats has some other commendable qualities too. It's a movie with some emotional sincerity, not just glitzy young actors going about their shallow business (like *She's All That* or *Summer Catch*). And it is nicely energized by its musical score, featuring The Goops ("Build Me Up Buttercup"), Elastica ("Line Up"), Weezer ("Susanne"), and even K.C. and the Sunshine Band ("Boogie Shoes"). Good laughs, good performances and a good score, what's not to like? Did reviewers actually walk into a movie entitled *Mallrats* expecting a thoughtful, Ingmar Bergman-style introspection? If so, no wonder they were disappointed.

Also, I would be terribly remiss if I did not report that at least a few critics found considerable depth in *Mallrats*. Graham Fuller, of *Interview* magazine, for one, saw fit to compare the film to the works of Shakespeare:

> *Just like* Midsummer Night's Dream, *it's got two couples... who repair to a mystical haven: Only in this case, it's a New Jersey shopping*

mall instead of the Athenian woods. Mallrats *also has an agent of mis-rule entrusted with reconciling these quarrelsome lovers and constantly botching it: He's played by Kevin Smith himself, who makes a low-rent Puck alongside Jason Mewe's Gen X Oberon."*[10]

So, with just two films under his belt, Smith's work had already been compared to *Waiting for Godot* and a Shakespearean comedy. Not bad.

Making the comparison to *A Midsummer Night's Dream* a bit more apt, it may be prudent to remind people that critics didn't happen to appreciate Shakespeare's comedy very much when it "premiered" either. It was called "the most insipid, ridiculous play"[11] by one self-satisfied critic. Scholars would also have us acknowledge that it was not until the latter half of the twentieth century that *A Midsummer's Night Dream* became recognized as a "complex and exacting work of art."[12] *Mallrats* may never emerge a critical darling, but neither has it waited some 400 years for popular acclaim.

Actually, as strange as it may sound to some, Kevin Smith's films do have elements in common with the comedies of Shakespeare. As Dwight Ewell, the classically trained actor who portrays Hooper in *Chasing Amy* observes: "In most of the Kevin Smith monologues, there is a rhythm there, you just have to find it. Reading Shakespeare is the same way. He uses iambic pentameter, which means when you're reading the lines you don't have to push to get the meaning out, you simply do the melody and the audience gets the meaning. Kevin's words are the same way. As an actor you don't have to do much—it's all in the words. Kevin's words are so lyrical and beautiful."

Brian O'Halloran agrees. "Thank god I had theatrical training, where you have to memorize an entire play, because Kevin's words have this great flow. If you listen to him, you can almost hear it in his conversational speech. His dialogue becomes very story-like, and you can almost feel the peaks and valleys. It is very song-like, very melodic, and there's always a point. It sort of works like this: let me give you the point, now here's the point, now here's the punch line to the point."

Jeff Anderson also suggests the dialogue of Kevin Smith is complex, purposeful and exacting. "It is like music. Once I start doing it, if one little word trips me up, my mouth keeps going and I'm lost."

Even in *Mallrats*, ostensibly a broad teen comedy, the dialogue, not unlike the Bard's, is a delightful dance, and is amusing not merely because of the delivery, but because of the very words themselves. The beast with two backs? The back of a Volkswagen? There isn't a whole lot of daylight between concepts.

"Some actors can't handle the dialogue," Ewell notes confidentially of Smith's writing, "because they don't trust themselves." But when it's done right, the Smith cadence is charming, amusing and downright Shakespearean. "Ben Affleck is very good with that dialogue," Ewell notes appreciatively, "very good."

Not surprisingly, considering the precision with which he selects his words, Kevin Smith is renowned throughout Hollywood as a director who strongly discourages improvisation on his sets. And that is precisely because his words are so carefully chosen.

Ethan Suplee explains the rule. "He wrote the lines, and that's what you're supposed to say. I never saw him give anybody a hard time about that, but there's a distinct pattern to how Kevin Smith writes, and if you improvise other things it throws off the prose aspect of it. It's cut and dry and he writes really well. It's intelligent, so there's no real need to change any of it."

"Kevin has a firm grip on the script and the characters," affirms Jeff Anderson. "I later found out, [while shooting *Now You Know*] that actors generally don't like to be given line readings, but when Kevin and I work together, Kevin would always do his director's thing and say, 'Do it like you're feeling anxious.' But I'd just tell him to read me the lines how we wanted me to say them. He'd give me the line, and I'd give it right back. We'd cut to the chase."

"Kevin is big on line readings," Pereira repeats. "He does that a lot with Jason Lee. Jason can listen to a line, internalize it, and give it back perfectly."

No actor would dare attempt to improvise lines in a Shakespeare play, and it's interesting that Kevin Smith holds his performers to the rigorous standard, respecting the written word to such a high degree.

On a lighter note, Shakespeare is also renowned for (presumably) writing 37 plays, the selfsame number that crops up often in Kevin Smith movies. But more importantly, both Shakespeare and Kevin Smith are known to have at least two other qualities in common: the ability to turn a naughty, bawdy phrase with the best of them, and a rather keen understanding of human nature.

Though Shakespeare wrote about kings and other noble figures and Kevin Smith writes about more common characters—like those in service industry—the colorful humanity of these *dramatis personae* is something both authors explore. In its core structure, love of language, ribald humor, and human characters, Graham Fuller is right about *Mallrats*: it isn't that far removed from *A Midsummer's Night Dream*. Both productions have been dismissed as trifles, but in the final analysis, such is the enduring fate of comedy. Most people think it is easy to make people laugh, and for some reason don't always take that ability seriously.

As in so many cases, the reviewers really just needed to lighten up when they watched *Mallrats*. As Jason Lee states on the DVD: "Critics, shmitics!"

ASKEW VIEWS

MAGIC EYE: Though Ethan Suplee plays a character vexed by those Magic Eye Posters that once dotted mall landscapes, the actor took the popular art somewhat less seriously.

"When I first saw those things, I had no idea you were supposed to look at it and some other image comes out of the chaos of the design. I never let myself get frustrated through, and thought if somebody did see something hidden there, they were creating it themselves. Then finally, someone said to me, 'Cross your eyes.' Not actually cross them, but let them relax until they naturally cross. Then I saw the picture, and it was this miraculous revelation."

ORIGIN: *Mallrats* heralds the first appearance of another favorite Kevin Smith comedy duo, Fanboy (Walt Flanagan) and Steve-Dave (Bryan Johnson). The more verbose of the duo, Steve-Dave, is based on a real person.

"He's the guy who actually used to own the comic book store before Kevin did," Johnson reveals. "Walter and I used to go there, and Kevin went there, and Walter could never remember if the guy's name was actually Steve or Dave. So the name Steve-Dave was coined. He wasn't an angry guy, like the character I portray."

As for Fanboy, Walt Flanagan has a pretty good idea of who the character should be. "He's the fanboy to the nth degree." Then Flanagan pauses with insight. "I'd imagine all he cares about is comics, but if you watch the movies it seems that all he cares about is Steve-Dave. He's constantly pumping up Steve-Dave's ego. Maybe he's more Steve-Dave's fanboy than anything else."

Johnson agrees, with delight. "Fanboy is needed to re-affirm everything Steve-Dave says. He's the ultimate bootlicker. It was Kevin who came up with that idea. He wanted the eternally outraged Steve-Dave, and then Fanboy always cowering behind him shouting 'Yeah!'"

BRENDA: During one scene with Shannen Doherty, Ethan Suplee's Willam looks at her with a piercing gaze and calls her "Brenda," the name of Doherty's character on the Aaron Spelling series *Beverly Hills 90210.*

"I did that take once," Suplee remembers, "and then Kevin whispered in my ear. He said I should call her Brenda. And I said 'What?' And he said, 'Yeah, call her Brenda.' To my knowledge at the time, she had no idea it was coming. I think that afterwards I found out she did know, but it was still pretty funny."

WALT FLANAGAN'S DOG: This is, perhaps, the ultimate of the Kevin Smith in-jokes. During a chase sequence in *Mallrats*, Jay notes of a pursuer that he is "faster than Walt Flanagan's dog." The line came from an event that happened doing shooting. After Flanagan had quit his brief tenure as production assistant, he had lots of free time.

"I was in Minnesota for four weeks with nothing to do. I'd be on the set for hours doing nothing but walking around different stores, and I saw this dog in the pet store that was so small. I think everybody on the crew had gone in to see it, because it was a pocket-sized rat terrier.

"I'd always wanted a dog, so I purchased it with about three weeks left in the shoot, which wasn't the smartest thing to do because then I had to keep a puppy in the hotel against hotel rules for three weeks. The people I was rooming with had kept their jobs on the film and were working these weird hours. They'd start at 6:00 p.m. and work till 6:00 a.m. and then they'd come home, and the dog would wake up.

"It wasn't the best conditions to train a new puppy. But I let her out in the mall, which was closed down for the shoot, and I'd go to an empty part of the lot and let her off the leash. She'd just tear around and looked like a little hockey puck, because she was so fast. That's where the joke came from. I don't know how it happened. It was such an inside joke, I guess Kevin just decided to keep it."

For the record, the dog's name is Brodie, and according to Flanagan, "She's a total lap dog," and was "still doing great" as of 2002, the time of this book's first edition publication.

CONDIMENTS: The character of Willam Black, the Idiot-Man-Child, undergoes a drastic transformation in *Mallrats*. Instead of Scott Mosier, Ethan Suplee portrays him. And, to Suplee's dismay, he's become a slob!

"I was in wardrobe and make-up and they said they were going to dirty me up," Suplee explains. "I thought it would be fine, but then this lady whips out a bottle of mustard. Then on top of that they dump on soy sauce, vinegar, and ketchup and I started to wonder if a little colored water wouldn't have done the trick instead. I mean, did I actually have to stink? The audience wouldn't be able to smell me, but I sure did. It was a pretty messy operation."

REFERENCES: *Mallrats* is chock full of references to Smith's favorite films, television shows, and comic books, including *Smokey and the Bandit*, *Jaws*, *Star Wars*, and *Superman* (particularly the Man of Steel's need for a Kryptonite condom if he wishes to have sexual intercourse with a mere mortal).

GENEOLOGY: As *Mallrats* opens, Brodie (Jason Lee) reflects on some messy anal fun and games played by his relative Walt. This is the same character Randal discusses in *Clerks* as having suffocated on his own genitals. Since Walt is cousin to both buddies, that makes Brodie and Randal related.

CONTINUITY: At the end of *Mallrats*, Jay and Silent Bob are seen walking down a long stretch of highway accompanied by an orangutan, as the song entitled "Susanne" plays on the soundtrack. Their adventure with the simian Susanne is the subject of *Jay and Silent Bob Strike Back*. Also, Silent Bob makes use of a bat-grapple gun in *Mallrats*, and that toy—as well as his Dork Knight utility belt—reappears in *Jay and Silent Bob Strike Back*.

KEVIN SMITH ON *MALLRATS*

"It was liberating making a movie that failed on such a grand level...You reach the point when the reviews are so horrendously bad and the critics are particularly vicious, that it's like, 'Where can you go but up?'"[13]

4

Chasing Amy (1997)

I FINALLY HAD SOMETHING PERSONAL TO SAY…

Finally, a comedy that tells it like it feels.
Sex is easy.
Love is hard.

CAST AND CREW

MIRAMAX PRESENTS A VIEW ASKEW PRODUCTION, *CHASING AMY*

Written and directed by: Kevin Smith
Produced by: Scott Mosier
Associate Producer: Robert Hawk
Line Producer: Derrick Tseng
Executive Producer: John Pierson
Cinematography by: David Klein
Edited by: Kevin Smith and Scott Mosier
Music: David Pirner
Production Designer: Robert "Ratface" Holtzman
Costume Designer: Christopher Del Coro
Bluntman & Chronic/Chasing Amy Artwork: Mike Allred
M.P.A.A. Rating: R
Running Time: 111 minutes

STARRING

Ben Affleck | *Holden McNeil*
Joey Lauren Adams | *Alyssa Jones*

Jason Lee | *Banky Edwards*
Dwight Ewell | *Hooper X/Lamont*
Jason Mewes | *Jay*
Kevin Smith | *Silent Bob*
Ethan Suplee | *Fan*
Scott Mosier | *Collector*
Casey Affleck | *Little Kid*
Guinevere Turner | *Singer*
Carmen Lee | *Kid*
Brian O'Halloran | *Exec #1*
Matt Damon | *Exec #2*
Alexander Goebbel | *Train Kid*
Tony Torn | *Cashier*
Rebecca Waxman | *Dalia*
Paris Petrick | *Tony*
Welker White | *Jane*
Kelly Simpkins | *Nica*
John Willyung | *Cohee Lundin*
Tsemach Washington | *Young Black Kid*
Ernest O'Donnell | *Bystander*
Kristin Mosier | *Waitress*
Virginia Smith | *Con Woman*

THE STORY SO FAR...

BLUNTMAN & CHRONIC COMIC BOOK co-creator Holden McNeil is blindsided at the Comic Con in Manhattan when he meets Alyssa Jones, a beautiful and feisty comic artist. When Holden learns that Alyssa is a lesbian, he must re-calibrate his traditional views about the sexes. But as his friendship with Alyssa deepens, Holden's business partner, roommate and long-time friend, Banky Edwards, begins to grow jealous of the bond forming between them.

When Holden and Alyssa's friendship deepens to romantic love, Banky uncovers a secret about Alyssa's past that shatters Holden's confidence. Despite sage advice from a black friend and artist named Hooper X (who writes the comic book *White Hating Coon*), Holden breaks up with Alyssa over the matter.

Jay and Silent Bob, seeking money from Holden because his comic book is based on their likeness, set McNeil straight in matters of the heart. But Holden draws the wrong conclusion, and in a tense summit with Banky and Alyssa, brings the matter to an unfortunate conclusion.

SILENT BOB'S WORDS OF WISDOM

"No, idiot. It was a mistake. I wasn't disgusted with her, I was afraid. At that moment, I felt small, like I lacked experience, like I'd never be on her level, like I'd never be enough for her or something like that, you know what I'm saying? But what I did not get—she didn't care."

THE STORY BEHIND THE MOVIE

After the disastrous reception heaped on *Mallrats* during its release in the closing months of 1995, many in the film industry wondered what would become of Kevin Smith. The story was an all-too-familiar one. A talented young filmmaker brimming with ideas goes to Hollywood only to see his edge blunted, his individuality reined in, and his creative muse tempered by interfering studios. The same "hot" director, once the talk of the town, retreats to obscurity, dreams shattered.

Fortunately, this was not to be Kevin Smith's story. Not by a long shot.

Instead, Kevin Smith and his View Askew colleagues simply went back to basics. They produced a small budgeted ($250,000) independent feature with the same team that had pulled it off so well before, including producer Scott Mosier and cinematographer David Klein.

Also along for the ride was a stable of talented actors who hadn't yet peaked, but were hungry to sink their teeth into meaningful roles, including Ben Affleck, Jason Lee, Joey Lauren Adams, Dwight Ewell, Ethan Suplee, and Brian O'Halloran. The result of the combined effort was a comedic and romantic masterpiece, *Chasing Amy*.

Funny and tender, touching and sharp, *Chasing Amy* was the movie that changed everything for Kevin Smith. It made a huge profit, won rave reviews, and became View Askew's new calling card to Hollywood at large.

"*Chasing Amy* made *Dogma* possible," producer Scott Mosier explains. "A lot of talented actors saw it, and it made them think about working on *Dogma*. *Mallrats* was not a great calling card to the Alan Rickmans of the world. But a film like *Chasing Amy* says that Kevin Smith can write great scenes and create an environment for actors where they produce good work. That's the kind of thing that is very attractive. *Chasing Amy* elevated us on all levels; as far as audiences, within the industry, and financially as well."

But before the film that has become known as Kevin Smith's "comeback" picture was released, there was an interesting period of development. At one point, the movie was set to follow hard in *Mallrats* footsteps as a broad, somewhat juvenile teen comedy.

Ethan Suplee remembers how he first heard about *Chasing Amy*. "A lot of Kevin's friends who worked on *Clerks* in some capacity came out and worked in Minnesota as production assistants on *Mallrats*. Some of them were into making movies too, and one, Vincent Pereira, was planning an independent film [*A Better Place*]. That happened really soon after shooting *Mallrats*. So I went back to Jersey and stayed at Kevin's house while I did a couple of scenes in Vinnie's movie.

"Then Kevin took me aside and said 'One day, all this will be yours,' and he was actually referring to a very early draft of *Chasing Amy* that took place in high school. I was going to play one of the main characters. But then *Mallrats* came out and did so poorly that Kevin totally rewrote *Chasing Amy*. But the vibe was still there that I would work with Kevin whenever he worked."

Vincent Pereira picks up the story from there. "I don't think I ever read that earliest version. I think Kevin only wrote a few scenes for it. But he had this idea that he was going to make a PG-13 movie that his mother could watch. Well, you've seen *Chasing Amy*, and that obviously didn't happen. But the original idea, before *Mallrats* was released, was to go down the same path and play it very broad.

"If I remember correctly, Jay and Silent Bob were trying to live as if they were really superheroes. Ethan was going to play a character that has two different gorgeous women on his arms every time you see him. He was going to be this real stud, and I think Kevin only wrote maybe two scenes of that version. Then, after *Mallrats*, he decided to go in a more subtle direction."

According to Pereira, once Kevin stayed on that path, *Chasing Amy* underwent relatively few changes in the scripting process. "There was going to be a subplot involving Holden and his ex-girlfriend, who happened to be a teacher, and that sequence had many of the characters Kevin introduced in the early version of the script. But those ideas were dropped very early on."

Interestingly, some sequences that were dropped from earlier View Askew films were resurrected for *Chasing Amy*, including the oral sex scars scene, which had appeared in the original draft of *Mallrats*. "The funny thing about *Amy* is that a lot of the good stuff in there came out of other scripts. Kevin found a notebook where he'd written some preliminary scenes for *Clerks*. He lost it before he actually wrote the screenplay, so he forgot all about it. About a year or two later, he found the notebook again and there's that wonderful deleted scene in *Chasing Amy* where Holden and Alyssa are at the dartboard talking about true love. That sequence was in the notebook, but it was a discussion between Dante and Randal. It was the exact same sequence, except with the two of them at the Quick Stop counter. I wish that scene were still in the film. That's the one thing Kevin's cut out of his movies that I believe should have stayed in."

Bringing *Chasing Amy* to final draft also involved opening up the story. "Miramax read it and sent a note to open it up a bit," Pereira recalls. "The whole confrontation scene in the hockey rink took place over dinner in an apartment, but Miramax said, 'Let's have them go out somewhere instead.' But the last draft wasn't tremendously different from the first draft."

The final script, a focused tale about a heterosexual comic book artist falling hard for an avowed lesbian, has been speculated about in the press for years. Some people believe it is an autobiographical work; that Kevin Smith wrote it as a love-letter to his then-girlfriend, Joey Lauren Adams, who had acquired more relationship experience than he had.

But other sources, including *Entertainment Weekly*, indicated there might be a dishier story to uncover. An article by Allison Gaines pointed to the fact that Kevin Smith and Scott Mosier became chummy with lesbian director Rose Troche and writer Guinevere Turner (director of *Go Fish*) during their stay in Utah during Sundance in 1994. The article vaguely intimates that either Smith or Mosier were infatuated with the lovely Guinevere Turner (who appears in *Chasing Amy*) and that somehow it all ended up on the screen.[1]

When questioned on the subject, Mosier was non-committal about the details. "It was in an *Entertainment Weekly* article. The information that's in there is fine."

Regardless of the story's beginnings, the final shooting script by Smith was a polished, yet blunt piece of work that seemed to understand the pain of the most intense human relationships and emotions. Ethan Suplee, for one, loved the results. "It was very honest in dealing with a much more intense subject matter than what Kevin had done before. It was much more true than I expected."

With a screenplay in hand, Smith, Mosier, and executive producer John Pierson made a deal with Miramax's Harvey Weinstein to finance the project.

"We went down to breakfast in Sundance with Harvey Weinstein," Pierson recounts, "and within a short amount of time, everybody agreed Kevin should make this movie, make it for very little, make it with exactly the cast he wanted, and exactly the way he wanted to do it."

And Pierson's role in the negotiations? "I was just sitting at the table nodding. I would love to hear an audiotape of that meeting, because I can't really call it up. I know Harvey was wearing this ridiculous skiing outfit..."

According to Pierson, the executive producer credit he eventually received on *Chasing Amy* was merely another example of Kevin Smith's kindness of spirit. "That was just Kevin being generous towards me, because I was very generous to him on *Clerks*. I didn't care about the money; I thought it was a great film, and I had a feeling this was going to be someone I would really like knowing. And I pretty much told him the first time I met him that I had a book idea and somehow he was going to be a part of it. Because of his participation in *Spike, Mike, Slackers and Dykes*—which to this day helps sell the book—I always felt our deal was completely fair.

"But that credit was him continuing to thank me. I love having my name on that film. I always thought it was a fantastic script, and he did a knock-out job bringing it to life. But I don't make the slightest claim that I was around to have an influence on that film. He was just really generous with the credit, and I'm happy to have it."

So, with $250,000 dollars to spend on production ($2,000 of which went to the creation of an authentic-looking comic book convention), producing *Chasing Amy* felt almost like old home week to the team, including producer Mosier.

"Once again we were in more of an isolated environment," Mosier says. "Unlike *Mallrats*, we were surrounded by people of our age, people of the same experience level, and so we were much more comfortable exploring exactly what we wanted to do and how we wanted to go about things. That was true from both of our standpoints: how I wanted to run a movie and how Kevin would direct it. We were able to grow and feel more confident about what we were doing. On *Mallrats*, we'd made mistakes here and there, but it was a good film to learn on because the mistakes aren't necessarily as apparent."

Smith too felt free and confident enough to go for broke on *Chasing Amy*:

> Clerks *had been over-praised.* Mallrats *had been over-bashed. We'd been at both ends of the spectrum. The third time is always supposed to be the charm so we were able to approach* Chasing Amy *from a very liberated position: what better could they ever say about us than they did the first time, and what worse could they ever say about than they did the second time?*[2]

The cast of *Chasing Amy* rehearsed for nearly a month (always Smith's preference when shooting a comedy wherein the dialogue and characterizations are so important). Though Miramax had pushed for a well-known female lead in the film, Smith fought to keep Joey Lauren Adams on the project. Previously known primarily as the girl who "deflowered" Bud Bundy (David Faustino) on Fox's *Married with Children*,[3] Adams soon came to inhabit the once-in-a-lifetime part of Alyssa, in the process creating a memorable character, and even writing a sexy torch song for one scene. Months later, the heartfelt performance would garner the actress a Golden Globe nomination.[4]

Joining the cast on *Chasing Amy* was a new face to the world of Kevin Smith cinema: Dwight Ewell. Born in North Carolina but raised in New Jersey, Ewell is a powerful and charismatic African-American performer who persevered through a difficult childhood. "My story is not very different from a lot of young black men," he says. "I had dreams of becoming something, but because of things happening in my environment, people told me I wouldn't amount to shit, or that I was just dreaming. I'd be one person out on the street, but then I'd come home and go read Shakespeare, like *A Midsummer's Night Dream*."

For Ewell, the decision to pursue acting came at an early age, and was cemented after one particularly harrowing incident. "I ran away from home and went to Philadelphia when I was sixteen. I hooked up with a drug dealer and he tried to kill me. I got in a car with him; I just didn't know any better. He offered me a joint, and when I couldn't feel my legs I realized it was laced with something. And he started saying, 'isn't it a shame: so young, so far away from home, don't you know I could do anything to you, and nobody would know where you are?' I was scared, but I had street savvy and I didn't let him see how frightened I was. I don't remember what I said to that man, but I got out of that car and decided I wanted to go back to school."

After studying at SUNY-Purchase, where Parker Posey, Stanley Tucci, and director Hal Hartley had attended, Ewell graduated well-trained and "sounding like a Shakespearean actor." He soon won roles in films such as Hartley's 1995 film *Flirt*, and in the short years since has appeared in more than thirty independent films. When interviewed for this book in 2002, Ewell had just finished shooting three films, including *Pagan*, *The Guru* (with Heather Graham and Marisa Tomei), and *Wheel Men*.

Ewell recalls with good humor his first meeting with Kevin Smith. "He came over to the house of a friend, and met me there. It was a really hot day so we went to sit out on the fire escape and I was reading from this book called Linda Goodman's *Love Signs*. It's sort of the bible of horoscopes, and Kevin and his girlfriend started laughing. It was then that my friend told me that Kevin was a filmmaker. I told him I'd just finished a film with Hal Hartley, and Kevin kind of interviewed me about the experience of working with Hal, and I told him everything I knew.

"Later on, Kevin and I joked about this conversation, because at the time he thought I was trying to school him on film. But I would never do that. I was just telling him about my particular experience. He had *Clerks* out at the time, and I'd never seen or heard of it. '*Clerks*?,' I thought, 'what's that?'

"Meanwhile, my film was premiering that night so I asked Kevin and his girlfriend if they wanted to come, so Kevin could meet Hal. So they came to the screening, met Hal, and after the movie was over, Kevin said to me, 'I liked you in the movie, but I don't think he used you properly.' Next thing I knew, it was a year later and I received a call saying that Kevin wanted me to read his new script. They mailed it to me and I loved it."

With one caveat.

"I liked the script a lot," Ewell clarifies. "Hooper is really funny, but I told Kevin there was just one thing that should be changed. Hooper seemed to be used as comic relief, only one-dimensional. All of the other characters talked frankly about their sexual encounters except for him. And Kevin understood immediately and said, 'Forget about that, I'm going to write something else.' Well, he came back with that scene in the record store and I loved it. Now I thought the character was really three-dimensional. I loved Hooper because you can't tear him down, even with words. He always has a reply to everything. He's not a victim. He wants to diss everything out, so people can't laugh at him."

Interestingly, Ewell based his interpretation of Hooper on an acquaintance. "I met this guy through a friend. He was black, 40 years old or so, and had this very dry sense of humor. On the outside he appeared very masculine; there was something very hard about him. But when he loved somebody, you could just feel it. He had a gruff voice, but you could tell he wanted to help people. It was a strange dichotomy. He was part of Hooper, the part who maybe hadn't seen his dreams fulfilled."

Also back in the saddle for *Chasing Amy* were Steve-Dave and Fanboy, the obnoxious comic book fans that had hassled Brodie at the comic book store in *Mallrats*. This time around, they would open the film, haranguing comic book writers Holden McNeil and Banky Edwards about the overtly "commercial" nature of their "juvenile" creation, *Bluntman & Chronic*.

To augment the reality of the scene, Kevin Smith actually used a negative review of *Mallrats* to formulate the blistering critique.

"Kevin showed me that review and was like, 'Can you believe this shit?'" Bryan Johnson remembers. "People are so full of venom."

How did Johnson find the necessary vinegar to play his vitriolic role so well? "I just thought of a person who is stunted in their own career, because it seems like there are a ton of jealous people out there who want to take other people down."

Walt Flanagan remembers it was difficult to maintain his composure as Johnson so expertly dressed down co-stars Affleck and Lee. "It was hard to keep a straight face, because we'd get to a certain point, crack up, and have to start over again. It was tough to keep going."

Unfortunately, this very funny sequence, which Johnson terms Steve-Dave and Fanboy's "finest hour," ended up on the cutting room floor. "The movie originally opened with Walter and me giving Ben and Jason shit," Johnson describes. "But then in the next scene, Mosier was giving them shit at the convention, so our scene had to go. It was too repetitive."

The shooting of *Chasing Amy* by all accounts went quite smoothly, save for a few incidents. For the scene of Alyssa Jones emotional breakdown outside a Jersey hockey rink, Joey Lauren Adams did sixteen takes, becoming increasingly effective and emotional each time.

And, at one point during the shoot, Scott Mosier nearly found himself in trouble with the long arm of the law for too closely following the tenets of guerilla filmmaking. "On *Chasing Amy*, we didn't have a production staff, so I did a lot of the physical work to get things done," he explains. "We were in a location we weren't supposed to be in, on a holiday, I think."

"It wasn't like we broke in, but we kind of tried to do something, hoping nobody would drop by. But we got busted, and for a minute the people who owned the building were threatening to have me arrested because I was in charge. The incident was a little more flavorful than that, but I don't think I should go into too much detail. We just had no money, and had to take some risks. Basically, I was a little more willing to take those risks then than I would be now."

For his part, Ewell enjoyed shooting *Chasing Amy*, except for his favorite scene in the script: the scene with Holden and Hooper gabbing in the record store. "That was uncomfortable. I had tape on the bottom of my boots so they wouldn't make any noise, a body mike inside my leather jacket, so I couldn't move, or it would rustle. And then on top of that, I had all of these CDs in front of me wrapped in plastic. If I picked them up, they'd rustle and the mike would pick up the sound. So I could only pick up the unwrapped CDs, which was difficult. I remember feeling very uncomfortable and insecure about that scene, but Kevin assured me that it flows."

Brian O'Halloran was a bit surprised to learn that his character, an MTV executive, went though some changes during shooting. "Initially, Matt Damon wasn't in that scene with me, it was just my character," he recollects. "But when Ben became involved, he wanted to get Matt in the picture and it was late in the casting, so Kevin didn't have a role for him. So he divided the executive part into two, and my agent called to tell me there was a change. My agent said there would be someone else with me, and I was like, 'who?' And the agent said 'Matt Damon.' And I said, 'Who the fuck is Matt Damon?' I'd never heard of him, but when I met him he was such a nice guy, and he had this beautiful girlfriend at the time. Matt is really a great and giving actor, and it was fun shooting with Ben and Jason Lee again."

Perhaps because the tone of *Chasing Amy* was more serious than *Mallrats*, old favorites Jay and Silent Bob only appeared in one scene in the film, offering sage advice to Ben Affleck's character, Holden. Though their appearance was brief, the scene remains one of the most important in the film.

Jason Mewes remembers a funny incident shooting the sequence: "I didn't know this until after we shot, but Kevin had told the crew guys to be patient with me. He told them I hadn't worked in a while, and said that we might be there all night because I had a long, long monologue. Kevin even thought we might have to do a line then cut, then do another line of my dialogue, then cut. But I breezed right through my stuff.

"Then Kevin's 'Chasing Amy' speech came up and we ended up doing *thirteen* takes because Kevin kept forgetting his lines. Afterwards, the crew started saying, 'Oh yeah, Kevin, we better watch out for this Mewes character; we're gonna be here all night...'"

After shooting the film, Scott Mosier and Kevin Smith repeated their editing collaboration, which had worked so well on *Clerks*. They cut the film during nine intense days. Then, David Pirner contributed an understated and highly effective musical score. The completed opening credits montage, like *Mallrats* before it, featured comic book creations, this time Jay and Silent Bob's alter egos *Bluntman & Chronic*, given life courtesy of Mike Allred. He also drew the more "personal" work of Holden McNeil, the comic book seen in the film's final frames, *Chasing Amy*.

What emerged from all of View Askew's hard work in spring of 1997 was a deeply emotional, touching, and very funny film that was beloved by audiences and critics alike. Kevin Thomas of the *L.A. Times* called it a "little movie with big truths," and a work of "fierce intelligence and emotional honesty." *Newsweek's* David Ansen reported that the film's characters were seductive with "their blunt and heartfelt eloquence."

Also supporting the film were *Time's* Richard Schickel, who found the film "smart and truthful" and Smith's old supporter, Amy Taubin, who thought *Chasing Amy* was the "funniest, most honest" sex comedy she'd ever seen. Financially, the film was a huge hit, raking in more than $12 million dollars on a meager investment of $250,000.

Even more delightfully, this was a Kevin Smith film that touched the heart as well as the funny bone. As Roger Ebert pointed out in his review, falling in love is often a painful experience. *Chasing Amy* speaks to the pain inherent in the situations where human beings try to connect in a meaningful way. Holden's confession of love (in the rain no less) is touchingly performed by Ben Affleck. And Alyssa's breakdown after her realization that Holden really is breaking up with her is also deeply sad and gut-wrenching. The nice thing about the film is that it was championed as a success by critics, but also judged as a positive contribution to society.

The gay community, in particular, welcomed Smith's efforts to portray it even-handedly and fairly, and Kevin Smith even made a prophetic statement in *The Advocate*, one that would take on ironic new meaning in 2001: "I'm sure there's a GLAAD award somewhere in my future."[5]

View Askew Historian Vincent Pereira was one of the many viewers who thought that *Chasing Amy*, so funny and yet so poignant, best expressed Kevin Smith as a creative artist. "I think it's Kevin's best film; his masterpiece. I think every director has a defining film. For right now, *Chasing Amy* is it. The only people who express problems with *Chasing Amy* are some of Kevin's youngest fans, who are more into the wild comedy. You go back to Woody Allen and it's the same syndrome: Why don't you make your earlier funny movies anymore?"

Dwight Ewell agrees that *Chasing Amy* has transcended its time and place to become something of a classic. "I believed in the messages the movie sent. There hasn't been another movie like it. A lot of people have tried to duplicate *Chasing Amy*, but no one can. It's a timeless piece, and I'm grateful that Kevin Smith saw I had the ability to be funny. I'm very leery of doing stuff where the humor is so forced and predictable, but Kevin's sense of humor is very intelligent; he doesn't spoon-feed it to you."

For Scott Mosier, *Chasing Amy* represented a mature look at complex relationships, ones that don't end with typical Hollywood predictability and pretense. As poignant as the film is, he feels it also carries a positive message. "Ultimately, if you look at the film from my perspective, it has a happy ending because it comes from a place of learning. Holden is a better person for being through that experience. That's what the end of that movie represents: that he's stronger and better and touched because of his relationship with Alyssa.

"Then, because of that, he's in a position to go out in the world and not make the same mistake. While it's emotionally sad to see that stupid mistakes made it impossible for Holden and Alyssa to be together, in the end the fact that he has grown through the experience is very positive.

"At the end of the movie you feel Holden gets it. He's going to be okay. I think it's a film about a guy who's trying to grow up and become a man. And finally he does."

THE NEXT SCORSESE?

In Spring of 2000, *Esquire* magazine ran a series of articles in which prominent critical voices looked at the next generation of filmmakers. One of those voices belonged to Andrew Sarris, the renowned film critic of *The New York Observer* and a professor of Film at Columbia University. In a brief, but pointed article, Sarris selected Kevin Smith as "the next Scorsese," a title which is quite an honor.

At the same time Sarris championed Kevin Smith as a filmmaker, he also noted his irritation with the young director for, basically, being so self-deprecating in his public persona:

> *I would be happier... if he stopped giving faux-naïf interviews about his alleged shortcoming as a "visual" director... For one thing, he shouldn't be providing ammo to reviewers who couldn't recognize visual style if it conked them on the noggin. For another, it is disingenuous... to claim that he is uninterested in the visual dimension of the cinema when he is... addicted to comic strips, a sure sign of an artist as much obsessed by how things look as how people talk.* Chasing Amy ... *works on all cylinders, visual as well as verbal, to deliver its explosive climaxes.*[6]

The interviews Sarris referred to were the ones in which the genial Kevin Smith off-handedly put down the look of his films.

In one piece, Smith called *Clerks* "shitty-looking," and in others berated himself for being unable to vet any material except for dialogue. Both those perceptions, with all due respect to the artist, are flat-out wrong. Regardless of cost, *Clerks* boasts a singular charm and visual style, a real authentic character and quality; and *Chasing Amy* is quite accomplished in its lighting, editing, and composition.

Vincent Pereira thinks he understands why Smith tends to belittle his own work in print. "It all comes down to his belief that if he bashes himself, then other people can't bash him for the same things. But I think he's gotten savvy to the fact that he has to stop it. If he doesn't bring it up, nobody else does either. It bugged me personally when he did it with *Dogma*. They went out and shot *Dogma*, and it had a bigger look. And then Kevin started bashing the visual style in interviews, and I thought, 'Oh Kev, you've got to quit it.' I think if people didn't know that Kevin Smith had a 'reputation' of not having a good visual style, you could sit them down in front of *Chasing Amy* and *Dogma* and it would never dawn on them in a million years to criticize his work."

Part of the problem, Pereira admits, may have stemmed from Smith's over-reported critical remarks concerning *Magnolia* in early 2000. The major news media picked up Smith's e-mail comments about the Paul Thomas Anderson film and things took off from there:

> They sent me an Academy screener DVD … I'll keep it right on my desk, as a constant reminder that a bloated sense of self-importance is the most unattractive quality in a person or their work.[7]

Smith also noted that watching the three hour-plus *Magnolia* was the movie equivalent of "root canal." Almost immediately, there was a backlash among some film buff sects, and a number of Paul Thomas Anderson fans went on the offensive.

"When this whole *Magnolia* flap came up, Kevin never said that he hated Paul Thomas Anderson or his films," Pereira clarifies. "He just didn't like *one* of his films. He loves *Boogie Nights*. But he didn't like *Magnolia*, and it was like this huge controversy. But then a lot of Paul Thomas Anderson fans were posting on the net saying how dare Kevin Smith say that about *Magnolia* when his films are technical disasters. And I'm thinking, 'technical disasters?' Where do they get that? How can you look at *Chasing Amy* and think that? Look at *Amy*, which cost $250,000, compared to *American Pie 2*, which probably cost $30 million, and tell me which film looks more accomplished."

John Pierson is able to put the controversy into a historical perspective. "The writer-directors who came of age in the 1980s—Spike, Jarmusch, the Coen brothers—they had been to film school and had either learned from classic films, or just had a more visual orientation. They figured out how to make films that looked great and had distinctive visual motifs that carried through their work.

"The current generation is not so much like that. There's a number of them, and I put Kevin, Todd Solondz [*Welcome to the Dollhouse* (1995), *Happiness* (1998), *Storytelling* (2002)], and Neil LaBute [*In the Company of Men* (1997), *Your Friends and Neighbors* (1998)] in the same category. I think all three are writers way before they're visual directors. I think they write their lines, and they've all worked with great actors, and they've all gotten great performances, but they want those actors to say those lines in a particular way, and they're much more concerned about that than exactly how it looks."

Jennifer Schwalbach, Kevin Smith's wife and confidante, concurs that visual style isn't nearly as crucial to the director's palette as what is on the page.

"The movies aren't his children," she explains. "They're movies, and they're very close to him, but when he looks at them, he's a writer first. He is a very emotional filmmaker who would rather have people focus on what the actors are saying and the emotions they are getting across, than how cool a set is. He's not trying to make a *Moulin Rouge*."

And yet *Chasing Amy* is a beautifully composed film, boasting visuals that effectively highlight the emotional story. Attentive viewers will note how a deep blue light—a cool shading—colors the funny and intimate scene with Alyssa and Holden in bed together as she discusses her motives for being with a man in general, and this particular man specifically.

That same blue light informs the later sequence in the hockey rink parking lot, but on its second appearance seems harsh and chilling rather than mellow, given the intensity of Alyssa and Holden's angry conversation. The identical lighting in the two sequences links them together in a subtle way.

Thematically, the scenes are purportedly opposite: intimacy versus anger, togetherness versus rejection and betrayal. But the reappearance of the blue light hints there is a connection; that the later sequence is an extension of the first; that whispered secrets and confidences sometimes give way to shocking turnarounds.

The hockey game also grants the film a touch of amusing visual panache. As Holden verbally corners and "checks" Alyssa, confronting her about her checkered past, the film promptly cuts to players on the ice literally checking each other in physical opposition. Funny too how the bells and whistles of the game punctuate especially powerful moments during the argument.

In *Clerks*, Smith maintained an appropriate distance from the humorous characters so that their turmoil came off as funny rather than sympathetic or even painful. In *Chasing Amy*, Smith's *modus operandi* is to make the audience closely identify with every scintilla of pain and yearning Holden feels. So Smith pulls a switcheroo on his established technique. Watch for Holden not in comforting medium shot, but in tight emotional close-ups as he confesses his love to Alyssa during a raging storm. Or notice his face when Alyssa rejects his invitation to a *ménage-à-trois*. The audience sees in agonizing proximity how a tear forms in his eye and rolls down his cheek.

These moments are deeply affecting for two important reasons. One is that Ben Affleck is a powerful and honest actor. Secondly, the situation is universal. We've all been in love and remember how much it can hurt, how deeply it can bruise. But frankly, neither of these two potent elements would work nearly as powerfully if Smith didn't understand where the camera should go; if he didn't have a keen sense of visualizing the drama.

Pereira also appreciates the manner in which Smith handled his third film (and the manner in which Mosier and Smith cut it). "In the case of *Chasing Amy*, Kevin played out a lot of the scenes in two-shot. Kubrick would do that a lot too. Look at *Eyes Wide Shut*; that film is composed of nothing but long shots. There's very little coverage in that film. It's two-and-a-half hours long, and it's a series of three-minute takes. The way Kevin shoots *Chasing Amy* is kind of similar. Look at that scene in the bar with Holden and Alyssa sitting at the table after Hooper and Banky go to look at *Archie* comics. It's a three-minute sequence that just plays itself out in two-shot. It doesn't cut, but why should it have to? What's interesting there is to see the chemistry between the two characters, to see them play off of each other. If you cut, you would lose that rhythm of the actors actually responding to one another.

"I get annoyed with movies nowadays that seem so cut happy. It's good to use coverage where appropriate, but today everything is covered to death, and there is so much cutting that it is actually distracting. *Lord of the Rings* was like that. In dialogue scenes, Jackson just kept cutting, not to different shots, but from one close-up to another close-up of the same actor from a slightly different angle. And I wondered why he couldn't let the dialogue play out. It kind of defeats the purpose of epic filmmaking.

"If you watch a great epic film like *Lawrence of Arabia*, it doesn't cut constantly. The whole point of having a wide frame is to let things play out, but a lot of filmmakers have forgotten that. It's distracting as hell. But *Chasing Amy* is subtle in the way it uses the frame; there's some nice camera stuff going on. It's just a really poetic film, in the use of music and everything, and I love the acting."

Other viewers found the film rewarding not just visually, but thematically too. Terry Teachout writes *Front Row Center*, a column about the performing arts for the magazine of the Library of Congress, *Civilization*, and penned an interesting column about *Chasing Amy* for *The New York Times*, noting the film was deeply Catholic in its approach to morality:

> ... I was struck by ... Alyssa's unexpected use of the word "sated"... it seemed to sum up the peculiar atmosphere of the film, all of whose principal characters are searching for valid moral coordinates in a post-moral world. Then I realized that Alyssa was speaking the language of conversion—one becomes sated with sin—and I asked myself, is there more going on here than meets the eye?[8]

In the remainder of her piece, Teachout expresses the idea that a relationship needs more than love to succeed, it also requires "grace." She even makes note of the fact that several characters in the film, including Silent Bob, identify themselves as being Catholic. This is an insightful reading of the film, and knowing Smith's religious background, one that's nearly impossible to resist exploring.

Yet *Chasing Amy*, as Teachout also notes, is a secular film, though perhaps informed by a Catholic mind-set. There may be a striving for grace in it, but, importantly, also a real lack of righteous judgment. Holden may feel inferior to Alyssa, and believe that she's been unforgivably promiscuous, but he never indicates she's a sinner in the eyes of God. Religions are prone to making just such pronouncements. In *Chasing Amy*, being gay is okay (notice that Holden has "zero" problem with Alyssa's homosexual experience), and that's not likely an attitude endorsed by the Vatican.

In contrast to Teachout's interesting and informed reading, one might argue equally cogently that *Chasing Amy* concerns a generation that is building its own morality out of the ruins of the old one, but having a hard time getting rid of some baggage, namely religious doctrine. Alyssa provides a perfectly reasonable explanation for homosexuality: Why rule out fifty percent of the population in selecting a mate? Isn't that dumb? Interestingly, the film doesn't refute her argument.

But it does note that religious upbringings (that of Silent Bob, and perhaps of Holden), may limit some people's ability to accept the decisions of others. It is that indoctrination in dogma, that judgmental quality of so many organized religions, that renders Holden (or Bob, in the case of his romantic quarry, Amy) unable to accept a woman who is forthright and honest about her sexuality. The movie is, like Scott Mosier noted, about guys who have to move past their stupidity and grow up.

Another rewarding element of *Chasing Amy* is certainly the deliberately self-reflexive nature of its screenplay. Kevin Smith, recently off a commercial project (*Mallrats*), now finds himself vetting a very personal film. In the screenplay, Holden McNeil finds himself similarly disliking his commercial art (*Bluntman & Chronic*) and finding career redemption in a personal project called *Chasing Amy*.

And, one of the best and most pointed moments in the film occurs when Holden asks Jay if he and Bob shouldn't be hanging out at the mall, and the loud-mouthed stoner replies: "We stopped that shit years ago." Nice.

ASKEW VIEWS

WE'RE GOING TO NEED A BIGGER BOAT: In *Chasing Amy*, Alyssa and Banky discuss "war wounds," scars received while performing oral sex, as an incredulous Holden watches. The set design, the staging and the discussion of old wounds all ape the famous "Indianapolis" scene between Robert Shaw, Richard Dreyfuss, and Roy Scheider in Steven Spielberg's 1975 film *Jaws*.

Observant eyes will note that the lamp hanging over the restaurant booth in *Chasing Amy* looks virtually identical to the one aboard the Orca in the film adaptation of the Peter Benchley best seller. "It's paying tribute to his influences, and Kevin is a huge *Jaws* fan," Vincent Pereira notes. "That scene was originally in *Mallrats*."

WALT FLANAGAN'S DOG: A comic book seen in the convention at the end of *Chasing Amy* advertises a book named *Walt Flanagan's Dog*, after the spunky rat terrier named Brodie who Flanagan trained in the Minnesota mall on the set of *Mallrats*. A comic book publisher in the films is named View Askew Comics.

THE DIVIDED ARTIST: *Chasing Amy* depicts Kevin Smith's third set of twenty-something buddies. In *Clerks*, it was the backwards-hat wearing Randal and Dante. In *Mallrats*, it was the stolid T. S. and the dixie-cup-bearing Brodie. In *Chasing Amy*, it's the backwards-hat wearing Banky and love-struck Holden.

"I think that they represent Kevin's comment on his friends," Pereira suggests. "He *always* has a friend with him. We worked at the Quick Stop together, and sometimes it was Kevin and Walter, and sometimes Kevin and Bryan. But he always has a real close male friend, and when he writes those characters, it's a riff on that."

Interestingly, Pereira suggests an alternative interpretation. "It's also a division of himself. One side of Kevin is the serious side, one is the slacker side."

IT'S A SMALL WORLD AFTER ALL: For a film that stands on its own so well, *Chasing Amy* is surprisingly rich in Askewniverse lore, and Smith's script refers to characters often mentioned or seen in the previous films. Alyssa mentions the Eden Prairie Mall by name, a reference to *Mallrats*. The screenplay also makes note of Caitlin Bree and Rick Derris (characters seen in *Clerks*), Brandi Svenning, Mr. Svenning, Shannon Hamilton, and Gwen Turner (characters seen in *Mallrats*), and even pauses for a brief sequence (with Cohee) outside Leonardo's Quick Stop.

Scott Mosier is happy, however, that despite cross-references, *Chasing Amy* has retained its own identity, and is only mentioned in passing in *Jay and Silent Bob Strike Back*. "It was better just to leave that alone," he considers, "and let *Chasing Amy* be what it was; let it end the way it did."

A LONG TIME AGO IN A GALAXY FAR, FAR AWAY: Just about every Kevin Smith movie ever made features overt reference to *Star Wars*. *Chasing Amy* boasts perhaps the funniest *Star Wars*-themed conversation of all: Hooper's racially-motivated diatribe against the Holy Trinity, noting that it is really about "gentrification."

"We shot that *Star Wars* dialogue in one day," Ewell remembers. "Some actors think there's a lot of film in that camera, so they can just keep doing take after take, and I don't think people thought I was going to get through it so fast. But it went really well. If we had to stop at all, it was to fix the lights or the sound."

THE ULTIMATE NUMBER: That number, thirty-seven, pops up again in *Chasing Amy*, this time in the opening credits. Banky and Holden's first comic was titled 37, and in headlines that open the picture, "Local Pair Have Drawing Pair" and "37 Pair Headed to Contender," the ultimate number appears.

A SPOONFUL OF SUGAR: If you watch Jay and Silent Bob's scene in *Chasing Amy* closely, you'll notice that in the background, Jay (Jason Mewes) is pounding down spoonfuls of sugar.

"Kevin wanted to do the sugar thing in *Clerks*," Mewes reports. "There was a scene where Jay was eating sugar, and then I spit out this big mouthful of it, but it got cut. So during *Chasing Amy*, Kevin was thinking of all this stuff to keep us busy, and he brought back that little thing from the first script. When I could, I would spit the sugar out..."

KEVIN SMITH ON *CHASING AMY*

"Holden was definitely the character closest to myself I'd ever written. Here's a guy who's a typical Nineties liberal male, who's like, 'Yeah, I'm from the suburbs, I got myself a black friend, me and my friends do this underground comic-book thing, I've got this girl I like and I'm very OK with her homosexual past.' It's in the arena where you imagine he'd be the most comfortable in—the heterosexual arena—that he completely malfunctions."[9]

5

Dogma (1999)

LEAVE IT TO THE CATHOLICS TO DESTROY EXISTENCE

Get touched by an angel.
Prepare thyself.

CAST AND CREW

LIONS GATE FILMS PRESENTS A VIEW ASKEW PRODUCTION OF *DOGMA*

Written and directed by: Kevin Smith
Produced by: Scott Mosier
Co-Producer: Laura Greenlee
Executive Producer: Jonathan Gordon
Cinematography by: Robert Yeoman
Edited by: Scott Mosier and Kevin Smith
Production Designer: Robert "Ratface" Holtzman
Music by: Howard Shore
Music Supervisor: Randall Poster
Costume Designer: Abigail Murray
Visual Effects Supervisor: Richard "Dickie" Payne
Special Make-up and Creature Effects Designer and Supervisor: Vincent J.
    Guastini, Vincent J. Guastini Productions
Stunt Coordinator: Gary Jensen
M.P.A.A. Rating: R
Running Time: 130 minutes

STARRING

Linda Fiorentino | *Bethany Sloane*
Ben Affleck | *Bartleby*
Matt Damon | *Loki*
Alan Rickman | *Metatron*
Salma Hayek | *Muse/Serendipity*
Chris Rock | *Rufus, the Thirteenth Apostle*
Jason Lee | *Azrael*
Jason Mewes | *Jay*
Kevin Smith | *Silent Bob*
George Carlin | *Cardinal Glick*
Bud Cort | *John Doe Jersey*
Alanis Morissette | *God*
Jeff Anderson | *Gun Salesman*
Brian O'Halloran | *Grant Hicks*
Janeane Garofalo | *Liz*
Betty Aberlin | *Nun*
Dwight Ewell | *Kane*
Guinevere Turner | *Bus Station Attendant*
Walter Flanagan & Bryan Johnson | *Protestors—Steve-Dave
    and Fanboy*
Jared Pfennigwerth, Kitao Sakurai& Barrett Hackney | *Stygian Triplets*
Dan Etheridge | *Priest at St. Stephen's*
Ethan Suplee | *Voice of Noman/Golgothan*
Ratface Holtzman | *Officer McGee*

THE STORY SO FAR...

PLAYING SKEEBALL IN NEW JERSEY, God is incapacitated by demonic forces known as Stygian Triplets, and the supernatural forces of good rally to rescue the divine entity. The problem is St. Michael's Church in Red Bank, New Jersey, and a new publicity campaign to revitalize interest in Catholicism (*Catholicism Wow!*). By offering a plenary indulgence—a chance to wipe away all sin—on the Church's anniversary, the avaricious Cardinal Glick has inadvertently opened the door for two exiled angles, Bartleby and Loki, to return to Heaven and thereby undo Creation.

Metatron, the voice of God, recruits Bethany Sloane, a divorced abortion clinic worker in Illinois, and stoner "prophets" Jay and Silent Bob to stop Bartleby and Loki before it is too late. But on their quest to reach Jersey, these unlikely saviors of mankind encounter a variety of friends and foes, including Rufus, the Thirteenth Apostle; Serendipity, a muse turned stripper; the Golgothan, a monstrous shit demon; and even the architect of the treacherous plan, Azrael the demon.

As Bartleby and Loki cut a swath of destruction across America, from corporate board meetings to mass transit, a faithless Bethany is forced to confront her religious beliefs, as well her secret role in the scheme of things. As Metatron reveals, she has a special lineage, and one that she must live up to.

THE STORY BEHIND THE MOVIE

Kevin Smith, a Catholic who once flirted with the Pentecostal Church and Calvary Ministries, and an avid reader of Milton and Dante, wrote the screenplay for *Dogma* in the August of 1994 for Miramax. The 148-page script, a satire about religion and a heartfelt statement about faith, would eventually lay the groundwork for Kevin Smith's most controversial film.

Like his other projects, *Dogma* underwent a long process of development before arriving on the silver screen. At one point, the screenplay was set to be a high school story, along the lines of *Mallrats* or the first proto-draft of *Chasing Amy*. Kevin Smith noted in the liner notes for the special edition DVD that some of this original thoughts on the project (conceived in Vancouver Film School, well before *Clerks*), included a male protagonist (a "jock"). But even early on, he knew *Dogma* would be a story of angels and demons, and biting, provocative humor.

"Originally it was an idea Kevin had called *God*," Vincent Pereira relates, "but by the time he finished the script it was called *Dogma*. Kevin told me about some scenes in it. In the original draft, the main character, Bethany, was a stripper—and that's how she met Jay.

"She was a stripper in Chicago, and Metatron came to her and ordered her to wait for someone who would 'come like Moses and identify himself as a prophet.'

"So the next day, she's working, getting ready for her strip tease in front of these little booths, where the partition slowly rises as the customer puts his money in. Her boss tells her she's got a customer, and it's Jay. He's already been there five times that day, and the boss warns that he's got a real mouth on him. So Bethany begins her routine, and as the partition slowly rises, Jay is already telling her everything he wants her to do. And finally, he says, 'I want to cum like Moses, and you can make yourself a profit.' She puts it together, asks him out to dinner, and he thanks God."

The script for *Dogma* was to have the longest gestation period of any View Askew production. It was, fans will notice, announced as the next picture at the end of *Clerks*, and later *Chasing Amy*. The reason of the delay was that there was some reluctance on the part of writer/director Smith and producer Mosier to tackle so grand a project early in their careers.

"I think Kevin knew we were going to make *Mallrats* second, but he'd written scenes for *Dogma*," Scott Mosier describes. "What happened was that Miramax had an option, and that was going to be *Dogma*, and *Mallrats* was this side thing where we were going to do this commercial film. There was no way we should have done *Dogma* second. We needed a movie in between to know what it was like to have an actual crew and the rest. The decision was mutual. I think we both knew there was no way we'd get the cast and money we needed for *Dogma*, so *Chasing Amy* became our transitional film."

When the script was completed, Miramax reviewed it and decided that, like *Chasing Amy*, some adjustments in settings might benefit the picture. "It was again a case of making things bigger," relates Pereira. "In the first scene, the dialogue between Bartleby and Loki occurs in a coffee shop, but Miramax told Kevin to give it more scope, and he switched it to an airport. The Golgothan and the Stygian Triplets weren't in the first draft either. They were all added to give the film more action, but thematically it was very consistent from start to finish."

The reaction to the script was very strong from all quarters. Ben Affleck read the script on a plane trip from New Jersey to Boston, before shooting *Chasing Amy*, and developed a fascination with it, becoming determined to play the part of the renegade angel, Bartleby. Another actor who loved the screenplay was Ethan Suplee.

"To me, that script was—and still is—the greatest thing ever written," Suplee enthuses. "There was a point in it where the Golgothan actually had dialogue scenes with Serendipity and talked about where he came from. Golga or Calvary, where Jesus was crucified, was also a site in that part of the world where they crucified criminals. And when they died, their excrement was released as their bowels opened up, and all that shit flowed into a pit.

Out of that pit, the Golgothan was born. I remember reading and wondering, 'Who can come up something that good?' It was the best script I'd ever read."

Furthermore, Vincent Pereira felt that Smith's intention in writing *Dogma* was noble. "Kevin is Catholic and his inspiration for writing *Dogma* was, I think, that he had in his life a priest who was very dynamic. He was an earthy guy, a great speaker, and Kevin realized religion could be fun, something that people aren't just obliged to go to because of guilt, but because they feel genuinely inspired. That's what *Dogma* was about. It wasn't anti-religion; it wasn't even anti-Catholic."

Smith sounded off on his intentions as well:

> *I think for me, the flick was my own celebration of faith ... I just wanted to do something that was pro-faith and expressed my spirituality—my Catholicism. And in the process I figured, you know, a few dick and fart jokes wouldn't hurt.*[1]

Working with their largest budget yet—$10 million—View Askew Productions ramped up to shoot *Dogma*, even as Smith and Mosier were aware that some audience members might consider the subject matter of the film offensive.

If any actors worried about being associated with a controversial film, it didn't stop them from appearing in *Dogma*, and the film boasted Smith's largest and most experienced cast yet. Although the role of Bethany was originally designed for Holly Hunter, and then Emma Thompson was briefly cast before begging off to have a baby, it was Linda Fiorentino, the femme fatale of *The Last Seduction*, who signed on as the troubled protagonist and "last scion."

Alan Rickman, Hans Gruber of *Die Hard* fame, agreed to portray the voice of God, Metatron. Ben Affleck recruited *Good Will Hunting* co-writer and friend Matt Damon to play Loki, Bartleby's angelic partner in crime. The hilarious Chris Rock signed on as Rufus, the thirteenth apostle, while indie-darling Janeane Garofalo was cast as a friend of Bethany's at the abortion clinic, and View Askew favorite Jason Lee was back as the film's antagonist, the rejected muse turned demon, Azrael.

In a small but significant role, comedy legend George Carlin made quite an impression in *Dogma* as the self-serving Cardinal Glick, and later returned for *Jay and Silent Bob Strike Back* and *Jersey Girl*. Lovely Salma Hayek (star of *From Dusk Till Dawn* and *Desperado*) took on the role of a muse turned stripper, and

Dwight Ewell also returned to the View Askew fold, along with Ethan Suplee, playing gang leader Kane and the Golgothan, respectively.

Clerks stars Brian O'Halloran and Jeff Anderson also appeared, the latter for his first role in a Kevin Smith film in more than five years. This time out, O'Halloran played another Hicks cousin, a reporter named Grant, and Anderson had a cameo as a gun shop owner visited by Loki and Bartleby. And, in a move that proved quite controversial, God was cast as a woman; singer/songwriter Alanis Morrisette.

"*Dogma*, to me, was our first movie with really big stars," Jason Mewes notes of the impressive cast. "It was Chris Rock, Alan Rickman, and Salma Hayek. I didn't really know Alan's work that well, but Kevin told me before we started shooting that I couldn't mess up my lines and forget my dialogue because Rickman was a British actor. He said to me that British actors are *serious*; that they're the ones who invented acting. So he told me to memorize my stuff."

Mewes took the advice to heart and memorized the entire script. Not just his own part; but all the parts interacting with Jay. But it wasn't just actor's pride that motivated Mewes to learn the dialogue. He ended up spending a lot of time in Pittsburgh, where much of the film was shot, because of a new friend—a girl.

"Kevin and I went out to Pittsburgh while pre-production on *Dogma* was happening," he relates. "We were scouting out locations, to look at the church there and see if Kevin liked it. I think we stopped at a college and Kevin did a Q & A, and we signed some stuff. But during those two days, I met this girl at a comic book store. While I was in there, I talked to her the whole time, because Kevin was shopping for laserdiscs, and when he does that it takes a really long time. So I ended up talking to her for a half-hour while Kevin shopped, and she was really cute.

"When we were leaving, she gave me her number and Kevin said, 'Invite her back to Jersey.' I said, 'No, she'll be scared.' But I did call her and asked if she could get off work for three days and come back to Jersey. She came back with us, and we hung out for four days. Then she took a train back to Pittsburgh, and we talked on the phone every night for two weeks.

"Anyway, I went back to Pittsburgh to hang out with her, and that was another reason I learned the script. There was nothing to do out there. So I would check out the sets being built and just read the script. Kevin and I rehearsed it, and suddenly I had memorized all of the dialogue."

Despite Mewes's extensive preparation for *Dogma*, dealing with the large, famous cast turned out to be something of a headache, at least from one person's perspective. "*Dogma* was a scheduling nightmare," reports Scott Mosier. "Actors can go from one set to another in L.A., but once you start flying people to Pittsburgh, you have to block it out like a week at a time. You can't have actors flying back and forth across the country fourteen times to be in a movie."

Another complication on *Dogma* involved visual effects. The film featured angels with wings, demons with horns, burning flames (heralding Rickman's supernatural arrival), people in flight, and not a small helping of blood and gore. This was the first time that a View Askew film prominently featured digital effects and prosthetics.

For Mosier, dealing with special effects added a whole new dimension to the producing game.

"It's all about hiring the right people," he says. "If you get the right people, they know what they're doing, and I don't really have to learn anything. If I have to learn a whole lot about CGI or digital effects then I haven't done my job right."

"My job really changes from film to film," Mosier contemplates. "It's mostly reactionary. You bring in a bunch of different people and then they generate a bunch of problems or what not for me to react to. Being a producer is like being a director of practical things; answering questions. I'm constantly making decisions and looking around, making suggestions. Mostly though, I'm in my office fielding telephone calls from different people, having meetings with the production staff and dealing with things so far as post-production. As the job goes on, I do more with talent, actors, and scheduling."

One of Scott Mosier's "right people," who designed and created many of the stunning "creature" effects in *Dogma* is Vincent Guastini, a veteran of films such as *Virus*, *Requiem for a Dream*, and *Hannibal*. After working with Bryan Johnson on *Vulgar*, Guastini came to *Dogma* with one mission: to create the best angel wings yet depicted on film.

"Kevin called me into his office, and said, 'Listen, I'd really like to go all out on this. I didn't like the wings in *Michael* [starring John Travolta], because you barely ever got to see them move.' Then he told me about the money." Guastini remembers. "It was decent. It wasn't horrible, but I knew it was definitely going to be a challenge."

The angel wings that emerged were based on Smith's notion they should look like those appearing in the *Justice League of America* comics. "It was a tall order," Guastini considers. "The main frame of the wings is aluminum, machine parts, welded metal with gears, and they were fully cable operated.

"On top of that was a foam build-up for the muscles, and on top of that, we had a stretching material called spandex which went over the wings to simulate the skin going over muscle. And all those giant feathers? They weren't feathers. You can't get them that big, so we had to sculpt them. We had three or four different sets of feather sculptures, and from those we took a mold and had them vacu-formed. So we vacu-formed as many feathers as we would need to build the main frame of the wings, and on top of that, each feather had a little spine that went down the center. It had to be sculpted and reproduced, and each feather had to have its own spine. Then we mixed in real feathers like you'd get at a feather supply place. It was all blended in, plus airbrushing and dyeing, so the real feathers would match the fake feathers in a seamless blend, and the wings would look absolutely authentic."

But even that wasn't the end of the process. "Kenny Walker was the main mechanical designer on the wings, and my animatronic supervisor, Gregory Ramoundos, put a team together and engineered how the wings were going to work," Guastini continues. "Usually, most wings only do one function. It's always a cheat. But these could not be cheat wings. They had to do everything at once. We had a second pair to back-up the first pair, in case one set went down. On top of that, any time you see someone flying over the steeple, with a double or Ben coming down, we had an open or "static" pair of wings. And those are the ones we actually used later, to blow up, so we didn't damage the animatronic wings. Due to movie magic and clever editing, it looked like those wings were really getting beat up.

"And towards the end of the shoot, I came up with this little mechanism, this little wing stump, to really get across the pain Ben was going through. I thought it would be really cool to have this bloody stump and a bone hanging out, while blood is coming out. People always comment about how painful that stump looks."

When complete, the angel wings in *Dogma* weighed some sixty pounds, and cost a considerable amount of money. Though Guastini notes that the wings were "economical," he is also quick to point out that the $5,000 price tag for them, related in the commentary of the *Dogma* DVD, is way off. The actual cost was much, much higher. "I'm a miracle worker," he notes, without going into specifics, "but I'm not that good."

Beautifully designed and executed, the heavy angel wings were nonetheless untested when it came time to shoot them.

"It was a situation where we wondered if they were going to work," Guastini remembers the first time the angels were deployed on set. "It wasn't that the wings were big and clunky, it was that no one had worked with effects before, and you have to keep practicing and adjusting, and all of that takes time. We had very little time to build the wings at all, and now we were on the set puppeteering them, and we'd never had a chance to work with Ben on them."

It was Kevin Smith, according to Guastini, who first managed to wrangle the wings. 'Kevin got behind the wing controls and started playing with them. And he got it! He said, 'Oh I see, you have to practice this.' And I said, 'Yeah.' You have to get magic moments—magic accidents—where it just all works, if you can catch it on film. And if you get it on the third take or the first take, you edit that moment into the film and you're on. Kevin was able to understand that. He turned around to me and said he wanted a puppeteer credit. And when a director wants a puppeteer credit, he gets it!"

Though the angel wings are no doubt the most extraordinary ever developed for the movies, they did have a downside, particularly in regards to Alan Rickman. The actor had a bad back and wasn't sure he could wear the sixty pound accouterment. Though for a time there was the possibility that the wings could stand on their own, on an aluminum stand stationed behind the actors, Smith felt that they wouldn't look attached that way. And, since Ben Affleck had worn the wings, Rickman was game to try too. Unfortunately, after shooting a few scenes, he aggravated an old injury and pulled his back out. A trip to the hospital was the result.

The Golgothan, the shit demon, was the second major special effects piece in *Dogma*. "Kevin wrote that into the script, and he's a big fan of *Batman*, so he wanted the Golgothan to look a little like Clay Face," Guastini explains. "I tried to approach the character as part of a comic fantasy. I took a little inspiration from *Ghostbusters* too. I took the funny and slimy characteristics from Slimer, and used the Marshmallow Man for bulk, and had Clay Face in there too. Then I added some shit horns, since it was a demon. And then we had to mechanize the whole suit and mimic dialogue. On top of everything else, we had to make shit talk and walk."

Attentive eyes will notice that the shit monster looks wet. That was also by design. "We had a local guy leading the Golgothan team, named Craig Hicks, and he was in charge of making different consistencies of shit," Guastini remembers. "It was made out of oatmeal and vegetables and all kinds of stuff. He had names for all of the shit too: baby poop, runny poop, all colors and varieties. But every time we had to put a stuntman into the suit [with the shit] it would really stink.

"We would store the shit in this warehouse in these big oil cans and during heat and condensation some of the containers would explode and shit would run all over the floor. There was no time to mix new stuff, so it smelled really bad. It was a mess, because everybody had to wear rain gear and ponchos every time we dealt with the shit monster. We had a shit team that just dealt with the monster after we locked the stuntman into the suit. He had on an animatronic helmet on it with all these radio-controlled servos, then we had to drop the shit on him, and it was just a nightmare."

At least some critics of *Dogma* complained that the Golgothan was too comedic-appearing, and somehow out of synch with the tone of the rest of the film; a rather unsubstantiated claim, considering the film's humor and comic book approach. Guastini has heard the feedback, but it doesn't concern him. "If people say it looks like shit, I win, because it's supposed to look like shit..."

Guastini's other contributions to the film were many, and not always as noticeable as the poop demon. His production team was responsible for Ben Affleck's metal chest armor (which one technician sanded for sixteen hours one day just to make smooth). Guastini Productions also engineered and built an animatronic Ben Affleck torso and head that ultimately didn't make it into the final film for the spectacular, exploding head shot that heralded Bartleby's exit from existence.

Guastini's team also crafted some thirty-to-thirty-five corpses (of Bartleby's victims) to litter the scene of the St. Michael's massacre. "Each of those victims had carefully designed heads and was painted," Guastini notes, "but nobody really gets to see all that work. There are people broken in half in cars and buses, and bodies on top of the cathedral."

While working on the effects for *Dogma*, Guastini heard an interesting revelation from Kevin Smith. "He told me he wanted to be a make-up effects guy before he was director."

And that would be fine with Guastini. "When I'm in dialogue with Kevin and we're talking about effects in his office, out at lunch, or on the set, he is so easy going, but also so precise in what he wants. He's a big fanboy, as big a fanboy of stuff from the 1980s as I am. When he writes his scripts, he interjects as many 1980s inspirations as he can into them, and that's why we click. We were both brought up by movies, especially 1980s movies, and it's a perfect marriage. He loves fantasy films and monsters."

One actor who got to work up close with the many special effects on *Dogma* was Brian O'Halloran. "*Dogma* was my first experience getting bloodied on film. I'd been in *Dracula* on stage, and the blood really flew there, but this was my first opportunity to do it in a movie. There was a lot of amazing stunt work in *Dogma* too. There was this whole ending scene with the reporter [Grant] that was bigger, a wider shot than what you saw. It was the first thing to be shot on the film. Stuntmen were being flown around and dropping from the top of the building behind me. I don't know what happened to those shots, but we had stuntmen and I had to coordinate how I would walk backwards. I'd take three steps back, then pause, and it was a lot of fun seeing these guys on rigs being thrown off the top of a church and hitting these bags below. There was a lot of set-up time on that."

Before it was finished filming, the production team of *Dogma* had shot at the Pittsburgh airport, St. Michael's Church, and back in Jersey. The opening sequence, which saw God ambushed by the Stygian Triplets, was shot at the Asbury Park Boardwalk, and the Bootlegger, a bar in Highlands, N.J., doubled for a bar in Chicago.

During the shooting of *Dogma*, Kevin Smith had to leave the set to do some publicity rounds for *Good Will Hunting*, the film he and Scott Mosier had executive produced for Affleck and Damon (for which he was later honored with a Humanitas Prize). He flew to Los Angeles on one such publicity run, and his life suddenly changed.

It was in the City of Angels that Smith first met a beautiful twenty-five-year-old reporter from *USA Today* named Jennifer Schwalbach. It was a Saturday, and the reporter for the paper's Life section didn't think the assignment would be anything special. In fact, she was a little peeved she had to do the interview on her day off.

"I had seen his films," Schwalbach relates, "but I wasn't some über-fan that was super-excited to go interview him. I liked *Chasing Amy* and vaguely remembered the other ones. This was before *Dogma* came out, so I didn't remember *Clerks* and had only the vaguest recollections of *Mallrats*."

But Schwalbach and Smith hit it off. And fast. "It was love at first sight," she explains. "I interviewed him for about an hour, and I started packing up my stuff, and he asked if I wanted to hang out and shoot the shit. And I said, 'Sure,' but I was secretly wondering if he was super creepy, or just a really nice guy, because we were in his hotel room. But it wasn't weird at all. We talked for hours and got to know each other. We really just connected, and laughed and traded stories, and told secrets. I walked out of there feeling giddy."

She wasn't alone. Smith was so taken with the reporter that when he next returned to Los Angeles, approximately a month later, he asked her out on a date. "He asked me to the Independent Spirit Awards, where he won for *Chasing Amy*, and we had a really fabulous time," Schwalbach remembers.

"It was weird for me, because I hung out with a totally different group of people. I wasn't really into film as much as I was into music. And then suddenly I'm at the Independent Spirit Awards sitting at a table with Harvey Weinstein and his wife. And they said to Kevin, 'You brought a journalist to sit at our table? She'll listen to our conversations! How can you do this to us?' And Kevin said, 'No, it's a date.' And they were really upset. 'Oh my god, he's dating a journalist! This is a nightmare for us!'"

Kevin remained in Los Angeles with Jennifer overnight, much to the chagrin of those still studiously lensing *Dogma* back in Pittsburgh, where he was expected back. "He was kind of M.I.A.," Schwalbach relates. "He was supposed to fly out to L.A., grab his award, and head back to Pittsburgh. And he just went missing. They expected him to be filming the next day, and I kept asking if he needed to check in with anybody, and he said no. It was wonderful."

From then on, Jennifer Schwalbach and Kevin Smith conducted a long distance romance, commuting back and forth from L.A. to Pittsburgh.

Finally, when filming was finished, they knew it was time to put the frequent flyer miles behind them and get together. As post-production began, Jennifer was introduced to the glories of Jersey life for the first time.

"It's heaven for Kevin there, and he loves it," she reports. "His friends are there and the 'burbs are like home to him. But I was an outsider. There just wasn't anything there for me. I didn't know a soul, I didn't have a job, and Kevin was living in this little apartment, and there was ratty-ass college furniture and boxes everywhere. He'd been so busy he hadn't even made the time to make a home for myself."

While Jennifer adjusted to the Garden State, *Dogma* was prepared for release. In post-production, Scott Mosier and Kevin Smith edited the film, and ended with a comic fantasy that lasted a whopping three hours and seventeen minutes. Thus it was not only the most expensive, most elaborate, and grandest of Smith's films to date; it was also the longest. But the editors knew they couldn't release a three-hour plus comedy, so they had to whittle away at the film, and pull it back in. The standard rule for comedy is that ninety minutes or less is a good length. *Dogma* had overshot that by quite a bit.

"The man was editing *Dogma* from the moment he woke up in the morning to 4:00 a.m. the next day," Jennifer Schwalbach, then a new arrival in Jersey, remembers of that period. "He didn't have time to take me on a tour of the 'burbs, or tell me where the best pizza place was; he was working all the time."

"Scott and Kevin did an absolutely great job of cutting it down from three hours to two hours," Pereira notes. "The film has a breakneck pace, and when some people argue that it's too long, I wonder what they would have cut out. The only way to cut the film would have been to drop whole sequences, and then I don't think it would have been coherent. But when people criticize the film, it's easiest for them to say it's too long."

Indeed, in many ways, *Dogma* is Kevin Smith's *J.F.K.* or *Malcolm X*. It's a big, sprawling film; an epic adventure packed with esoteric but fascinating information on a variety of religious subjects. For some viewers, however, it was a bit too ambitious a trip, and some of the wordy, technical information about matters such as the Last Scion, plenary indulgences, and transubstantiation were simply too much to process in one viewing.

Published reports on such matters indicate that on a first viewing, audiences only "register" about 80 percent of what actually happens on screen. In a fast-talking, dialogue-laden movie like *Dogma*, that may not have been enough to make the story comprehensible to some.

"I have a whole theory about *Dogma*," confides Pereira. "It's not that's it too long. It's that it's too short. There's so much information that's given to the audience, and the two-hour cut removes any chance for the audience to breathe. The audience tries to process it all, and sometimes people feel there's something off about the pacing; that it's too long.

"In fact, it needs to be twenty minutes longer. The original cut of the film had some transitions that got cut out; some chances for the audience to breathe and take it all in. I think if the film still had those moments intact, and the audience were able to sit back and let the information sink in, the film would feel shorter because you're getting the chance to process."

"*The Deer Hunter* was three hours long," Pereira argues. "In the book *Final Cut* [the 1999 book by Steven Bach, subtitled *Art, Money and Ego in the Making of Heaven's Gate, the Film That Sank United Artists*], he talks about how the studio previewed a two-hour version of the film, and the audience didn't like it. Then they previewed the three-hour version and the response went way up. Even though the movie was longer, it needed that length to breathe. I think *Dogma* may have suffered from that. Of all Kevin Smith's films, it's the one that would have benefited from a bigger budget. It needed another $5 million and another twenty minutes of running time. I still think it's a great accomplishment, but it was hugely ambitious considering the scope the budget allowed it to have."

Since *Dogma's* release, many Kevin Smith fans have pined away for a new special edition of the film, the original Mosier-Smith three hour, seventeen minute cut. In Hollywood today, people don't always give audiences credit for being willing to sit three hours in a theater. However, under the right circumstances, like *J.F.K.*, *Malcolm X*, *Lord of the Rings*, or even *Dogma*, many moviegoers are willing to commit that much time because the director's vision is a thoughtful one.

It is important to note, however, that even at two hours long *Dogma* was released in 1999 to great acclaim. The sound mix from Skywalker Sound was impressive, and Howard Shore's brilliant, rousing score made the action seem even bigger. Indeed, if you called the View Askew offices in 2002 and happened to be put on hold, you would hear Shore's score and be drawn into its majesty.

Considering his fine work here, and on *Lord of the Rings*, Shore's 2001 Oscar for best score was definitely earned (and probably many times over).

On the critical front, Roger Ebert gave *Dogma* "thumbs up," *Entertainment Weekly* heralded it as one of the "ten best films of the year," and *The New York Times'* Janet Maslin again waxed enthusiastic about View Askew's work. But, as most people who lived through the experience recall, the film also attracted more than its fair share of negative publicity.

Months before *Dogma* was even released, in the early summer of 1999, it was attacked by conservative elements of the far religious right. The Catholic League, the group responsible for pressuring ABC to cancel *Nothing Sacred*, a TV series about a progressive man of the cloth, made Kevin Smith's fourth film its latest target.

Leading the charge of moral indignation and outrage was William A. Donohue, the president of the Catholic League for Religious Civil Rights. Importantly, Donohue hadn't even bothered to see the film before condemning it.

Apparently, originality isn't important to self-appointed guardians of morality, because Donohue's strategy to protest *Dogma* appeared cribbed from Billy Graham's old play-book. A quarter century earlier, it was Graham who had vigorously objected to William Friedkin's film version of *The Exorcist*—claiming it was evil, and even causing people to become possessed by Satan. In equally fiery terms, Donohue laid out his objections to the movie:

> *Joseph and Mary have sex and a descendent of theirs is a lapsed Catholic who works at an abortion clinic; God is played by a singer known for her nude videos and songs about oral sex; the Thirteenth Apostle resembles Howard Stern, the Mass is compared to lousy sex.*[2]

Disney, the parent company of Miramax, which planned to release the film, had faced this kind of censorship before and buckled.

"Disney is an easy target for this kind of protest. It's their Achilles' heel,"[3] noted Harvey Weinstein. *Nothing Sacred* was not the only precedent. In 1994, the same year *Clerks* ran in theaters, Miramax released a British film called *Priest*, about a gay Catholic man of the cloth, and it too was picketed. Disney deemed the film "inappropriate" because of its content involving "Roman Catholics," and didn't release it under a Disney imprint.[4]

When it looked like Disney was again going to cave to censorship (allegedly at the behest of Michael Eisner, who may not have wished to see theme park attendance drop because of protesters), the resourceful brothers Weinstein swooped in. They put up $12 million of their own cash to buy the rights to *Dogma*, so Disney would no longer be attached to any of the controversy. The Weinsteins then shopped for a new distributor, and after turn-downs from Columbia, MGM, and Universal, the film was sold to Lion's Gate Films, an outfit headquartered in Vancouver, BC.

Though his screenplay won an Independent Spirit Nomination for the year, Smith had other things to worry about. For one thing, the CBS television network objected to the film's ad line, "Get Touched by An Angel," claiming it infringed on the copyright of their white-bread inspirational series, *Touched by an Angel*.[5] But more disturbingly, the protests were reaching a fever pitch.

"It was terrifying," Schwalbach explains. "It was so shocking to me that we needed armed bodyguards—when I was pregnant—if we ever went out in public. We'd get all these horrible little suggestions from Miramax, like, 'Be sure to look under your car before you get in it. Look behind you when you go anywhere.' And I thought, 'This is horrible, are you serious?' When Kevin would walk out on stage, they'd tell us, 'You don't know who is in the audience, so you might want to have a guard.' But it was just a movie! Then the hate mail started coming, and we couldn't have mail sent to our house or the office because of mail bombs, and I was just disgusted and very angered by the entire experience."

Donohue's Catholic League picketed *Dogma* during its premiere in the New York Film Festival in October of 1999, but the attacks only emboldened Kevin Smith, according to his wife. "Kevin is never one to hold back about what he's feeling, so we poked back a little bit."

What did Smith do to "poke back?" He joined the opposition.

"The movie came out at our local theater," Schwalbach explains. "And it was on the news that some people were going to protest *Dogma*. So we said, 'Let's go,' and started making signs that read 'Dogma is Dogshit' and things like that. It was Bryan Johnson, myself, and Kevin. I started throwing back drinks before we left because I thought the protesters would immediately recognize Kevin and we'd be chased out of town. But it was completely the opposite. There were five yokels there singing, and we walked up . . . and they wouldn't let us use our sign because it said 'shit.' They were just hooting and hollering, and had no idea who Kevin was."

Then the first news team arrived.

"A reporter came up and asked if Kevin was Kevin Smith. He said, 'Oh God no, I get that all the time. I'm here to protest this movie, it isn't right.' And she looked at him, then a picture of him on her clipboard, and just didn't put it together. Basically that was the point. The protesters and others were trying to stir up a controversy, but hadn't even seen the movie enough to recognize Kevin. How can you be so offended by something that you haven't seen, and aren't educated about? But the whole thing was tired. It went on for months, and people wanted to sue us. It was really ridiculous."

Ironically, the controversy surrounding *Dogma* only made more people see the film. By 1999, Ben Affleck was a huge and influential movie star, and he used his authority and popularity to support the film:

Dogma is a lot more accessible than any sermon. This movie has a real chance of getting younger people talking about faith. If the Inquisition were around, they would undoubtedly brand Kevin a heretic and light him on fire.[6]

Other collaborators were just as quick to come to Smith's defense. "I did anticipate the protest," notes Pereira, "because I'd seen what the same people did to *The Last Temptation of Christ*, which was probably the most pro-Christian movie ever made, and these idiots shot themselves in the foot by protesting it."

O'Halloran also feels bad that people couldn't understand what Smith was trying to do, and instead saw only their own fear. "When these mini-controversies come up about Kevin, like GLAAD and the Catholic League on *Dogma*, he isn't really intending what these people are thinking. They don't realize that it really does bother him that people take things the wrong way and lose their sense of humor when it comes to comedy. They forget what comedy means. All Kevin is doing, all we're doing, is questioning; that's all. But some people don't like that."

Interestingly, many religious sources crossed Donohue and actually supported Kevin Smith's film. Richard A. Blake, writing for *America*, praised the film:

He [Smith] has created a profoundly spiritual film, but he does not speak the church language of those of us who have absorbed several decades of dull, unimaginative sermons and ponderous ecclesiastical abstractions. Dogma takes aim at an audience that has not yet learned to take the suffocating face of religion as the norm.[7]

Douglas LeBlanc of *Christianity Today* also found some things to admire. He noted the film was "flawed, but oddly touching" and that "Kevin Smith shows nascent gifts as a visual stylist and a storyteller."[8]

Still, there were some holdouts who objected to *Dogma*, not because of the controversy—but merely because they found the film to be weak. "The real problem is that *Dogma* isn't as funny as it thinks it is. The speechifying about religion is dull to a surreal degree," wrote Jeff Giles of *Newsweek*.[9] "*Dogma* is a smugly gory film," complained Karl Stevens in *The Christian Century*. "The violence seems to be incorporated only because it is part of the common aesthetic of Smith's generation."[10]

Worst of all, *Entertainment Weekly's* Bruce Frett wrote a column entitled "Unholy Mess" on December 1, 1999, in which he devised a new holy commandment, one dictating that Kevin Smith "shalt not" direct any more films.[11]

As is typical of the witty Scott Mosier, he had a pithy response to all the controversy and negative vibe surrounding *Dogma*. "People took it awfully seriously for a movie that had a rubber poop monster in it."

In this case, View Askew really did have the last laugh. Not only was the film highly regarded by America's mainstream critics, it generated more than $30 million at the box office, making it Kevin Smith's most profitable movie yet. It was also the third-highest grossing film the weekend of its release. Accordingly, Smith and Mosier re-upped with Miramax in an "expansive three year, first-look deal" covering film and TV projects.[12]

In addition, Smith was awarded the "Defender of Democracy" award from the People for the American Way for his efforts to shepherd the controversial *Dogma* from page to stage, to theaters.

Thanks, Mr. Donohue.

MORALITY PLAY IN FOUR COLORS

When it was released theatrically in 1999, *Dogma* commenced with a disclaimer noting that it was not the filmmaker's intent "to offend." Ironically, Smith's disclaimer was highly amusing because it gently mocked disclaimers in general, noting they were designed to "save one's ass." That's the essence of Smith's self-deprecating comedy style and in many ways the perfect opening for *Dogma*. The disclaimer releases tensions, makes one laugh, and leaves one ready for the silliness—and remarkable intelligence—that follows.

Despite the Catholic League's protestations to the contrary, *Dogma* seems to be a highly pro-faith and moral film. In fact, it is a post-modern morality play, cloaking its overt didacticism in a slew of very funny fart and dick jokes.

More than five centuries ago, the morality play was a school of theater that in essence represented "dramatized sermons."[13] The common theme of the morality play was the war for control of the immortal human soul; the battle between good and evil, God and the Devil. Characters in morality plays often had names that expressed their vital traits, such as Gluttony, Sloth, Chastity, Virtue, Vice, etc.

It isn't a stretch to see how *Dogma* fits into this long-standing tradition. Bartleby and Loki, for instance, take great glee in turning humans to "the dark side," convincing a nun (Betty Aberlin) to leave behind her vows, and then punishing them for their infractions. In doing so, they endanger the human soul and chock up one more score for evil.

And look at the names of the characters in *Dogma*. Salma Hayek's muse is called Serendipity, and Bethany and friends run across her at a strip club by pure happenstance, only to learn important information about their quest from her. *Serendipity*, of course, is defined as the faculty of making valuable discoveries by accident. So in a very real sense, the role the character Serendipity plays in saving the world is dictated by her very name.

Loki, the angel played by Matt Damon in *Dogma*, also lives up to his name. In Norse Mythology, Loki is known as a terrible troublemaker, a mischief-maker, a trickster, who is ultimately punished by the gods for his behavior (an unsanctioned murder). In *Dogma*, Loki is the more playful of the two angels. As he torments the head of the Mooby board of directors, he presents him a voodoo doll and leads him to fear that it possesses supernatural powers. Of course, Loki is really deceiving him. "I don't believe in voodoo!" he laughs playfully.

On the bus journey to New Jersey, Loki takes great amusement in his entrapment of a young adulterer (Scott Mosier). He toys with him before killing him, thus sharing the same characteristics as the mythical Loki, and in fact, suffering his very fate: exile. Only here, *Dogma*'s Loki is punished for his unsanctioned decision not to commit murder. He once (a very long time ago) showed mercy, at the behest of Bartleby.

Metatron, played by Alan Rickman, represents the voice of God, a necessity in interactions with humanity because man's frail ears could not withstand the sound of the divine voice. *Meta* is a prefix that means "transformation or change" and *tron* is a Greek suffix denoting an instrument. Put those two together and you have an "instrument of transformation." Of course, that perfectly suits Rickman's character because he hears the word of God in one ear, and then must transform (or translate) it with his own instrument, his voice.

The other characters are similarly named to represent Christian symbols or characteristics. Bethany may be named after Mary of Bethany, a character in Luke (10:39) who listened to the teachings of Christ. It is Bethany's job, in *Dogma*, to hear the will of God, and heed those teachings.

The Golgothan is named for a place, a terrible site where criminals died, and in the process voided their bowels. Thus the Golgothan is literally emblematic of his birthplace's primary characteristic: he is composed of shit.

Even Cardinal "Glick" seems to be a play on two words: *glib*, meaning "superficial" and *click*, meaning a sort of unpleasant, short sound. This fits his character because this is, after all, the man trying to dumb-down Catholicism to make it more "user-friendly." His words, though not merely clicks, are unpleasant sounds that have little significance.

Then of course there's Silent Bob. His name speaks for itself.

Perhaps more significantly, *Dogma* might be considered a modern morality play because its purpose is didactic. Kevin Smith's screenplay explains the importance of faith, decries how an idea can become first a belief, and then, ultimately, dogma. In the end, the film is pro-faith most simply because the characters that work against creation, and therefore against God, are punished for their trespasses. Bartleby commits the mortal sins of vanity and hubris. He can't conceive that God might prefer man to angel, and so is ready to betray God and un-write the universe in defiance of that preference. His punishment, like something out of David Cronenberg's *Scanners*, is an exploding head.

Another interesting facet of the film is the ambiguous climax. Do the murdered men and women at St. Michael's (including Cardinal Glick?) remain dead, or does God restore them to life when she "cleanses" the crime scene? And, what of Bartleby and Loki? What will be their "eternal" punishment for nearly destroying creation? By leaving those answers to the viewer's imagination, Kevin Smith is permitting a personal interpretation of *Dogma* (and again establishing that he prefers the realistic school to the formalist school of filmmaking). If audiences believe that God is a wrathful, punishing entity, they can believe the guilty are punished. Contrarily, if audience members believe in a loving and forgiving God, there is an opening for their view as well. Much of *Dogma* is similarly open-ended.

Despite some provocative and positive messages, *Dogma* remains a controversial work of art because Kevin Smith is not willing to equate "dogma" with "faith." He sees and describes an important difference. He believes one can have faith without necessarily believing in every edict handed down from the Vatican (or any organized religion).

In *Dogma*, for instance, a savior is found in an unusual place: an abortion clinic. Homosexuality is not a sin, yet the disowning of another human being is. The New Testament is "false" in that it ignores a black apostle, and hence it is bigoted too. And finally, the very act that saves all of creation is one that would make the late Jack Kevorkian and other advocates of euthanasia proud—pulling a terminal patient (John Doe Jersey) off of life support. Each of these issues—abortion, homosexuality, racism, and euthanasia—is a hot-button one for the Church, and by confronting them head-on, Smith seems to be expressing a critical point: Faith in God does not necessarily mean an unquestioning support of everything espoused by man's organization, the Church. God's laws and man's "dogma" are separate things.

It's probably also fair to state that Donohue and the Catholic League didn't appreciate Smith's attempts to make Jesus Christ an understandable, sympathetic and, yes, likeable figure on pure human terms. But that was Smith's bag, to make a film that "celebrated" faith and didn't treat it like a "funeral."[14] In the superhero mythos, the best and most popular figures are those who have some flaws, some connection to humanity. Batman has his anger, Peter Parker his angst, and so forth, and without these characteristics, the heroes would be boring—invincible drones with whom no one would identify. In *Dogma*, Smith discusses Jesus as if he is the ultimate superhero.

When Metatron speaks of the young Jesus Christ, who had to face his fate—to die on the cross for all mankind—it is strongly suggested that Jesus rebelled against the notion; that he had moments of self-pity and agonizing doubt. Sadly, that level of pure humanity flies in the face of a rigid dogma that wants people to consider Christ wholly divine, infallible, and nobler than the best in human nature. Of course, that interpretation leaves Jesus wholly unbelievable and unsympathetic. Smith takes the opposite approach, relating how Jesus was really the culmination of all man's best characteristics—graced with divinity—but still identifiable as a human being.

Smith's understanding of superhero mythos is ideally suited for this material, and *Dogma* succeeds because of this radical re-characterization of a religious "super" hero.

That Smith re-writes familiar Church beliefs with humorous new interpretations (a thirteenth apostle, a female God, and the idea that Hell is a place where *Mrs. Doubtfire* plays continuously) no doubt fails to win him new friends among the religious right. Religion is, for these folks, something to be treated only with righteous solemnity and reverence, and comedy's goal is always to make one laugh, to be irreverent. There is probably no religious comedy in the world that would satisfy the Catholic League, but that's okay. Comedy remains accessible; religion not necessarily so.

Dogma is also a great and funny adventure. In many senses, it is filmed like the most majestic comic book ever imagined, filled with colorful angels, monstrous demons, and an outrageous shit monster that could challenge the Incredible Hulk. This "comic book" interpretation of religious concepts fits in with Smith's earlier films and makes *Dogma* a more accessible film than it might have been, despite a screenplay that is, alas, more knowledgeable about Christianity than most viewers are.

Before this crazy ride is over, the audience is expected to have processed ideas such as Divine Mandate, Plenary Indulgence, Transubstantiation, Papal Sanction, and the Last Scion, a wordy chunk of material. For that reason, *Dogma*, already a good film, improves dramatically on repeated viewing. And, one has to admire the audacity of Smith's common-man, genre approach. His comic book background reduces difficult religious conceits to concepts no more arcane than the Fortress of Solitude or the Phantom Zone. It's clever and endearing, and grants an all-together new perspective on faith. If the Bible were a (Marvel) comic book, it might very well look and play like *Dogma*.

Yet it is the quieter moments in *Dogma* that speak most clearly of Smith's evolving sense of film style. The scene wherein Metatron walks on water, approaching the despondent Bethany on the shore of a quiet lake by moonlight, is nothing less than wondrous. The location is perfect and idyllic, and the shot is beautifully composed. As the soundtrack reaches an emotional crescendo, the film rises to and honors its important subject matter. It may seem belittling to compare a quasi-Biblical scene of cosmic importance to a pop culture movie, but for me, this scene always evokes the grandeur of *Star Wars*, when a wistful Luke Skywalker awaits his calling under the setting suns of Tatooine.

Kudos also go to Matt Damon. His character goes from angel of death to doubting Thomas with great skill. "I've heard a rant like this before," he reports in a stunning scene with Bartleby, and Damon finds exactly the right pitch for the material. Loki wants to return home to Heaven, but he understands that there are limits. That there is something greater than his own needs and that he and Bartleby can only go so far.

On the down side, Bethany is an interesting character, but it may be a mistake that she is never permitted to be funny. Linda Fiorentino is a fine actress, but her performance ranks as the least interesting of the "straight man" characters in the View Askewniverse. Like Jeremy London in *Mallrats*, she doesn't seem totally in tune with the cadences of Smith's dialogue, and often comes across as whiny or mopey.

By contrast, Brian O'Halloran and Ben Affleck have really mastered this style of "straight man" character, bringing a solid foundation of self-awareness and *joie de vivre* to their similar roles in *Clerks* and *Chasing Amy*. Granted, Bethany is facing remarkably tough stuff in *Dogma*, but the audience is not completely on her side; at least not in the way it identifies with Rufus, Jay or Silent Bob, or even, for that matter, Bartleby and Loki.

It may just be the so-called superhero syndrome. Being "special" (or super) may be a drag for a time, but wouldn't it also be really cool to be invisible, super-strong, or the savior of all humanity? Fiorentino's portrayal seems to have no joy in it, and that's a shame. Bethany, unlike Smith, seems to treat faith as a funeral.

Dogma is an ambitious, entertaining, and thought provoking movie, and many critics and audiences found it to be Kevin Smith's best motion picture yet. This author is firmly in that camp that prefers *Chasing Amy*, but it would be impossible not to appreciate and respect the audacious nature and beautiful execution of *Dogma*.

ASKEW VIEWS

SACRED COW: One of the best sequences in *Dogma* involves Bartleby and Loki punishing idolaters who worship the golden calf named Mooby. The star of TV, film and other media, Mooby the Cow also sports a line of fast food restaurants (seen in *Jay and Silent Bob Strike Back* and *Clerks II* as well) and a gaggle of merchandising to boot. Many viewers and reviewers assumed that Mooby symbolized Mickey Mouse, and by proxy, Disney. But that wasn't necessarily the intent, as Vincent Pereira explains.

"Mooby wasn't a jab at Disney per se, it was more a jab at corporate America. People speculated that it was about Disney, especially after everything that went down, but I don't believe that was Kevin's intention. He was just showing people how little kids are brainwashed by corporate America into buying things they don't really need."

PUT 'EM UP: In a complete departure from his role as Hooper, Dwight Ewell plays a violent gang leader named Kane in *Dogma*. One of the requirements of the role was a scene (eventually cut) that involved firearms.

"It was cool playing Kane, but I hate working with guns," Ewell reveals. "In that scene, they had policemen on the set and everything, standing all around you. As soon as you fire the weapon, you have to freeze in that position. After the takes are over, they rush in and get the gun out of your hands."

METHINKS THEY PROTEST TOO MUCH: Bryan Johnson's Steve-Dave and Walt Flanagan's Fanboy make their strangest appearance yet in *Dogma*, picketing at an abortion clinic in Illinois.

Johnson explains how that came about. "Realistically, where are you going to put Steve-Dave and Fanboy in *Dogma*? Maybe they were traveling together and were so full of piss and vinegar that they stopped at this abortion protest.

"It's funny, because if you notice, we're set apart in that scene. Everybody else is gathered together in support of one another, and we're just off by ourselves, having our own personal protest."

THE STRAIGHT POOP: Those listening closely to the monstrous Golgothan may recognize the tones of actor Ethan Suplee. "There was some computer enhancement of my voice," the actor says. But nonetheless, he regards the demon as his favorite character in the View Askewniverse. "There's just a special place in my heart for an excremental shit demon..."

A LONG TIME AGO IN A GALAXY FAR, FAR AWAY: The *Star Wars* references fly fast and thick in *Dogma*. One scene in a dinner featuring Jay, Silent Bob, and Bethany evokes the famous Mos Eisley cantina scene from George Lucas's space opera. Another cut sequence sees Matt Damon's character Loki pontificating (with hilarious results) about the religious significance of such Lucas characters as IG-88 and the Ewoks.

NO TIME FOR LOVE, DR. JONES: Other than *Jaws* and *Star Wars*, the *Indiana Jones* films are those most referenced in the cinema of Kevin Smith. In *Clerks*, Randal quoted *Temple of Doom*'s sidekick, Short Round. In *Dogma*, Silent Bob throws Bartleby off the moving train and then deadpans "No ticket." This is the same line Indiana Jones spouted in *The Last Crusade*, when throwing a Nazi officer from an in-flight dirigible.

In the *Clerks* cartoon, the fifth episode re-stages the *Temple of Doom*, making Randal slave to an Egyptian, quasi-Thuggee cult until rescued by Dante and his little league team.

HE'LL TAKE YOU FOR A RIDE: Keen eyes will notice that the bus line in *Dogma* is named Derris, after that chick-magnet from *Clerks* and *Chasing Amy*, Rick Derris.

A VERY VIEW ASKEW WEDDING: Kevin Smith & Jennifer Schwalbach tied the knot while *Dogma* was being mixed at the Skywalker Ranch and Schwalbach was eight months pregnant.

"I'm not a very traditional person," Schwalbach notes, "and wasn't very concerned with the details. We'd been up to Skywalker so many times during *Dogma*, and the last time we were up there it was so beautiful and breathtaking. We were there with Mosier and his then-girlfriend Monica. And we said, 'Let's do it,' and put it together in a day. It was exactly what we wanted and from what I understand, we were the second couple ever to be married there.

"Kevin and I had a special moment that I hope everyone who gets married goes through. We had thrown our lives together, we were having a child, and we didn't think we could become any closer. It was more than I ever expected or hoped for, and he feels the same. We just love being married."

KEVIN SMITH ON *DOGMA*

"... It was just kind of an offering up of what I consider myself to be, a contemporary Catholic. I'm Catholic, I go to church, but I'm not one of these people who condemn others for not believing in the same thing I do. So isn't it possible to be a guy who makes a movie chock-a-block full of dick and fart jokes and still have faith in God?"[15]

6

Jay and Silent Bob Strike Back (2001)

A JAY AND SILENT BOB MOVIE? WHO WOULD PAY TO SEE THAT?

Hollywood had it coming.

CAST AND CREW

DIMENSION FILMS PRESENTS A VIEW ASKEW PRODUCTION, JAY AND SILENT BOB STRIKE BACK

Written and directed by: Kevin Smith
Produced by: Scott Mosier
Co-Producer: Laura Greenlee
Executive Producers: Bob Weinstein, Harvey Weinstein, and Jonathan Gordon
Cinematography by: Jamie Anderson
Edited by: Scott Mosier and Kevin Smith
Production Designer: Robert "Ratface" Holtzman
Costume Designer: Isis Mussenden
Visual Effects Supervisor: Joseph Grossberg
Special Make-up and Creature Effects: Vincent Guastini Productions
Music: James L. Venable
Casting: Christine Sheaks
M.P.A.A. Rating: R
Running Time: 103 minutes

STARRING

Jason Mewes | *Jay*
Kevin Smith | *Silent Bob*
Ben Affleck | *Holden McNeil/Himself*
Jeff Anderson | *Randal*
Brian Christopher O'Halloran | *Dante*
Shannon Elizabeth | *Justice*
Eliza Dushku | *Sissy*
Ali Larter | *Chrissy*
Jennifer Schwalbach | *Missy*
Will Ferrell | *Marshal Willenholly*
Jason Lee | *Bruce Brodie/Banky Edwards*
Judd Nelson | *Sheriff*
George Carlin | *Hitchhiker*
Carrie Fisher | *Nun*
Seann William Scott | *Brent*
Jon Stewart | *Reg Hartner*
Jules Asner | *Herself*
Steve Kmetko | *Himself*
Tracy Morgan | *Drug Dealer*
Gus Van Sant | *Himself*
Chris Rock | *Chaka*
Jamie Kennedy | *P.A.*
Wes Craven | *Himself*
Shannen Doherty | *Herself*
Mark Hamill | *Himself/Cocknocker*
Amy Noble | *Baby Bob's Mother*
Harley Quinn Smith | *Baby Silent Bob*
Ever Carradine | *Baby Jay's Mother*
Brian Andrew Saible | *Baby Jay*
Gavin Brooks | *Baby Jay Voice*
John Willyung | *Passerby*
Jake Richardson | *Teen #1*
Nick Fellinger | *Teen #2*
Vincent Pereira | *Customer*
Ernest O'Donnell | *Cop*

Marc Blucas | *Guy*
Matthew James | *Dude*
Jane Silvia | *Bookish Girl*
Carmen Lee | *Redhead Beauty*
Dan Etheridge | *Deputy*
Diedrich Bader | *Security Guard*
Scott Mosier | *AP; Willam the Idiot-Man-Child*
Jason Biggs | *Himself*
James Van Der Beek | *Himself*
Bryan Johnson | *Steve-Dave*
Walter Flanagan | *Fanboy*
Renée Humphrey | *Trish*
Joey Lauren Adams | *Alyssa*
Dwight Ewell | *Hooper*
Alanis Morrissette | *That Woman*

THE STORY SO FAR . . .

RANDAL GETS JAY and SILENT BOB ARRESTED for peddling pot outside the Quick Stop, and the two stoners complain about their situation to Brodie, who is now running a comic book store in Red Bank. He informs them that a movie is being made by Miramax, one based on Holden McNeil and Banky Edwards's old cult comic book, *Bluntman & Chronic*. Jay and Silent Bob know nothing about the deal, and haven't been paid for their likeness rights.

The stoners visit Holden McNeil, who tells them about the Internet and a site called *Movie Poop Shoot.com*, where nerds are blasting Jay and Silent Bob and the *Bluntman & Chronic* project. Jay and Silent Bob are angered about the rap against their good names, and decide the only way to stop the online bitching is a pilgrimage to Hollywood to shut down the movie.

Jay and Silent Bob hitchhike cross-country, and after a few harrowing adventures with a hitchhiker, a nun, and the cast of *Scooby Doo*, stop at a Mooby restaurant to eat breakfast. There they meet Justice, a beautiful girl who claims to be from S.A.A.C. (Students Against Animal Cruelty). She and three friends, Sissy, Missy, and Chrissy, are on their way to a pharmaceutical company in Boulder to free animals from captivity. But that's just a cover. Justice is actually part of a gang of jewel thieves who plan to use the Garden State stoners as patsies.

Before long, Jay and Silent Bob have stolen an orangutan named Susanne, had numerous run-ins with the law (and a Federal Wildlife Marshal, Willenholly), and disrupted the Miramax Studio lot. Masquerading as Bluntman and Chronic, Jay and Silent Bob finally catch up with Banky Edwards, even as Willenholly and the jewel thieves close in on them.

SILENT BOB'S WORDS OF WISDOM

"As we are not only the artistic basis, but also obviously the character basis for your intellectual property, *Bluntman & Chronic*, when said property was optioned by Miramax films, you were legally obliged to secure our permission to transfer the product to another medium."

THE STORY BEHIND THE MOVIE

In the dog days of August 2001, the fifth film of Kevin Smith and View Askew's "New Jersey Chronicles" appeared on the screens across America and took the weekend box office by storm. Replete with a gaggle of celebrity cameos and a laugh-a-minute pace, *Jay and Silent Bob Strike Back* was essentially a big budget ($20 million) party, a celebration of all things Jay and Silent Bob. Featuring state-of-the-art CGI special effects and satirical looks at movies such as *Scream*, *Good Will Hunting*, *E.T.*, and *Planet of the Apes*, *Jay and Silent Bob Strike Back* brought the five-strong film franchise to a close (at least until 2006...) with hilarious style.

"After *Dogma*, and how stressful it had been, we thought we were safe with *Jay and Silent Bob Strike Back*," reports Jennifer Schwalbach. "Kevin needed to make a movie like *Jay and Silent Bob* that was very funny and irreverent and light-hearted and ridiculous."

"I thought the script was hysterical," adds Brian O'Halloran. "A road trip with scenes from *Scooby Doo* and *Planet of the Apes* was great. You could tell that it was a movie made for the fans, and yet it could still stand up on its own."

And stand it did. *Jay and Silent Bob Strike Back* won the weekend box office sweepstakes (a first in View Askew history), raking in over $11 million. It also poked wicked fun at a current phenomenon in contemporary America: fanboy posters on the Internet.

Alas, it's a fact of life in the twenty-first century. Movie fans of all ages now flock to message boards and chat rooms to bash films, albums, TV

series, and books. These attacks are often misspelled, inappropriately capital-
ized, poorly worded, and launched behind the all-protective veil of anonymity.
People can say anything on the net, with no consequences or accountability,
and unfortunately some people have exploited the freedom the technology
offers merely to vent personal frustrations.

For artists working in this environment, the negative, persistent, and
often thoughtless assaults are hugely frustrating. And, yes, Kevin Smith has
been the target of some of the crap (to wit: the *Magnolia* flap). So, to the
delight of many, *Jay and Silent Bob Strike Back* seems tailor-made to skewer
those "militant" movie fans that hide behind jocular handles and lob attacks
at filmmakers. To its credit, the film does so in the funniest manner imaginable.
Specifically, Smith reveals these accomplished "critics" to be twelve year-old
boys; or better yet, people with the mentality of twelve year-old boys.

"The Internet is a great communications tool," explains Vincent Pereira,
"but everybody suddenly thinks they can be a film critic. And their idea of
criticism is to come up with the best one liner as they bash something. There
are a lot of personal attacks, and for some people, it's become a tool to let out
their pent-up frustration. The anonymous attacks are hard to deal with."

Kevin Smith seems to be of two minds when it comes to the net. He has
lauded it as being a "valuable" tool to build and communicate with his audience,[1] and is known to be a rabid surfer of the web. But at the same time, one
senses he is not particularly pleased that some users of the Internet have
resorted to irresponsible, inaccurate attacks:

> *When people say negative things about me on the Internet, I kind of lose*
> *my cool and basically hire P.I.'s to track these people down, because they*
> *always hide behind anonymous names.*[2]

Accordingly, it is one such attack on the good name of Jay and Silent
Bob at the web-site *Movie Poop Shoot.com*—a dead-on parody of Harry
Knowles's popular, controversial and ground-breaking *Ain't it Cool News*
movie site and its "talk backers"—that precipitates the wild events of Smith's
latest film.

This "hook" then introduces a series of cameo performances from the
likes of Carrie Fisher, George Carlin, Marc Blucas, Tracy Morgan, Deidrich
Bader, Matt Damon, Gus Van Sant, Shannen Doherty, James Van Der Beek,
Jason Biggs, Jon Stewart, Seann William Scott, Chris Rock, Jamie Kennedy,
and Mark Hamill.

Playing the supporting roles in *Jay and Silent Bob Strike Back* are *American Pie*'s Shannon Elizabeth, Ali Larter (of *Varsity Blues* and *Final Destination*), *Buffy the Vampire Slayer*'s rogue slayer, Eliza Dushku, and *Saturday Night Live*'s comedic powerhouse, Will Ferrell. In the ultimate in-joke and reference to 1970s television, Ferrell is named Marshal Willenholly—a tribute to the three leads in Sid and Marty Krofft's *Land of the Lost*: Marshal, Will, and Holly. Another *Land of the Lost reference*: Chris Rock's character is named "Chaka"— the handle of the Pakuni ape boy from that 70s Saturday morning classic.

Before Jay and Silent Bob have finished their odyssey across America, Miramax, Hollywood, and even films adapted from comic books are thoroughly roasted. On that last count, Hollywood's inability to produce a "faithful" film from a comic book is noted with specific references to *Batman & Robin*.

"I think Hollywood tries to make films for everybody," notes Walt Flanagan of the superhero movie quandary, "and when you try to make things for a wide audience, you take a risk of watering them down; changing the aspects that appeal to certain people in the first place. If you're really in love with a character and want to do the movie, I don't understand why Hollywood wants to change it."

On hand for the less-than-successful premiere of the fictional *Bluntman & Chronic* movie are the many stars of Smith films past. Dwight Ewell returns as Hooper, Joey Lauren Adams is back as Alyssa, Renee Humphreys re-appears as Trish the Dish, and Scott Mosier re-creates the role of Willam "Snowball" Black. And, of course, Bryan Johnson and Walt Flanagan make a triumphant re-appearance as the forever-discontented Steve-Dave and Fanboy. Star Ben Affleck also returns to the fold playing Holden and himself, and fan favorite Jason Lee performs double duty as Banky and Brodie.

One of the few familiar faces missing from this grand bash is actor Ethan Suplee. "I was working and couldn't get out of what I was doing," Suplee notes with disappointment. "I was working on a movie called *The First 20 Million is the Always the Hardest*."

Despite Suplee's absence, shooting the film proved to be something of a class reunion for many View Askew stars. For Brian O'Halloran and Jeff Anderson, the stars of *Clerks*, it was a chance to play Dante and Randal again, and to return to the Quick Stop, the setting where the whole adventure began, after more than eight years earlier.

"Returning to the Quick Stop to shoot was a lot of fun," O'Halloran reminisces. "It was strange though. This time we had tractor-trailers of equipment, dressing rooms, and people taking your costume. It wasn't just five of us in the store going, 'Ready? Yeah, let me finish my Gatorade.' It was a little overwhelming."

"They could have literally built that store on a soundstage in L.A.," O'Halloran acknowledges. "But I'm so glad Kevin went back to Jersey. It was nice coming back and doing scenes in the store. It was like coming home."

For Jeff Anderson, it was a little disconcerting to return to the familiar setting, but with so many changes. "Good Lord, it was a different scene! I'd missed my plane the day before, so I had to take a red-eye. I flew in, and had to film that morning, so I asked the driver to take me to the store so I could see what time I needed to come back.

"We pulled into the U-turn and I saw police cars blocking the street, and there were groups of people standing there, and trucks and trailers. And I thought, 'This is definitely different.' I came back to shoot around ten in the morning and the crowd was three times larger. It was maybe two hundred feet from my trailer to the actual store, and I was just signing autographs the whole way, and people were snapping pictures.

"I even remember that at one point in the convenience store, between set-ups, I counted 60 people crammed inside. I turned to Brian and said: 'do you remember doing *Clerks* when we actually had to clap the scene and throw the clapper on the floor because we had no available hands to clap?' Now the store was packed with people, and I didn't know what half of their jobs were."

But if shooting *Jay and Silent Bob Strike Back* was a reunion for some, it was a new ball game for others, specifically Jennifer Schwalbach, who was cast in the film as sexy "tech girl" and jewel thief, Missy.

"I had never acted in my life," she reveals. "I had never even taken an acting class. But I thought, 'If Bryan Johnson and Walt Flanagan can act, I can too.' At the time, I knew that Kevin would be on the set all day, and wanted to be included in some way so I could see him. I wanted to be in the movie and Kevin asked me if I could handle it. I said, 'Of course I can!' Bryan, Walt, and Mosier—they all just jump in there, and I don't see them in acting classes. So I wanted to be one of the girls. I picked Missy, Kevin was happy, and Miramax was supportive."

But, Schwalbach admits, some folks were a teensy bit worried there would be trouble with a director's wife on the set of a major film production every day. "I tend to be a little sassy, and I'm constantly getting into trouble telling somebody off," Schwalbach says. "The Miramax people were terrified I'd go on the set and that Kevin and I would fight when he tried to tell me what to do. But that couldn't have been further from the truth. I didn't know what I was doing. I didn't even know camera right. So I didn't give him any guff at all, and I think everyone was completely shocked and thankful for that. I went in terrified, and was so grateful for any direction or rehearsal time Kevin gave me."

Jennifer also found support from her co-stars, Eliza Dushku and Ali Larter. "The other girls were so amazing, and that's not a line of shit. They were incredible."

Which might not have been the case. "Kevin gave me this whole speech going in. 'The other girls may not like you and might be really mean to you because you're my wife and because you're not an actress. You know, who does this chick think she is, the director's wife?' So I went in terrified.

"But I started spending time with Ali and Eliza, and we immediately hit it off. We threw back a couple of beers, tossed a football around the parking lot and had an instant bond. If it hadn't been that way, it would have been a terrible experience, because I spent so much time with them. We would work all day together, and then go out at night. And they'd play with Harley. Eliza taught Harley how to do her first high-five."

Jennifer also remembers the shooting of *Jay and Silent Bob Strike Back* as being something akin to a revolving door, because so many performers dropped in for a day or two, finished their parts, then left. "There was a new actor on the set every day: Ben and Matt, and Jason Biggs and James Van Der Beek, and so on. So Kevin had no time to coddle me through my performance. 'Get your clothes on and get your ass out there and do it!' I was at the bottom of the totem pole. My close-ups were shot last; everything for me was shot last. I didn't get any special treatment at all because I was his wife."

But, at least for Scott Mosier, the scheduling of *Jay and Silent Bob Strike Back*'s large celebrity cast was not as much of a stumbling block as scheduling *Dogma*. "It was not hard, because we shot in Los Angeles," he relates. "Everyone lives there, so it was easy to deal with the cast. There's much more freedom surrounding L.A., than say, Pittsburgh, because there you had fly actors in and fly them out. You'd lose days here and there."

For Jason Mewes, who now resides in L.A., shooting the film there was a great experience. "It was nice to work every day. When I'm out-of-town shooting other movies, I don't have anything to do because I don't know everybody. So usually I'd sit in a motel and not do much, but this was cool. I loved watching the other actors. Will Ferrell was so much fun. It was great to work with him, but it was also great to just sit back and watch him work too."

While shooting *Clerks*, way back in 1993, Kevin Smith and his crew had dealt with a wily cat who escaped the Quick Stop, but on *Jay and Silent Bob Strike Back*, they not only worked with animals, but children too. Unfortunately, in this case, it was his own child, Harley Quinn Smith, who proved the most difficult to direct.

"It was a complete nightmare," Schwalbach remembers of the scene in which Harley was tapped to portray a young Silent Bob in front of the Quick Stop. "I wanted her to play that part, for obvious reasons. It was a once-in-a-lifetime opportunity for her to play her father, and I thought it would be wonderful to have that on film for the rest of her life. So I insisted that there be no back-up baby actors.

"So there we were in New Jersey, and it was early in the morning; it was freezing cold and it was raining. And Harley is a bit like me: she wanted to do her own thing. She didn't want to sit in the stroller, she wanted to talk, and we kept telling her to stop. After months of us begging her to talk, she's chattering away, but has to play a silent character. So she's yammering away, and wouldn't wear the hat.

"It was so frustrating, but Kevin and I learned a good lesson about parenting that day. We had not only the entire crew, but all of these onlookers, his fans, who came out to watch. And we tried to keep our cool as parents in front of this huge crowd. She wasn't even two. But it was raining, and was probably about 35 degrees out. And it was 6:00 in the morning. And it just took hours. At one point, they were even considering switching kids and having Harley play Jay. She would not shut up! But I really wanted her to play her father, so they finally got it together, and it was a genius bit of editing that did it. If you watch closely, you'll see that Harley is holding a bagel in one hand during part of it, and then not in another. They had so few seconds where she was behaving that they just left the bagel in. They had no choice during editing!"

One of the main characters in *Jay and Silent Bob Strike Back* is an orangutan named Susanne. For Jason Mewes, it was both fun and difficult working with the simian. "That ape was cool! It was neat to watch how she interacts with people. But it also sucked because we weren't allowed to play with her or mess with her. Her trainer said that when you mess with an ape that's trained, you confuse them. They have to work with you, so you're like a prop to them. If you start messing with them, all they want to do is play, and they won't act.

"So we had to do a scene with her and they had to take her away. Every once in a while, Kevin and I would forget the rule and start messing with her. Then we'd remember to watch it. But we'd slap her hands and she'd slap you back."

In the film, Jay imagines a *Planet of the Apes*-style scenario in which Randal is hunted by gorilla soldiers, and Dante undergoes experimental brain surgery at the hands (and scalpels) of two chimps. For Brian O'Halloran—who wore a head appliance featuring an exposed brain in that scene—it proved to be a bit harrowing to shoot.

"I had to get up really early to be in make-up for two-to-three hours putting on that brain skull," O'Halloran sets the scene. "It was amazing how they were able to match my hair color and make it look so real. So anyway, I came to the set with my exposed brain and there were a lot of *Hannibal* jokes, because the movie had come out not long before.

"So I approached the trainer and asked if I could meet the chimps, because I was nervous about working with live animals. In fact, it wasn't until that morning I knew there would even be live chimps. I thought it would be guys in costumes like in *Planet of the Apes*, like Zira and Cornelius, poking at me. Jeff had taped his scenes a week earlier and told me about these stunt men in *Planet of the Apes* costumes so I just assumed that's how it would be with me."

It wasn't.

Instead, O'Halloran was to work with a brother and sister team of chimpanzees. "They had been training these chimps with a plastic brain, teaching them to touch it. And they did really well, so when they saw me with my exposed brain, they immediately wanted to touch it. So I went up to Jonah [the male] and they put him in my arms. He was really heavy; I mean he was solid muscle, like a small adult. Then I went over to his sister to say hello and Jonah got really jealous that I'd put him down, and started jumping up and down on a cabinet."

Jonah's temper tantrum got O'Halloran thinking, and made him a little nervous. "They were supposed to have surgical implements in their hands, and I was going to be tied down on the autopsy table. The trainer told me he'd be just out of camera if anything went wrong during the scene, but that didn't really help. If something went wrong, he'd be too far away. But the make-up guy who was watching my brain told me that if anything happened, he'd get me out. I told him just to cover my face, because I didn't have my hands free to cover my eyes in case they wanted to poke them.

"So we're ready to go for picture and they roll action and tell me to scream. So I scream, and it freaks out the apes. They won't touch my brain. At one point, as I'm screaming, Jonah puts his hands over my mouth. But they just won't touch my brain. So they tell me not to scream, and I just pretend—mouthing the scream—and the chimps still won't go near the brain.

"By now we're all starting to get nervous that these chimps are freezing up. And I wonder if there's anything they might like instead of the slime on my brain. And I ask if there's honey on the set, and they bring it over from craft services. So they pour honey on my brain, because apes like honey.

"On the next take, Jonah really starts going for the brain. The sister didn't want anything to do with it, but then they started poking me with their fingers. At one point, Jonah leans in and licks my head."

The *Planet of the Apes* parody also proved interesting for Jeff Anderson. "It was their first day of shooting, I think, for *Jay and Silent Bob Strike Back*, and we went out to some field in California, and it was early in the morning, and it was cold. I was in my trailer eating breakfast and they bring me my hockey shirt, all ripped and torn. Then they take me out to this field, and I remember I'm standing there and here come the *Planet of the Apes* characters on horsebacks, and they have mechanical [animatronic] faces that move.

"So they line me up with a dozen or so slave people. And Kevin gives the direction: 'Let the slaves go first, and then Jeff, you run up from behind, pass them, and run through this field.' The field was pretty much cropped and cut down, so we all line up, Kevin calls action, and the slaves start running. But they stop after about five feet into the field.

"I started running into the bushes, and I'm wondering why these guys stopped. So I keep running and suddenly I'm in these sticker bushes. But these poor slaves are only wearing loin clothes, and they're impaled on these branches. And here I am, still in my old *Clerks* mentality, thinking 'Don't waste film! It hurts like hell, but keep running!' I actually ran out of one of my sneakers, and these bushes were just chewing up my feet. When I stopped, they yelled cut, and everybody was wondering what was up with the slave people—and they were breaking out in hives already."

Then came the rub. "I walk out of the bushes and there's this guy dressed like me. He was my stunt double! And I think, 'Now you tell me?' I've been jumping into the pricker bushes, I'm all cut up, and I have a stunt double sitting and watching this on the monitor?"

Another film referenced by *Jay and Silent Bob Strike Back* is one of Kevin Smith's all-time favorites: *Star Wars*. In fact, Carrie Fisher (Princess Leia), and Mark Hamill (Luke Skywalker) appear in the film, and Smith even gets to indulge in a light-saber-style duel. As Hamill told *USA Today*:

> As we were filming the movie, and I'm in this outfit, I said 'Kevin, this is your big, giant play set—and I'm your action figure...Kevin had gone from playing the ersatz toy versions of Star Wars characters in New Jersey to a big Hollywood set. Now he was playing...on the grand scale.[3]

As for working with Carrie Fisher, Smith had this pithy remark: "Won't say the words *Star* and *Wars* in the same sentence. Not in the same paragraph—even if they're separated by 98 words."[4]

For the climactic battle between Jay (as Chronic) and Mark Hamill (as Cocknocker), *Jay and Silent Bob Strike Back* featured a dramatic bong-saber duel, like something out of *Star Wars* and *The Matrix* combined. Jason Mewes, for one, was thrilled at one more opportunity to perform stunts.

"For that flip where Jay says, 'Call me Darth Balls!,' they put me in harness with cables, and were trying to teach me how to flip," he explains. "That was fun, but really tough. I thought it would be easier than it was. We did it a few times, and I got it, but not that good. It just didn't pan out."

Another scene that didn't quite pan out was the parody of cartoon favorite *Scooby Doo*. According to f/x guru Vincent Guastini, the scene in the original script was far different, and much more outrageous than what eventually appeared. "*Dogma* had the angel wings, and that was the effect everybody would talk about," Guastini recollects, "and when I read *Jay and Silent Bob Strike Back*, I felt that the *Scooby Doo* scene would be the show stopper, so it was my main concentration.

"The scene was that Jay gets high and hits the dog's dick with a bong. The dog gets a hard-on and basically attacks Jay. Jay and Silent Bob try to get away from it by hiding in a van, and the dog hops on the windshield and starts humping the window. The dog's eyes go crazy and it blows its load all over the windshield, and the dog flies off while they're driving. It was the most hysterical scene in the whole film, as far as I was concerned."

To make it happen, the artist built an elaborate, animatronic dog for the sequence. "I made the dog's tongue come out and touch its nose; I made the eyes bulge. It had every single movement that a real dog would have, plus five more on top of that. It was so highly-detailed that the testicles on the dog actually swelled, the shaft swelled, and the dog could blow its load.

"So I kept asking, 'Are you guys sure this is going to make it into the movie?' Then, the day before we were going to shoot the thing, I'm hearing about lawyers getting nervous about the *Scooby Doo* image and licensing. So, in one weekend, they were going to make a decision. By Monday, the dog would either be in or out.

"Well, Monday came and the word arrived: the dog was out. I'll be honest, I cried. I cried like a big baby. That's how personally I take my work. Kevin and Scott saw me on the set and hugged me and told me they were really sorry."

And, to this day, Guastini is convinced the movie would have been funnier with the original Scooby-attack. "As great and funny as the movie was, I thought the Scooby scene needed that."

Legal issues were also a concern for Guastini while creating the gorilla soldiers for the *Planet of the Apes* satire. "I was in something of a quandary, because Miramax was a little worried, and I believe I was hearing through them that 20th Century Fox wanted to make sure that I didn't come too close to what Rick Baker was doing on the *Planet of the Apes* remake. But they also didn't want me to get too close to the old movies, so I had to come in somewhere in between.

"My main inspiration was *Planet of the Apes 2* [from the art book *Millennium*], which had very 'heavy metal'-style apes [rendered by artist Luis Roya]. I wanted to go heavy metal, and the main gorilla in the film is actually animatronic, with moving eyebrows, but it went by so quickly that you didn't get to see it that much. It wasn't about the effects on *Jay and Silent Bob Strike Back*, it was about getting the point across quickly in funny little gags."

That said, the ape hunt was no picnic. "It's one thing to have a stuntman in a hot mask in the California sun, out in a field, it's another to have animatronics and servos on top of that. The gorilla had a battery pack on too. And then you had to coordinate with a horse galloping across a field. It has to stop on cue, on a dime, the camera has to zoom in, the gorilla has to make an expression, then take a shot with a rifle. It was a really difficult thing to coordinate, but we just went for it. I could have just put a rubber mask on the rider, but that's not me. It's too easy. That's what I'm always killing my crew on: giving more than what's asked for."

Other Guastini effects in *Jay and Silent Bob Strike Back* included an orangutan "suit" to double for little Susanne. An eight year-old boy (son of another stuntman) wore the suit in some sequences, such as *The Fugitive* riff at the dam.

At other points, a foam body was sewed into the suit for more dangerous stunts, such as the *E.T.*-style bicycle flight on the Miramax lot (past a sign that reads "Ben Affleck IS the Moonraper").

Guastini's firm also designed Cocknocker's oversized, maniacal fist (laden with acrylic nails), Dante's exposed brain, and Sean William Scott's rather unattractive braces.

By all accounts, shooting the effects-laden *Jay and Silent Bob Strike Back* was nothing less than a hoot. "Everybody who worked on that movie was crying when it was over, saying it was the best experience they'd ever had," Schwalbach reports with pride. "We had barbecues at our house, and we'd invite the entire crew over, and they'd say, 'My God, the director never has the crew to his house!' But everybody walked away from that movie having a wonderful experience, and we benefited completely. Our daughter got to be on the set every day, and Eliza Dushku played with her, and trainers would let her play with the monkeys, and all kinds of stuff."

According to Schwalbach, the experience of being in a Kevin Smith movie also increased her respect for her husband. "I had never really been a part of something Kevin had worked on. I visited the sets of *Dogma*, or when he was doing a commercial, but never really paid that much attention. But having been in the movie was a really wonderful thing for our marriage, because I understood why he couldn't come home for lunch. I understood why he was working twelve hours a day.

"I got it before, but now I really got to see with my own two eyes the experience that Kevin has making a movie, the incredible pressure that he has on his shoulders: writing it, directing it, acting in it, and having to deal with the problems and joys of everyone on his set. I really admired him for being able to handle it so gracefully. There's always a line of 45 people wanting to ask him a question or two. It was really a very healthy thing for me to have been a part of that."

An early publicity photo of Joey Lauren Adams.

A candid shot of View Askew favorite Jason Lee (right).

"You're way too conservative for her." Holden McNeil (Ben Affleck) and Banky (Jason Lee) discuss the provocative Alyssa Jones outside their loft in *Chasing Amy* (1997).

Minority report: Alyssa Jones (Joey Lauren Adams) and Hooper X (Dwight Ewell) meet Holden and Banky at a comic convention minority panel in *Chasing Amy*.

"What's a nubian?" Hooper (Ewell), Holden (Affleck), and Banky (Lee) debate the role of African-Americans in comic books.

She wants you. No, not you! Alyssa (Adams) performs a sultry torch song at the Meow Mix.

Who me? A case of mistaken identity as Alyssa's lover (Carmen Lee) and Holden (Affleck) watch Alyssa perform on stage.

"Now that's a shared moment!" Alyssa (Adams) and her lover (Lee) smooch.

Alyssa Jones (Adams, center) literally gets in between Holden (Affleck, left) and Banky (Lee, right).

A pseudo-date? Holden (Affleck) and Alyssa (Adams) get close over drinks.

Wake up call: Holden (Affleck) and Alyssa (Adams) are discovered in the loft after spending the night together.

They're back! Jay (Mewes) and Silent Bob (Smith) offer sage advice about love lost in their *Chasing Amy* cameo.

Hooper (Ewell) and Holden (Affleck) have a tete-a-tete about sexual experience in a record shop during a pivotal moment in *Chasing Amy*.

In all, it was a joyous send-off for that stoner duo, Jay and Silent Bob. And make no mistake, that's what it was at the time; a send-off. "I think this is it. I'd rather get out while the getting's good,"[5] Kevin Smith noted in an interview for *Hollywood.com*. Later, he admitted he'd miss the duo, but really had no choice except to leave them behind:

> If I had any balls whatsoever, I'd make nothing but Jay and Silent Bob flicks for the rest of my life. However, being a critical whore, I've gotta move on and "grow" beyond those characters. But no matter what I wind up making in the future, a part of me will always yearn to make another flick with Jay and Silent Bob.[6]

Released by New Dimension, Miramax's sister "genre" arm, *Jay and Silent Bob Strike Back*, the stoner swan song, screamed into theaters on the weekend of August 28, 2001, facing off against the work of other cult directors including Woody Allen (*Curse of the Jade Scorpion*) and John Carpenter (*Ghosts of Mars*). But, for a film that was supposed to be fun and games, it ended up stirring perhaps the strangest controversy of Kevin Smith's career. Even before the film was released, there was another protest not unlike the one that had dogged *Dogma*.

Specifically, Scott Seomin, the media director for the Gay and Lesbian Alliance Against Defamation (GLAAD), complained that *Jay and Silent Bob Strike Back* was a film that was hostile and derogatory to the gay community. "I've never seen something so horrific,"[7] he reported in one periodical.

In a letter addressed to Kevin Smith, dated July 26, 2001, Scott Seomin went further. He wrote:

> We were overwhelmed by the potential negative impact for the film with what we would assume is a large share of its target audience: teen and young adult males. We will be public and aggressive in our condemnation and will provide substantiation for our opinions.[8]

Seomin's comments were picked up all throughout the media, and before long, a Kevin Smith film was again at the center of a publicity firestorm.

"It's getting to the point in this country you can't make a joke," Smith fired back to *The Washington Post*. "You're always offending somebody."[9]

But Seomin and GLAAD proved firm in pursuing their belief that the Smith film portrayed gays in a bad light. They believed the film's humor came at the expense of a stereotyped people; that it promoted the ridicule of gay men, that it offered new defamatory vocabulary to use against gay men, and that the movie substituted the word "gay" for things seen as stupid or wrong.[10]

Feeling that the movie could not adequately address the concerns of GLAAD, Scott Seomin and the group instead requested a $10,000 check from Smith, to be donated to the Matthew Shepherd Foundation.

"Kevin and I are the most gay-friendly family that could exist," Jennifer Schwalbach says. "We have so many gay people in our lives, and we're so thankful for them. It was so shocking and offensive to us that we had Scott Seomin, the head of GLAAD, and the person who started this whole shit storm, come over to talk to us about it. I needed to confront him, I was so offended. With the Catholic protest, I wasn't affected by it because religion isn't a part of who I am, but this really hit me. My family has a lot of gay people in it, and I was outraged. I insisted Malcolm film the entire thing, because it was a scam job. It was extortion. We gave them $10,000 dollars out of our pocket. We would have gladly done so in a more natural setting, but this was like, 'We're going to twist your arm for cash.' And he [Seomin] came in, and I had to tell him how I felt, and it was really emotional, and he didn't do anything or say anything to make me feel any better about it. But at least I got to vent. I'd been venting to Kevin, who was equally outraged.

"It was pointing the finger at the wrong person. As a woman, I have to be able to laugh at myself; at the jokes that people make about women, and if they're not mean-spirited, go along with it. Because if you can't laugh at yourself, you'll probably have a mighty sad existence. And I think that was the case here. It was too bad. It was mean-spirited."

Vincent Pereira also believed that the wrong target had been selected by GLAAD. "Kevin is not a gay basher. You can see it in *Dogma*. One of the greatest and most subtle moments happens during the Mooby scene. Bartleby is going through the offenses of the various executives on the Mooby board. And the one offense that damns this executive is that he disowned his gay son. An angel sees that act as an unpardonable offense. You can't get any more pro-gay than that."

On the other hand, Vincent Pereira does believe that there are some people who don't understand Smith's humor, and misinterpret the jokes in his films. "Kevin is not a homophobe, but reading his web site, GLAAD may have had a point so far as a few people were concerned. Some of his younger fans perhaps didn't understand that the film is satire. I know absolutely that it is not Kevin's intention to put people down and that intelligent people can see that *Jay and Silent Bob Strike Back* isn't a gay bashing movie at all, but there are those people who don't see the satire. It's flared up a couple of times on the web site, and people get banned very quickly, but it is terribly disheartening to see kids bashing gay people. They think it's cool."

"But," Pereira adds, "I thought *American Pie 2* was much more homophobic than *Jay and Silent Bob Strike Back*, and nobody protested that."

The controversy surrounding *Jay and Silent Bob Strike Back*, like the *Dogma* protest, may have merely drawn more attention to Kevin Smith's film. It had a big opening weekend, and continued to play well into September, before the tragic terrorist attacks that left a nation stunned on September 11, 2001. When the film was released on DVD and VHS some months later, on February 26, 2002, it topped the rental and purchase charts for several weeks.

Jay and Silent Bob—always a magnet for controversy—"had left the building."

ALL GOOD THINGS

Jay and Silent Bob Strike Back was designed to be the curtain call for two of cinema's true originals, the New Jersey stoner duo played by Jason Mewes and Kevin Smith. Their final adventure (at least until *Clerks II* in 2006 . . .) is a film with not much on its mind but out-and-out fun. In some interesting ways, the film speaks to its historical context (the advent of the Internet's down side; the proliferation of entertainment news channels and programs; the slew of uninspired Hollywood sequels and remakes, etc.), but it's really just a knock-down, drag-out funny film. For fans of the View Askewniverse, it is nostalgic (and sometimes touching) to see Randal, Dante, Brodie, Hooper, Banky, Holden, and the rest of the gang back in action.

In the years to come, *Jay and Silent Bob Strike Back* may be of primary interest, surprisingly enough, for its visual aplomb. The first scene of the film features one of the greatest visual jokes to come down the road in years.

Outside the Quick Stop in the 1970s, Jay's mother says "fuck" about two hundred times, and as her child takes tentative baby-steps out of his stroller with momentous effort, Jay voices the word for himself for the first time. Then the film dissolves to twenty or so years later. It's the exact same shot, and a grown-up Jay is standing in the very same place, singing "fuck" in a variety of original ways.

It's the comedy equivalent of Stanley Kubrick's masterful transition in *2001: A Space Odyssey*, as primitive ape first picks up a bone and uses it as a tool, and then tosses it into the air. The bone, through a jump cut, transforms into a spaceship in Earth's orbit centuries later. All of man's technological development, from primitive ape to space-shuttle-piloting human being, is encapsulated in that single cut.

In the Kevin Smith film, Jay's transformation from infant to adult charts a similar evolution, only the tool in this case is a cuss word; a cuss word the adult Jay has mastered like no other man alive. It's a funny, funny moment, and the perfect use of the dissolve brings roars of laughter every time the scene is shown.

Jay and Silent Bob Strike Back also features the best damned *Planet of the Apes* satire yet put to film. In fact, it's a hell of a lot better than Tim Burton's horribly weak "re-imagining." The scene featuring Jason Mewes on the beach before the ruined Statue of Liberty intoning "Damn youse! Damn youse all to Hell!" proves so faithful in composition and art design to the original 1968 film that it's actually difficult to tell the two apart. And Vincent Guastini's soldier gorilla on horseback is full of character and individuality, a more convincing villain than any seen in the remake and a nice alternate interpretation of the Apes characters. *Spaceballs* executed a *Planet of the Apes* joke like this back in 1987, but Smith's crazy parody blasts Mel Brooks' version from the pop cultural map.

As far as "gay bashing" is concerned, *Jay and Silent Bob Strike Back* is really pretty innocuous. Kids have been substituting the word "gay" for "stupid" since before Kevin Smith was a kid on the playground. It may not be nice or even PC, but it is reflective of the truth in our culture. Sometimes women get termed "bitches," men are called "dicks," and "gay" is substituted for the word "stupid," so just about everybody can complain about something if they look hard enough. It is far worse to censor an artist (for mirroring real life, to boot) than to endure a few jokes like this. And, it's a little sad and disconcerting to see a progressive, helpful organization like GLAAD seeking to assert control over artistic content simply because said content doesn't favor the organization's preferred world view.

Those who complained about the movie might be wise to review some of the film's dialogue. "Don't be so suburban," George Carlin's hitchhiker chides Jay and Silent Bob. "It's the new Millennium. Gay, straight, it's all the same now. There are no more lines."

That, it seems, might have been a point GLAAD would be happy to see made in a mass entertainment.

And really, why look to anti-heroes Jay and Silent Bob to model appropriate behavior anyway? That's like asking the Three Stooges to legislate public policy.

With a joke-a-minute pace, a wicked and witty premise about Hollywood and the Internet, and more celebrities than your eyes can register, *Jay and Silent Bob Strike Back* is the most enjoyable comedy of 2001 hands down.

ASKEW VIEWS

KITTY LITTER: Those sleek, black cat suits worn by Missy, Sissy, Chrissy, and Justice looked terrific on film, but were difficult to wear, according to Jennifer Schwalbach.

"It was freezing cold all the time, and these cat suits were so thin. They were like nylon suits. They were some cheap-ass material and we'd be out at 4 a.m. running around in them, freezing to death. And we could not get too close to the heaters, otherwise the suits would go up in smoke."

Making matters worse, there was only one suit per jewel thief; no back-ups. "Those suits are not easy to get on, and not easy to get off." She reports. "And since there's only one, you have to move very carefully. Mine, they had to alter, so they stitched me into it. Unfortunately, I had the worst stomach flu in my life, and was having to go the bathroom literally every ten minutes. So they'd stitch me in, then rip the suit off to me, I'd go to the bathroom, get back into the suit, and get sewed back in. It was a nightmare. I was so sick I didn't even care that two hundred people on the set knew I was living in the bathroom."

RAP MEWES-IC: Fans of the New Jersey Chronicles will note that Jay's profanity-filled raps have become more elaborate over the course of five films, and that's fine by Jason Mewes. Even though he's never done any professional singing, he reports that he's written songs and would like to pursue his interest in music.

But even if the first rap in *Jay and Silent Bob Strike Back* was easy to master ("It just flowed."), Mewes found the later one, eventually cut from the film, more difficult.

Mewes explains, "If you watch the outtakes, you can see the one they didn't show, at the convenience store out west. 'Balls, balls, in your mouth!

Balls! Where? In your mouth!' That was tough, and I had to do it a few times. At one point, I messed up and said, 'Where, where? In *my* mouth!' And then I realized what I said and was like, 'Yuck. I messed up.'"

DAME DENCH: One of the funniest lines in *Jay and Silent Bob Strike Back* is Dante's exasperated remark that he can't believe the filmmakers behind the *Bluntman & Chronic* movie hired "Judi Dench" to play him. But that was just one permutation, as O'Halloran remembers.

"It was either that, or 'I can't believe they got Freddie Prinze Jr. to play me.' But I think it was better with Judi Dench."

TOGETHERNESS: The fact that Walt Flanagan and Bryan Johnson are good friends sometimes adds to the impression that Fanboy and Steve-Dave are constantly together. Unknowingly, the actors encouraged this notion on the set of *Jay and Silent Bob Strike Back*.

"In the movies, we're constantly portrayed as hanging out together," explains Johnson. "So I wonder if people look at us and say, 'These motherfuckers really do hang out all the time!' Every time we're seen, we're together.

"When we did *Jay and Silent Bob Strike Back*, according to SAG rules, the production has to pay for a room for each of us. But we didn't know that. So I signed in at the hotel and just assumed that Walter and I had one room. So Walter stayed in my room for three days. Then someone asked us why we didn't take Walter's room, and we were like, 'Walter has a room?' People must really think we can't stay away from each other. He had his own room, but we had to sleep side-by-side."

FREEZE FRAME: The colorful, 1960s TV version of *Batman* starring Adam West and Burt Ward is the basis for some of the *Bluntman & Chronic* sets in *Jay and Silent Bob Strike Back*. In particular, the Bluntcave resembles the Batcave of that classic series, down to a similar "atomic pile" in the background.

"It was stunning to see how much work they'd put into the set," Walt Flanagan notes. "But you don't see it that much in the movie. All that effort and you don't even get a real panoramic shot of the Bluntcave! But you can see it great on DVD."

THE ULTIMATE NUMBER: The number 37 crops up repeatedly in Kevin Smith's films. In *Jay and Silent Bob Strike Back*, a poster at their condo heralds Missy, Chrissy, and Sissy's "37th" successful jewel heist. Later, on the set of *Bluntman & Chronic*, Jay and Silent Bob appear during, according to the clapper, Scene 37.

SHE AIN'T ALL THAT: Early in *Jay and Silent Bob Strike Back*, it is noted that everything went downhill for Miramax after its release of *She's All That*. According to John Pierson, that joke relates to a real-life incident:

"When *Dogma* started test market screenings, at least two were in Philadelphia, and *She's All That* had either just opened big or was about to open big. The fact of the matter was that it was thrown in Kevin's face. 'Look, you're getting okay scores here, but it's no *She's All That*.'" Pierson pauses before continuing, "How could anybody compare *Dogma* to *She's All That*?"

KISS-KISS, BANG-BANG: One of the spicier moments from *Jay and Silent Bob Strike Back* was cut from the theatrical version (and restored for the DVD outtake section). Specifically, it was Jennifer Schwalbach's steamy kiss with co-star Ali Larter.

"Ali and I had become such good friends, and we knew from the beginning we would have to do it," Schwalbach explains. "The worst stuff got cut out and wasn't even on the DVD. It was that bad. It was ... dirty. And I thought 'Good God, no.' But they had cleared the set, and it was just Kevin and Mosier and a few other people, so it wasn't hard or awkward. We just did it. Then Kevin started to get paranoid that everybody thought he was a total pervert. But the whole thing was un-pervy and sterile. There wasn't porn music playing in the background to get us in the mood, and no one was plying us with drinks."

But if the love-scene was easy to do, stunts were a killer. "Ali accidentally whacked me in the face with her fake gun," Schwalbach reveals. "In fact, I got hit in the head by several things during the filming of that movie. A light would fall, find me, and then hit me. It was the most random thing. But the movie was so fun, a blow to the head didn't even matter."

KEVIN SMITH ON *JAY AND SILENT BOB STRIKE BACK*

"We were trying to do a live action *Looney Tunes* with more dialogue ... Scott Mosier, my producer summed it up best. He said, it's kind of like *The Muppet Movie* on acid."[11]

7

Clerks (2000)

THE ANIMATED SERIES

CAST AND CREW

FROM MIRAMAX HOME ENTERTAINMENT

Based on Characters created by: Kevin Smith
Developed for Television by: David Mandel, Scott Mosier & Kevin Smith
Produced by: John Bush
Co-Producer: Chris Bailey
Supervising Producer: Brian Kelley
Executive Producers: Bob Weinstein, Harvey Weinstein, Billy Campbell, David Mandel, Kevin Smith, and Scott Mosier
Film Editor: John Royer
Art Director: Alan Rodner
Animation Producer: Saerom Animation Inc.
Executive in Charge of Production: Bob Osher, Miramax Television
Music: James L. Venable
Voice Casting: Jamie Thomason
From Woltz International Picture Corporation and Touchstone TV.

FEATURING THE VOICE TALENTS OF

Brian O'Halloran | *Dante*
Jeff Anderson | *Randal Graves*
Jason Mewes | *Jay*
Kevin Smith | *Silent Bob*
Alec Baldwin | *Leonardo Leonardo*

THE STORY SO FAR...

EPISODE I

Teleplay by: David Mandel and Kevin Smith

The Story: The construction of a new deluxe "Quicker Stop" by billionaire megalomaniac Leonardo Leonardo threatens Dante and Randal when it looks like R.S.T. Video and Quick Stop will be closed. The clerks break into Leonardo Leonardo's office by night and team up with Jay and Silent Bob, now selling fireworks, to destroy the competition.

Guest Voices: Charles Barkley

EPISODE II

Teleplay by: David Mandel and Kevin Smith
Story by: Paul Dini, David Mandel, and Kevin Smith
Directed by: Nick Filippi

The Story: Randal and Dante lock themselves in the Quick Stop milk room freezer after the store is robbed. Bored and cold, they reminisce about previous adventures. When they run out of old stories, they resort to flashing back to sitcoms like *Happy Days*.

Guest Voices: Charles Barkley, Gwenyth Paltrow, Gilbert Gottfried

EPISODE III

Teleplay by: David Mandel and Kevin Smith
Directed by: Chris Bailey

The Story: After introducing a new African-American character to the show named Lando, Randal and Dante mishandle a container of frozen burritos and visit a new pet shop next door. When Leonardo Leonardo samples the rotten burritos and becomes violently ill, Randal thinks the monkey at Patrick Swayze's pet shop—Gerbils, Gerbils, Gerbils—is responsible for the outbreak.

Guest Voices: Charles Barkley, James Woods, Gilbert Gottfried, Al Franken

Episode IV

Teleplay by: Steve Lookner, David Mandel, and Kevin Smith
Story by: Steve Lookner
Directed by: Steve Loter

The Story: Dante and Randal challenge each other to switch jobs for a day, but Randal has trouble with the Quick Stop. When Jay slips on Randal's spilled soda, he gets a high-priced lawyer to sue Dante and Quick Stop in the People's Court, presided by Judge Reinhold.

Guest Voices: Judge Reinhold, Kenny Mayne, Dan Patrick, Charles Barkley, Grant Hill, Reggie Miller

Episode V

Teleplay by: Brian Kelly
Directed by: Nick Filippi

The Story: Dante and Randal attend their high school reunion, but run afoul of Leonardo Leonardo and Randal's old girlfriends, all of whom have become lesbians. When Randal gets the high score on an old arcade game called "Pharaoh," the government abducts him and forces him to work as slave labor. Dante's pathetic little league team saves the day and rescues Randal.

Guest Voices: Michael McKean, Charles Barkley

Episode VI

Teleplay by: David Mandel and Kevin Smith
Directed by: Steve Loter

The Story: Dante and Randal go to a convention and are deluged by fans that think the *Clerks* cartoon is a sell-out! The duo vows to take the series back to its independent film roots, come hell or high water. Meanwhile, a fair is in town and Caitlin Bree is cheating on Dante again. And some mysterious guy named Morpheus keeps telephoning Dante and calling him "Neo."

Guest Voices: Kevin McDonald, Mark McKinney

THE STORY BEHIND THE SERIES

In the summer of 2000 *Clerks: The Animated Series* came—briefly—to network television. Though it was pulled by its host network ABC after just two half-hour episodes, the series has since been released on DVD and VHS and has, like virtually all Kevin Smith productions, acquired a rabid cult following. There has even been talk of a big-screen resurrection: an animated *Clerks* feature film to be called *Clerks: Sell Out*.

However, if things were just a little different, *Clerks* would never have been a cartoon at all. Instead, it would have been a live-action series—a sitcom—and Kevin Smith, Scott Mosier, and View Askew would have most likely had nothing whatsoever to do with it.

"When we were shooting *Mallrats*, ABC was interested in doing a *Clerks* TV show," Scott Mosier recalls of this strange chapter in View Askew history.

But the notion of a twenty-two-minute, live-action *Clerks* sitcom was news to Jeff Anderson. "It was after *Clerks* came out, I guess, and they were shooting this live action pilot. I had just come out to L.A. for the Spirit Awards, and it was my first time there. I met up with these agents—and they were all asking where I'd been. They wanted to know if I wanted to audition for the *Clerks* TV show. And I was like, 'What the heck? Sure!' So they set up an audition, but then told me that the part of Randal had already been cast. So I actually went in and auditioned as Dante."

"We both auditioned as Dante," Brian O'Halloran notes with amusement. "Because Jim Breuer from *Saturday Night Live* had been cast as Randal."

Or rather, a pseudo-Randal.

"He was named Randal, but he wasn't really like Randal at all; more of a new, third character" Mosier reports of Breuer's interpretation. "And they added all of these new locations to the show, like an ice cream parlor and a tanning salon."

Jeff Anderson continues the story. "At the time, a CNN news crew was following me around town for the *Showbiz Minute*, and were doing a kind of 'young actor comes to Hollywood' story. Probably on my second or third audition for the part, the news crew cleared it with the people I was auditioning for that they could come in and tape it. So it was my third audition ever, I'm reading for Dante in the *Clerks* TV show, and it's all happening on CNN. No pressure there!

"I went in and I'm sure it was the world's worst audition, because I was laughing. I read the part of Dante, but not as the Dante you saw in the movie. I did my own Dante, which was kind of a pain-in-the-assy Randal—which is exactly what I wanted to do. I didn't get the part.

"Kevin heard through me, I think, about the pilot, because I told him I was auditioning for it," explains O'Halloran. "He got involved with it at that point as an executive producer. But he read the script and didn't like it at all."

"I called Kevin about the show," adds Anderson. "Miramax owns the name *Clerks*, I guess, and they did this pilot without Kevin. After I auditioned, Kevin and Scott came to town and were attached to the pilot as consultants. Later, I called Kevin again and told him that my audition was terrible, and that the script was terrible. And Kevin said, 'Yeah, Scott and I are out now.' They were in for about four days before they bailed out!"

"Kevin had a different sensibility about it," Mosier notes diplomatically, then on further thought adds, "The pilot was terrible; almost unwatchable."

O'Halloran's description is less flattering. "It was such an abortion of a show. They set it in a 7-Eleven type of convenience store. It was a very big, corporate type of place. And the set looked like a bubble gum set you'd see on *Saved by the Bell*. You could tell it was a fake set."

"I saw the pilot later," adds Anderson, "and boy was I glad I didn't get the part. It really was like *Saved by the Bell*. It was sort of edgy, but everyone was acting as though it were a kid's show. I was glad not to be associated with it."

But the idea of a *Clerks* TV show done well was one that still carried major appeal to many producers in Tinsel Town. And at least one old friend too. "Harvey Weinstein wanted there to be a TV series," O'Halloran reports, "even after that one was aborted. He was hot on the idea, and I think it was then that Kevin first offered the idea of doing a cartoon, because he wanted to do bizarre scripts, have more freedom, and not do a sitcom version."

"This is the PG material that my mother always wanted me to do."[1] Kevin Smith told *The New York Times* of the proposed series.

But Jeff Anderson wasn't so sure that a cartoon would work either. "I thought everybody had lost their minds about this movie. But then Kevin called me again and asked me to play Randal on the animated show. I thought it would be bizarre, but wonderful."

"I was ecstatic," O'Halloran notes of the concept. "I'm a huge cartoon fan to begin with. I just love animation so much, so when I heard we would be doing a cartoon I knew the potential it had to offer was enormous."

"And then I heard that the show was going to air on ABC in prime time and thought, 'Holy crap!' I thought it would be a Saturday morning show, not a *Simpsons*-type thing. Then it clicked, and I realized how long *The Simpsons* had been on. I knew if it came off, and was popular, which I thought it would be, this could be huge."

Others shared that belief, and there was something of a bidding war to see which network would finally carry the show. "When UPN made their initial offer, they were going to purchase thirteen episodes, with all thirteen going to air, but we wanted to go with ABC because it was a bigger network," O'Halloran explains.

Indeed, in the year 2000, ABC seemed like a good, solid bet. "At the time, it was in third place, and seemed to be doing more edgy television," Scott Mosier explains. "I guess they figured if they were in third, they had nothing to lose. So they had a show set in a mental institution, *Wonderland*, and they were going to do the *Clerks* cartoon."

Writing the scripts for the new series were Kevin Smith, *News Radio* scribe Brian Kelly, and *Saturday Night Live* alumni Steve Lookner and David Mandel.

"We went to ABC and did the first table reading for the cartoon," recounts Anderson. "It was my first time in the situation where we were doing our *Clerks* thing in front of guys in three piece suits who had befuddled looks on their faces."

"We were reading the scripts to the bigwigs at Disney and ABC," O'Halloran joins in. "We'd met Steve Lookner and David Mandel at that point, and the scripts were a little longer than twenty-two minutes. They're usually about thirty-five minutes, so you have enough material to trim down from, and we got a really great response."

The result of the readings was a deal for a TV series. There would be a *Clerks* cartoon, and it had a guarantee of six episodes. From that point, it was a matter of transforming Dante, Randal, Jay, and Silent Bob into animated characters.

"When it came to production, we went out to L.A. and I saw the production offices, and there were these great start-up sketches," O'Halloran describes. "The artists were looking at me, taking photos, and we discussed what they wanted. They did all these passes on the characters and I loved Chris Bailey's style of animation. He had such a great idea and edge as to how he wanted to stylize those characters. There was something lovable about the animation."

"They locked down Brian pretty early." Anderson relates. "Jay went through a few changes. I kept asking to see myself, but I never saw the sketches. So I pulled the writers aside and said, 'Give Randal some muscles and a tattoo and some piercings.' Then I finally saw the drawing and thought, 'That's not me.' But everyone else said, 'Oh yes it is,' and I thought, 'Dammit!'"

One of the new characters created specifically for the *Clerks* cartoon was a millionaire arch-villain named Leonardo Leonardo. As O'Halloran recalls, the clerks' new nemesis wasn't easy to cast.

"They had originally hired Alan Rickman, I believe, to play Leonardo Leonardo. I think Kevin had based that character on Hans Gruber, the villain Rickman played in *Die Hard*. But for some reason it just wasn't coming across in the vocalizations. So they interviewed quite a few people, and I think they met Alec Baldwin up in Toronto. I never got to meet him, because it was late in casting, but I think he recorded the dialogue up there. He has such great comedic timing. People don't think of him as being really funny, but he is. His timing and vocalizations were great."

Anderson and O'Halloran agree that recording the scripts for *Clerks* turned out to be the most fun, and most hilarious, job of their careers. "Everybody believed in that show, and would tell you that it wasn't like work at all," Anderson confides. "We'd show up at the studio, horse around, and have all these cool people in there doing voices with us."

"Recording was so much fun," O'Halloran concurs. "We worked with so many people I admired, and the shows just got better and better. We got more comfortable, and we taped the shows in sequence, so we were getting used to the process. You don't realize how much, as an actor, you have to be animated for an animated series. There's got to be more fluctuation and emotion in a voice so that when you see the animation it goes together well; it isn't just a voice quietly saying a line."

"They should have left the recorder on constantly, because the things we'd come up with and just change on the spot . . . it was hard to believe I got paid to do that job," Anderson laughs. "Initially, I sort of read Randal how he would be in the movie *Clerks*, but once we got into actually recording the show, Kevin encouraged me to bring him up a little, to put more energy into him. I would always get a kick out of Kevin doing cartoon Randal. He'd get this kind of squeal to his voice."

"We had great directors," O'Halloran adds. "They always wanted to do a couple of takes to nail it down. David Mandel was the primary vocal director of the episodes, and he would encourage us to try new things and do things different ways. After about the third episode, we knew exactly what they wanted and were able to have an immediate sense of what the script required vocally."

As the stars, writers, and directors of the *Clerks* cartoon grew more confident about their work, the recorded scripts and storyboards were shipped to Korea to be animated. "It takes about eight months to put out an episode," O'Halloran notes. "So you have to do it in batches. You do all the recordings, and then send over all the episodes in a batch, and it still takes that long."

Unfortunately, the higher-ups at Disney and ABC began to perceive content problems with the show. In their eyes, it was simply too racy. ABC "reportedly gave Miramax a difficult time,"[2] according to the press, but that modest description was apparently an understatement.

"After our readings, they would tell us, 'You can't do that.' And it was pretty tame stuff they objected to. Then they'd finally okay it, the cartoon would get drawn, and when the network got the stuff back, they'd make changes again," Anderson explains with frustration. "You can't do that with an animated show once it's been drawn. You know you're way off track if you're making people re-draw scenes."

The result of this interference was that *Clerks* missed its debut. "For a long time we were going to premiere after the Super Bowl, so we believed ABC was really behind the show," O'Halloran remembers. "Then the Super Bowl got closer and the first episode wasn't even done because they were asking us to re-do scenes."

"They moved us back to the summer," Mosier reveals, "which meant we were on with reruns."

When *Clerks* finally did appear in the summer of 2000, it aired on Wednesday nights at 9:30 p.m. Unfortunately, it was pretty well ignored by viewers and poorly reviewed by the critics who took note. "Why put them on a broadcast network, where they can't talk nearly as dirty as they did in the movie?" questioned *People*'s reviewer, Terry Kelleher. "Can you say ill-conceived?"[3]

"That's like saying *South Park* is ill-conceived because the characters can't say 'fuck' on TV," notes historian Vincent Pereira.

Still, those who tuned in to the short-lived series found much to appreciate and chortle about. "The first night the show was on, I was out with a friend of mine and we were in a hotel lobby," Anderson remembers. "We ran into the bar and flipped on the TV, and when the show came on, we were just fascinated by it. I couldn't go anywhere; I just had to sit and watch the whole show."

With the addition of *Clerks: The Animated Series* to the ever-expanding View Askewniverse, the grungy, discontented register jockeys of the 1994 film *Clerks* were re-invented and re-tooled with one purpose in mind: to skewer popular culture (particularly film and television). Smith's films have always been laden with references to contemporary culture, but his *Clerks* cartoon is a rapid-fire barrage of zingers aimed straight at Hollywood. In many ways this approach signals the direction of *Jay and Silent Bob Strike Back*. That movie featured parodies of *Scooby Doo, E.T., Scream, The X-Files*, and *Planet of the Apes*, to name but a few. Any one of those sequences would have been right at home in the cartoon.

Tracking the references in *Clerks: The Animated Series*, it's amazing to witness their breadth and scope. *Marathon Man, Silence of the Lambs, Access Hollywood, Aliens, The Secret Diary of Desmond Pfeifer, Batman* (all in episode 1), *The Flintstones, Schindler's List, The Real World, Happy Days* (all in episode 2), *Outbreak, Jaws, Dirty Dancing, Road House, Point Break* (episode 3), *The People's Court, Law & Order, J.F.K., Beverly Hills Cop, Pokemon* (episode 4), *The Last Starfighter, Indiana Jones and The Temple of Doom* (episode 5), and *The Matrix* (episode 6) are among the many productions parodied, often brilliantly, always mercilessly.

These self-aware jabs at Hollywood, this acknowledgment of Generation X pop culture touchstones (like the *Happy Days* episode in which the Fonz jumps the shark), lands *Clerks: The Animated Series* in the realm of such hip programming as the much-missed *Mystery Science Theater 3000*. Straight, narrative content has been rendered secondary to a slew of canny references to the culture Gen Xers grew up worshipping. It is a hysterically funny TV series, but one undeniably aimed right at Smith's own age group. Those outside it, like the baby boomers, may not really get the jokes, because, ostensibly, they don't understand the significance of *Happy Days* to the audience that grew up with it in the 1970s.

But ABC didn't seem to get the jokes either. The racy material reportedly confused Bob Iger and Michael Eisner. ABC also objected to one of Smith's more colorful jokes about Dr. Seuss (and an erotica book called *Horton Hears a Hymen*), as well as comedic material about the Challenger explosion and the Holocaust.[4]

Even worse, ABC pulled *Clerks* from its schedule after airing only two episodes. Why? Between the time period the program was conceived and then finally ready to air, the network went from being last ranked to first with the help of Regis Philbin.

"This milquetoast game show, *Who Wants to Be a Millionaire*, was so successful and they didn't want to risk losing their first place," Scott Mosier notes. "It ended badly. We were all calling each other names."

"*Millionaire* changed the complete dynamic of what ABC was going for," O'Halloran explains. "They thought they could air *Millionaire* three times a week and it would be their savior, but now they're paying for that decision. They ran that show into the ground."

And, in the process, killed *Clerks* before it could find an audience. "If you watch those six episodes, you get the feeling it's the beginning of something good," notes Pereira. "Look at the first season of *The Simpsons*, and then what it ultimately became. The pacing was different, the design was a little different. I believe that had *Clerks* been given the chance to develop, it would have grown in the way *The Simpsons* or *South Park* did. I think by the fifth episode of the show, you could already see where it was heading."

O'Halloran and Anderson, who were having the time of their lives shooting the series, were dismayed by the way the series was treated. "They jerked us around," O'Halloran says. "It put a bad taste in our mouths. When you go into television, episodic work, you have to realize they can just pull you any second."

Anderson offers his own post-mortem. "Fox or UPN would have been the place for the show, because those networks really don't have anything else."

Others have suggested that Comedy Central might be the right home for the series, but O'Halloran isn't so sure. "At the time, Comedy Central didn't have the budget to spend on *Clerks*. The cartoon cost $750,000 to make per show."

Mosier puts it more succinctly. "If we'd been on Comedy Central, we all would have made about three dollars per episode."

O'Halloran was especially disappointed by *Clerks'* cancellation, because he'd caught a glimpse of things to come. "When we fulfilled our six episode contract, I asked Kevin what was next and he gave me some of the synopses of future shows, and they were just so funny. It would have been great to be able to do it."

Still, fans shouldn't lose hope. The idea of another *Clerks* animated production—whether a TV series or a feature film—is not yet dead. "Harvey Weinstein is a huge fan of the series," O'Halloran reveals. "He would rather Kevin make an animated feature than *Jersey Girl*. He's saying we shouldn't worry; that once we do a feature film, we'll find another episodic outlet for the show, even if it's HBO. Cable is starting to become more and more a contender, sweeping the Emmys and such, and it offers more freedom."

"There is talk of doing an animated feature," Anderson confirms. "Kevin says that he and Mandel, who wrote the TV show, are working on the script. I'd love to do it. On the TV show, I was always waiting any minute for someone to bust in and close us down because we were having so much fun."

While the stars and fans of *Clerks: The Animated Series* wait for the feature, there's opportunity to reminisce about their favorite moments on the short-lived series.

"I always liked that Randal began referring to himself in the third person. If the cartoon went any further, it would have been the undoing of Randal. In the *Real World* episode [episode 2], he was saying, 'You kicked out Randal? You can't kick out Randal!' That's where it gets scary, when Randal starts referring to himself in the third. Kevin said if the Jay Leno shorts [short films starring Dante and Randal produced for the *Tonight Show*; see chapter eight] go further, that's where we're headed."

"I liked the fifth episode," O'Halloran reports. "Dante's little league baseball team and the *Temple of Doom* thing is just really funny. And I loved the idea of Randal's ex-girlfriends all becoming lesbians."

"I always liked the courtroom episode too," Anderson laughs. "That one actually made it on the air. I always appreciated the line: 'Show me where they touched you. Show me on the doll where they touched you . . .'"

ASKEW VIEWS

TAKE THE FIFTH: In *Clerks*, episode 4, Randal represents Dante in court against Jay's attorney (named Pierson), and calls various personalities to testify, including filmmakers George Lucas, Woody Allen, Spike Lee, Joel Schumacher, and Steven Spielberg. He questions them about the quality of various productions, including *The Phantom Menace* and *Hook*. But if Jeff Anderson had his way, there would have been one other witness on the stand: Kevin Smith.

"I always said why the hell isn't Kevin testifying, so I could ask him what the hell was up with *Mallrats*?"

NC-17: The stars of *Clerks: The Animated Series* had so much fun recording their dialogue, that at one point they conceived a wicked idea, O'Halloran remembers. "It was the type of fun where Jeff and I got together and decided that if the show went on, we'd record an entire episode wearing only our underwear. Then we'd have the pleasure of knowing that people are watching this episode all over the country, and we were almost naked when we did our lines."

UN-PRESIDENTED: The *Clerks* cartoon, even more than Kevin Smith's films, are packed with references to popular films and television. One of the funniest such jokes occurs in episode 4, where there is a straight-faced riff on Donald Sutherland's powerful, information-laden scene with Kevin Costner in Oliver Stone's meditation on the murder of President Kennedy, *J.F.K.* In this case, Randal fills in for the Costner character.

Speaking of presidents, in episode 2, when Randal and Dante flash back to their first meeting at the Quick Stop in the 1980s, the character first seen walking down the street is none other than an animated Ronald Reagan. Likewise, in the 1970s introduction of Randal and Dante, the first character to appear is a cartoon version of Jimmy Carter.

WOMEN'S LIB: At the start of episode 3, a letter writer named Jen Schwalbach complains in a missive to Randal and Dante about the lack of substantive roles for women on the show.

Well, at least she didn't ask them for ten grand.

PART II

STATE OF RED (2003–2011)

8

Jersey Girl (2004)

SUN EVEN SHINES ON A DOG'S ASS SOME DAYS

Cast and Crew

MIRAMAX FILMS, VIEW ASKEW PRODUCTIONS, BEVERLY DETROIT, AND CLOSE CALL FILMS PRESENT *JERSEY GIRL*

Written and directed by: Kevin Smith
Produced by: Scott Mosier
Co-producer: Laura Greenlee
Executive Producers: Jonathan Gordon, Bob and Harvey Weinstein
Cinematography by: Vilmos Zsigmond
Edited by: Scott Mosier and Kevin Smith
Production designer: Robert Holtzman
Costume designer: Julie Polcsa
Music: James L. Venable
Casting: Diane Heery, Avy Kaufman
M.P.A.A. rating: PG-13
Running time: 102 minutes

Starring

Ben Affleck | *Ollie Trinke*
Liv Tyler | *Maya*
George Carlin | *Bart Trinke*
Jennifer Lopez | *Gertrude Steiney*

Jason Biggs | *Arthur Brickman*
Raquel Castro | *Gertie Trinke*
Jennifer Schwalbach Smith | *Susan*
Mike Starr | *Block*
Stephen Root | *Greenie*
S. Epatha Merkerson | *Doctor #1*
Carol Florence | *Doctor #2*
Matt Maher | *Delivery Guy*
Jason Lee | *PR Exec 1*
Matt Damon | *PR Exec 2*
Charles Gilbert | *Sweeney Todd*
Will Smith | *Himself*
Harley Quinn Smith | *Tracy*
Betty Arberlin | *Teacher*
Matt McFarland | *Boy #1*
Sarah Stafford | *Girl #1*
Paulie Litowsky | *Bryan*
Christian Fan | *Boy #3*
Victor Chavez | *Boy #4*
William Mace | *Boy #5*

THE STORY SO FAR ...

A PRECOCIOUS LITTLE GIRL, GERTIE TRINKE tells her classmates and teacher the love story of her father and mother, Ollie and Gertrude. Once upon a time, Ollie was the toast of New York, a music industry publicist at the very top of his game. Then, one fine day, Ollie fell head over heels in love with the beautiful Gertrude, and—after introducing this woman to his curmudgeonly father, Bart, in Highlands, New Jersey—married her. Very soon, the couple was expecting their first child.

Unfortunately, tragedy struck these lovebirds when Gertrude died of an aneurysm during childbirth. This turn of events left Ollie no choice but to move in with his father, and to take care of his daughter, Gertie, alone. His professional life, however, quickly imploded when he made negative comments about the "Fresh Prince," Will Smith, at a press conference. In a heartbeat, Ollie's career was over.

For years, Ollie lived as an outcast in New Jersey, eventually taking a job as a garbageman with his dear old dad. But all the while, he had hopes of returning to the big game in New York City and resuming his career in public relations. One day, Ollie met a video store clerk and graduate student named Maya, who helped restore his confidence. Then, with a little help from former associate Arthur Brickman, Ollie believed he might finally return from purgatory.

There was only one problem.

Ollie was not the same man he once was. His life in New Jersey had become filled with love and friendship, and young Gertie did not want to leave that life for a new one in the city.

In the end, Ollie had to make a choice about what kind of life he wanted to lead, and where he wanted to lead it.

THE STORY BEHIND THE MOVIE

KEVIN SMITH'S MUCH ANTICIPATED sixth feature film, the first one not to feature Jay and Silent Bob, was called *Jersey Girl*, and the writer/director once described it in print as a "chamber piece about fatherhood."[1]

Smith's wife, Jennifer Schwalbach, felt very enthusiastic about the screenplay in 2002 because, for one thing, it offered another instance of the director having something very personal to say.

"*Jersey Girl* is the movie I wanted Kevin to do after *Dogma*, because I thought it was that good," Schwalbach told me when the film was in preproduction. "It's really him expressing himself as a parent. And we don't think that anybody can be offended by it . . . though there might some group out there looking for money!

"It's a very quiet film," Schwalbach reported. "There are no stunts or bright colors or loud music, and it's very real. It may be the first and perhaps only PG-13 movie that Kevin does. There's little to no need for swearing, and there isn't anything racy or scandalous about it. Basically, if you're not crying within the first thirty pages, you're a robot. It's a tearjerker.

"It tells this very beautiful story between a husband and his wife, but is basically about the husband facing life with his daughter, and not knowing what to do, kind of winging it, and learning on his own. It's him getting to know himself, and getting back to his roots to raise his daughter in the way he thinks his wife wants him to.

"It's Kevin's love letter to Harley," Schwalbach continues. "It sounds so ridiculous coming from me, his wife, to someone writing a book about Kevin, but I could not ask for a better father for my child. Kevin touches me so deeply when I watch him with her. Not only does she look exactly like him, but she has so many of his personality traits. The two of them are just two peas in a pod, and it's so wonderful to watch the two of them together. And he's so brilliant and funny, and a completely different parent than I am. It's so nice for me to sit back and watch him give her the things I never could. I'm the mom, and I put the Band-Aids on her boo-boos, but he brings out this very creative, very different part of her personality, and it's amazing to see. And I think she's going to grow up to be just like him.

"I think *Jersey Girl* is a peek into our love," Schwalbach says, "but it's really so much more about fatherhood. I think he'll come back to us."

Contextualizing *Jersey Girl* in terms of View Askew film history, producer Scott Mosier reported that the project was "funny" and emotional, and very "close" in feeling to *Chasing Amy*. He also reported that as "adults," the creative team could no longer avoid telling "this kind of story."

A ten-week shooting schedule was slated for August in the city of Philadelphia, and the film saw the return of Ben Affleck to the fold, in a leading role. The actor too was impressed by the sheer emotionality of Smith's new script. "It's smart and interesting and unusual in a way that was appealing to me," Affleck reported. "It also had some events that were unexpected story-wise, which I thought was great. It grabbed me and surprised me when I read it. I was really invested in the characters."[2]

Ben Affleck's high-profile love of the time, Jennifer Lopez, would also appear in the film in an extended cameo as Gertrude, as would Affleck's costar from *Armageddon* (1998), Liv Tyler. Tyler played Maya, a character who seemed like an adult version, perhaps, of *Mallrats'* Trish the Dish.

Working with Smith for the first time, Tyler expressed a fascination with the specificities of the director's creative equation.

"Well, I love the fact that he deals with the profane and sacred, together, often verbally in the same sentence," she reported. "And *Jersey Girl* is about redemption. It's a religious movie on a certain level. At the same time, he's a trash-meister; he loves reveling in the scatological stuff and profanity and sexual playfulness."[3]

Also joining the cast was *Dogma* veteran George Carlin, who would appear as Affleck's crusty but good-hearted father. "Kevin wrote it with my voice in mind. And he knew that I knew this type of person by indirect association from growing up in a working-class, Irish, New York community," the comedian explained. "Bart Trinke, per se, is not Irish, but he could easily be. This is a working-class guy who has, more or less, old-fashioned concerns and values. I know those guys. I was around them plenty. And playing this role made me more confident in my abilities. I just called on the imaginary grandfather in me."[4]

The shooting of *Jersey Girl* occurred largely in Philadelphia, with some shooting also scheduled in Manhattan. By most accounts, the shooting went smoothly, save for a tidal wave of tabloid interest in—or perhaps obsession with—the real-life romantic pairing between Affleck and Lopez. Together, the couple became known in the gossip mill as "Bennifer" and the preferred topic of every tabloid paper and TV show in the nation, and possibly in the world. The fascination with all things Bennifer occurred as *Jersey Girl* was lensing, and at first it looked like the coupling would be a significant boon to the film's opportunity at the box office. As Kevin Smith noted:

> We got Ben and Jennifer at a perfect time. They were falling in love in real life and falling in love on film. I don't know that they had to act that much.[5]

But interest in celebrity couples quickly burns out, as Affleck and Lopez learned the hard way. Their earlier film together, *Gigli* (2003), premiered to blistering reviews, and a backlash against Bennifer ensued. Held back until 2004, by the time *Jersey Girl* came out, the couple had separated—and everyone seemed sick to death of the duo. Naturally, the press's oversaturation of Bennifer and then the violent backlash over the couple made *Jersey Girl* a tough sell. Smith described the problem aptly:

> No matter how hard we tried, the marketing seemed to say, "Remember the movie [Gigli] with those two people you can't stand anymore that came out a few months ago? Here's even more!"[6]

In fact, no matter how many interviews Kevin Smith granted to the press, he seemed to be in the unenviable position of attempting to distance himself and his new movie from *Gigli* and the entire Bennifer debacle. But as Scott Mosier related, the director had no choice. "Once the other movie came out and our name was getting thrown into those articles, whether you want to do it or not, it was important for us to go out and say, 'We're not that movie. We have nothing to do with that movie. Our movie is a completely different experience.'"[7]

Ben Affleck himself had to go through a period of reassessment regarding his career and his work, not to mention his public face as a star. He later reflected on the Bennifer situation that "Our relationship was written about so much that it just alienated people...I'll sort of disappear for a good long time, and not be...this person."[8]

The immediate collateral damage however, was *Jersey Girl*, which underwent a late re-edit to minimize Lopez's role, and which faced guarded, suspicious audiences. Already, the film had something going against it in the fact that it was Smith's first ever so-called "adult" movie, dealing with "having a job or career, getting married, having a kid."[9]

Even before the Bennifer breakup and backlash, there was a lot of doubt that fans of Jay and Silent Bob would follow Smith to his new film. Smith worried vocally in the press that he might be perceived as a sellout for leaving behind the concerns of his more juvenile admirers.

When released, *Jersey Girl* indeed proved divisive and received mixed reviews from the critical community. *Interview* magazine called the film "surprisingly moving,"[10] while *Variety*'s Joey Leydon expressed disappointment and noted that the "pic overall resembles a 'very special episode' of a routine sitcom."[11]

USA Today's Mike Clark took a more even-handed approach. He noted that "Smith is looking more and more like a developing major talent, so it could be years until we get a handle on this movie's legacy. This is not only defensible as a cute one-shot, but also as a positive sign for the future. For now, look for both fans and detractors to overstate their cases."[12]

Ultimately, *Jersey Girl* didn't do terrible business, but neither did it grow the fan base or Kevin Smith's box office clout. Still, the director expressed happiness that the film—a tribute to fatherhood—was seen by his own father before he passed away:

> He was moved by it and understood it was obviously a big shout-out to him.[13]

Until *Cop Out* in 2010, *Jersey Girl* was probably considered Kevin Smith's most mediocre film, an assessment that may be true, but certainly doesn't reflect the amount of heart that went into its crafting.

FORGET ABOUT WHAT YOU THOUGHT YOU WERE, AND JUST ACCEPT WHO YOU ARE

Kevin Smith boasts two distinctive modes of communication, as many film critics have keenly observed: earnest and irreverent. *Jersey Girl* finds a heavy focus on the earnest portion of that filmmaking equation, which, alas, siphons off some of this film's energy. And while the message of *Jersey Girl* is delightful and worthwhile—lauding the seemingly magical spell children seem to cast upon adults, even curmudgeonly ones—even the dedicated Smithian viewer may still end up missing the director's trademark irreverence. It's still present to a degree, of course, but blunted by the film's nature as a sentimental story about family. Still, it's not as if the film were falsely advertised.

To put it another way, *Chasing Amy* brilliantly concerned the agonies and ecstasies of falling in love, but never seemed schmaltzy or rested upon bromides and clichés. That film's observations about romantic love not only felt fresh, but true, and at times actually caustic. There was nothing canned, processed, or obvious about Smith's approach to the topic in that remarkable film. As John Pierson might note, *Chasing Amy* transcended its form and genre, the romantic comedy.

Contrarily, *Jersey Girl* doesn't accomplish the same feat, transcending the family comedy. It feels too cute by half, and the conclusions it reaches about parenthood—while undeniably true—feel pat and comfortable, not blazingly original, or anything folks didn't already know going into the movie. Just because a movie is about family doesn't mean it has to play things safe.

And yes, I get it.

I'm a devoted father myself, and so I understand that this project represents Kevin Smith's love letter to his daughter and to the sustained acrobatic act of meaningful fatherhood. And yet one can see and appreciate this point of view fully and still the wish the film featured more edge, more sharpness. The first fifteen minutes of *Jersey Girl* certainly seem to promise that level of energy and attitude. The film opens with flourishes and spikes of beauty, wit, and tragedy, but after that rarely treads into any kind of courageous territory about fatherhood. Instead, it makes jokes about changing diapers and asking little boys, "What are your intentions?" And the critics who made the observation are correct: this quality feels abundantly like sitcom material.

Disappointingly, Smith doesn't depict the controversial world of public relations much more ingeniously, either. During Ben Affleck's big moment as Ollie Trinke—publicist extraordinaire—the film doesn't even allow the audience to listen to the character's accomplished, opinion-altering rhetoric, the words that so dramatically sway the people at a local town hall meeting.

Instead, the film offers up a sentimental montage in place of ideas, and then Ollie's explanatory testimony that he feels like he's back in the game. Yet the audience doesn't get to follow along, see (and register) why Ollie is good at PR, or even why he loves it. What is it about this particular experience that makes him want to uproot his entire life at this juncture? If we actually had the opportunity to hear his talk, we might have a better insight into the man and his desires. We would understand the pull of his career better if we saw him in action; and therefore the outcome of his decision—the crux of the drama, here—would seem more in doubt.

A more truthful, edgier film might have acknowledged that Ollie loves his daughter, but resists being a dad because—like many men—he doesn't view success as something he can achieve at home, for instance, or in a domestic setting. But again, the film settles for familiar sentiments and mainstream answers to pressing questions about fatherhood, and thus *Jersey Girl* feels like it could be the product of a different, less probing director altogether.

Late in the film, *Jersey Girl* attempts to mine tension from the notion that Ollie may miss Gertie's school program. In fact, obstacles are almost literally thrown in his path, and he must run to her school to make it there on time and prove his love for her. Again, this sequence simply feels artificial and manufactured. The point is that whether Ollie makes the show on time or not, *he has already selected his daughter.* But the film reaches for melodrama, for an infusion of artificial suspense, when it simply doesn't need to go that route.

In Hollywood today, there's a belief that for a movie to appeal to a wide audience, it has to be homogenized. It must be largely inoffensive, reinforce conventional middle-American values, and appeal to the lowest common denominator. Kevin Smith boasts so many fans primarily because his films *don't* hew to any of those conventions, for the most part. *Clerks* concerns two men talking about life and growing up, no holds barred. *Dogma* affirms religion and faith through the crucible of doubt. *Chasing Amy* deeply explores the gulf between men and women, and their different perspectives on love. Even mainstream films such as *Mallrats, Clerks II,* and *Jay and Silent Bob Strike Back* are quirky, colorful efforts enlivened by Smith's willingness to probe the edges of societal acceptability and to use language in a unique, colorful fashion. *Jersey Girl* doesn't feel like any of those films. You've seen it all a hundred times before.

In the final analysis, the movie feels a lot like *half* a Kevin Smith movie, which is better than none, I suppose, but not nearly as good as getting the full monty.

None of this criticism is meant to suggest that *Jersey Girl* represents some historical super-debacle, or that it doesn't generally entertain—merely that it entertains in a fashion that a dozen other films also entertain. It doesn't feel special; it doesn't feel distinctive. *Jersey Girl* blunts Kevin Smith's rough edges and feels remarkably generic, despite beautiful intentions. Except for much of Maya's dialogue regarding porn and the married man, the Kevin Smith aesthetic is tamed to an unfortunate degree. His voice just doesn't shine through the way his fans may wish it might.

Perhaps the film also fails to a significant degree because Ollie Trinke doesn't seem to represent the difficulties and diffidence of Generation X the way characters such as Randal, Dante, or Brodie do. Their perpetual struggle is to find purpose or meaning in an adulthood or profession that seems absurd and without purpose. Here, Ollie has already solved that problem. He's not against the system or the establishment as it exists. In fact, he's an enthusiastic part of it until he gets thrown out for having a very bad day. But Ollie never feels like the outsider that he should, and he doesn't question "the way things are" in any meaningful way.

And, as much as I admire Ben Affleck as an actor, he appears almost too buff in *Jersey Girl*, too physically perfect. Throughout seven years of mourning, you don't maintain an Adonis-like physique like his unless you work out literally *all the time*. And you don't work out all the time if you have no money, or you're depressed, or you're still grieving the death of your wife. Even physically, Ollie Trinke doesn't ring true as a believable character.

In my opinion, one big shift would have provided *Jersey Girl* with the real edge that many admirers associate with Kevin Smith. Imagine—just for a moment—if Jeff Anderson had played Ollie. In that eventuality, the arguments between father and daughter would have authentically sizzled, and we would have wondered where Ollie's priorities truly lay. Anderson can play acerbic and harsh to the high heavens, and isn't afraid about his words coming out like he's always a nice guy. He's not a movie star with an image he's protecting.

With Affleck in the lead role, it's a foregone conclusion which path Ollie will choose, and this fact ultimately robs *Jersey Girl* of what little tension it possesses. Not all fathers choose their children over their careers, after all, and it seems that *Jersey Girl* could have played more truthfully and more edgily with this dynamic.

Parts of *Jersey Girl* are really terrific. The film looks fantastic and appropriately autumnal, thanks to the accomplished cinematography of Vilmos Zsigmond. And certainly Raquel Castro is a tremendous find as Gertie. She actually looks like Jennifer Lopez's daughter, and has an easy grace before the camera. Additionally, the death of Lopez's character is not only powerful, but palpably upsetting. The movie works on all cylinders when it charts her demise, whether you love or hate Bennifer.

Yet by the time the film gets to Ollie racing to Gertie's school program, and a prim and proper principal character fainting over the "violence" of *Sweeney Todd*, a fatal dose of saccharine—of earnestness—has robbed the *Jersey Girl* of too much life force, too much irreverence, too much truth.

Just because a film is about children and parents, that doesn't mean it has to be sickly sweet. On his finest days, Kevin Smith tells the truth whether it is comfortable or not. His final shot—*of Ollie and Gertie dancing in a spotlight*—is a beautiful, romantic image, but because *Jersey Girl* is so toothless and earnest, such a happy outcome is never in doubt, the way it should be.

Jersey Girl is not the "bad" film some critics and fans complained it was, but neither is it the blazing original we see so frequently in Smith's canon.

9

Clerks II (2006)

I'M NOT EVEN GONNA POINT OUT THE IRONY, HERE

With no power comes no responsibility.

CAST AND CREW

THE WEINSTEIN COMPANY AND VIEW ASKEW PRODUCTIONS PRESENT *CLERKS II*

Written and directed by: Kevin Smith
Produced by: Scott Mosier
Co-Producer: Lauren Greenlee
Executive Producers: Bob and Harvey Weinstein, Carla Gardini.
Cinematography by: David Klein
Original music: James L. Venable
Edited by: Kevin Smith
Production Designer: Robert Holtzman
Costume Designer: Roseanne Fiedler
Special effects: Charlie Belardinelli
Casting: Smith & Webster/Davis Casting
M.P.A.A. Rating: R
Running time: 97 minutes

STARRING

Brian O'Halloran | *Dante*
Jeff Anderson | *Randal*

Jason Mewes | *Jay*
Kevin Smith | *Silent Bob*
Rosario Dawson | *Becky*
Trevor Fehrman | *Elias*
Kevin Weisman | *Hobbit Lover*
Zak Knutson | *Sexy Stud*
Jason Lee | *Lance Dowds*
Earthquake | *Husband*
Wanda Sykes | *Wife*
Jake Richardson | *Teen #1*
Ethan Suplee | *Teen #2*
Ben Affleck | *Gawking Guy*
Sarah Ault and Lalida Sujjavasin | *Catholic School Girls*
Gail Stanley | *Elias's Mom*
Bruce Macintosh | *Elias's Dad*
Scott Mosier | *Concerned Father*
Walter Flanagan | *Pack-Smokes guy*
Grace Smith | *Milk Maid*
Malcolm Ingram | *Fat Guy Dancing in Bathroom*

SILENT BOB'S WORDS OF WISDOM

"I got nothing."

THE STORY SO FAR...

WHEN THE QUICK STOP IN LEONARDO, NEW JERSEY, BURNS DOWN, clerks Dante and Randal take jobs at the fast-food restaurant Mooby's, and Jay and Silent Bob also take up residence outside it. After some time there, Dante develops a friendship and brief sexual relationship with the manager, Becky. Meanwhile, he is also engaged to Emma, who wants Dante to move to Florida to manage one of her father's car wash franchises.

On the day Dante is to move away from Jersey permanently, he and Becky discuss their own relationship and whether it can have a future. Meanwhile, Randal feels abandoned by his longtime best friend and continues to act irresponsibly. He flames a wheelchair-bound blogger on the Internet, attempts to reclaim the term "porch monkey," and disses modern movie franchises such as *The Lord of the Rings* and *Transformers* to their fans. Randal's inappropriate behavior culminates with a live sex-act show involving a donkey.

The bestiality show lands Randal, Dante, Jay, and Silent Bob in prison, a perfect place for the slackers to reflect upon their lives and the future.

THE STORY BEHIND THE MOVIE

Following the box office and critical disappointment of *Jersey Girl*, Kevin Smith did what many film directors have done in a similar situation. He sought safe harbor. In particular, he returned to the View Askewniverse and Jay and Silent Bob for the long-hoped for sequel to his first film, *Clerks*.

Although many critics and fans interpreted Smith's return to the New Jersey Chronicles as career retreat, Smith himself saw it as the fulfillment of a sacred promise. In particular, he had told his star and friend Jason Mewes that if Mewes could stay clean and off drugs for a year, he would make another movie involving Jay. Mewes lived up to that arrangement. As Smith reported:

> *He's been sober for a year and a half. I've got a promise to keep.*[1]

But if Jason Mewes desired a return to the character that had made him a star, other performers in the *Clerks* saga weren't entirely certain it was wise to return to that world. Jeff Anderson observed that making the sequel wasn't an "easy decision"[2] for him, in part because even after twelve or thirteen years, he still received fan letters about the original. That was a legacy he didn't want to see tarnished by an inferior product. And Anderson also wasn't sure how to make a sequel work.

"What do you do? You can't do black-and-white, 'cause then you're trying to do the same thing," he observed. "You can't do color because it's too different. I needed a little convincing that it was the right idea. Even [Kevin's] wife told him it wasn't a good idea. Lots of people close to him told him it wasn't a good idea, and he said, 'No, I really think we can do this.'"[3]

On a budget of $5 million—still a much higher sum than the cost of the original film—there seemed to be little to lose. Accordingly, Anderson, Brian O'Halloran, and Mewes all returned to their famous roles, joined this time by actress Rosario Dawson as the manager of a fast-food restaurant called Mooby's, the new setting for the action.

And delightfully, Smith again found he had something personal to say about his famous Generation Xers:

> I've got nothing to say about fast food. But I've got everything to say about getting past that period of life where you've been one person for ten or fifteen years and suddenly you have to change.[4]

The return to the world of *Clerks* over a decade later, perhaps more than anything else, revealed how much had changed for the director and his cast and crew. The new film did not shoot primarily in New Jersey, for one thing, and the catering team was probably bigger than the whole film crew on the original film.

Brian O'Halloran noted that it was odd not shooting in New Jersey, but that he had also hoped to enjoy the good weather in L.A. during principal photography. Unfortunately, that didn't happen.

"We were down here for the fabulous, sunny weather, which during one week of shooting was nonstop rain for three days straight. We had this one scene where I'm making out with Kevin's wife... The scene ended up on the schedule for three days straight. There was so much making out!"[5]

After initial toying with calling the film *The Passion of the Clerks*, based on Mel Gibson's 2004 lightning-rod production *The Passion*, it eventually was simply titled *Clerks II*. It opened in more than 2,000 theaters in July 2006 and was greeted warmly by longtime fans of the View Askewniverse.

The reviews of *Clerks II* were also generally very positive. In *The San Francisco Chronicle*, Peter Hartlelaub wrote: "Whatever your expectations, they will almost certainly be exceeded by Smith's hilarious and creative return to low-budget cinema. The continuing adventures of Dante and Randal are just as amusing as the first *Clerks* film, and the story line has an unexpected sincerity that will remind this movie's aging slacker target audience of *The Breakfast Club* and Smith's best film, *Chasing Amy*."[6]

At *Salon*, Stephanie Zacharek noted that "Smith is a sweet-spirited film-maker, and a blessedly unsnobbish one. And even though *Clerks II* is loaded with coarse humor (as any sequel to *Clerks* would have to be), it also gets at some subtler ideas, about how we're shaped by where we come from, and how, even when it seems we're going nowhere, we're still on our way to becoming *something*. And *Clerks II* may be the sweetest movie ever to feature an act of bestiality."[7]

One famous movie critic, however, disagreed vehemently with Zacharek about the bestiality... and he made royal a stink out of it. Legendarily, *Good Morning America* critic Joel Siegel walked out of a screening of *Clerks II* at the forty-minute point, and loudly proclaimed that he hadn't walked out of a film in thirty years.

Later, Siegel defended his unprofessional behavior in *The New York Post*: "It was so foul and mean and repulsive. I finally realized I could not say anything positive... I wasn't ready for this kind of smut... I hope he doesn't make any more movies."[8]

The matter took an even weirder—and graver turn—when less than a year later, Siegel passed away, and Smith was left feeling guilty for fighting a "deeply cancerous man" in what the director termed a "lose/lose" situation."[9]

In toto, the whole back-and-forth between Siegel and Smith closely resembles the kind of trouble that Randal Graves himself might have gotten into, were he a real person.

IT MUST BE NICE TO HAVE A JOB WITH SO MUCH DOWNTIME

The midlife crisis is the subject of *Clerks II*. In this case, counter jockeys Randal and Dante have moved to the world of fast food at Moobys but resolutely failed to find fulfillment or a real, meaningful path to adulthood and career commitment.

Lacking real meaning in his life and on the verge of losing his best friend, Randal has grown increasingly caustic and contrary over the years, and Dante has settled for a dream (of running a car wash franchise in Florida) he doesn't really care about.

Much like his characters in *Clerks II*, Kevin Smith appears to be at a career crossroads with this film. After the critical and commercial failure of *Jersey Girl*—a deeply personal project—he has done what he once swore he would never do: returned to the familiar Askewniverse and the role of Silent Bob as he nears the "grown-up" age of forty.

That's the reason, perhaps, *Clerks II* felt like many critics to the equivalent of a career retreat. Because *Clerks II* is a good and very funny film, that assessment is probably overly harsh, but at the least, *Clerks II* is back in Smith's comfort zone: a bawdy comedy about disaffected characters dealing unsuccessfully with adulthood, and a film rife with geeky movie references (from *Transformers* to *Lord of the Rings*).

But despite the familiarity of the enterprise, *Clerks II* is resolutely the product of a confident director who, while hitting all the requisite notes for a sequel, also finds plenty of occasions for inspiration, such as a Bollywood-style musical number, or a totally unexpected and bizarre riff on a famous movie scene from *The Silence of the Lambs* (1991). The bottom line is that *Clerks II* boasts quite a few surprises, and so audiences will thoroughly enjoy revisiting these characters and their world.

In particular, Randal is a very affecting character this time around. Here's a guy who believes in friendship above all, and yet can't really express his feelings of friendship. Instead, his feelings of hurt and pain about his friendship with Dante seem to cause him to grow ever more cynical and harsh. This is something you actually see in a lot of Generation Xers as the realization hits them, mid-thirties, that their lives aren't exactly what they hoped they would be.

While success has come to the Lance Dowds of the generation, others have been left behind . . . in minimum wage, customer service jobs. There's little else to hold on to but the belief that there are, at least, friends who see you for what you truly could be, and who will stand beside you in times of crisis.

When Randal believes he could lose Dante, the façade of confidence drops, and we see this beloved character as a scared, bitter, and self-hating guy. He turns his angst and cruelty toward even the innocent, such as the wheelchair-confined blogger, or the young and hopelessly naive Elias.

As for Dante, he's hit the jackpot in terms of a girlfriend, Emma, and a new job with greater responsibilities and financial rewards. But importantly, it's a jackpot he doesn't really desire. Instead, he's taking the path that seems expected of him by society: settling down with a respectable job and woman. Dante seems willing to accept a life of mediocrity, and again that's something of a trademark Generation X dilemma. Should we pursue our dreams and be what we want to be? Or should we tamp down our hopes and be exactly what our parents were before us?

Even Jay, a character usually entirely lacking self-awareness, stands at a crossroads in *Clerks II*. He realizes he can't keep doing what he's been doing, either. He's been to jail, gone to rehab, and found solace in religion (Christianity). Suddenly, he's gazing at the rest of his life, not just passing the time in a haze. Ultimately, Jay decides that the best way to succeed and do what he wants to do (meaning hang out . . .) is to invest his money wisely. In other words, he finds his own distinctive path. He acknowledges what makes him happy (being with Silent Bob outside the Quick Stop) and charts a path to reach that life goal. This is perhaps not what many of us would choose, but it is a validation of Generation X and the "go your own way" aesthetic. We'll get to our individual destinations the way we want, and "use" the established system only so much as it can get us to that point.

Clerks II climaxes with Dante and Randal also embracing responsibility—becoming small-business owners—but as with Jay, there is the feeling that this is what they want to do, not a surrender to economic or family realities. *What they want is a place where they can be together*, doing what they do. And that, in the final analysis, is a victory, too: bromance for life.

One senses this is the very place Kevin Smith strives to get to: the place where he is comfortable making his own films his own way, with the cast and crew he loves. He need not aspire to anything beyond his own artistic enjoyment and creativity. Critics, shmitics, right?

In the decade-plus between *Clerks* and its sequel, what did not change about Kevin Smith is his apparent obsession with movies and with the specificities of language itself. From the reclamation of the pejorative term "porch monkey" to a debate about the *Lord of the Rings* movies, *Clerks II* reveals a fixation on the forms and surfaces of life. What do our words really mean? What do movies such as *Transformers* really tell us, if anything, about ourselves? And how does this new generation of blockbuster differ from *Star Wars*, Smith's eternal obsession? Again, this debate also involves the middle-aging of Generation X. Pop culture has moved on to elves and Autobots, while we cling to our light sabers.

As usual, Smith asks some tough questions about why people get so offended by words or by films that don't jibe with their own wisdom. Therefore, *Clerks II* emerges as a kind of comedy of manners and political correctness. Is a dislike of *Transformers* or *Lord of the Rings* an insult to good taste? Or a welcome commentary on the state of modern blockbusters? Why do we fear words? As usual—right down to the donkey show—a Smith film seems to be about the very powerful idea of pushing limits, and asking us to reconsider our own limits. What's on the other side of decorum, and what do we learn about ourselves in broaching it?

If *Clerks II* fails on any level, it's simply that the characters somehow seem diminished and less special in full-color photography. The film doesn't boast a distinctive or signature look the way the original did, or the way *Chasing Amy* did. At times, in fact, *Clerks II* looks like a TV version of *Clerks*, "now in color."

That drawback established, the film's final, epic pullback in the Quick Stop, which features a transition to black-and-white, is a nostalgia-provoking, powerful image that reconnects the viewer to the original film in a trenchant and emotionally deep way. Suddenly, it's as if no time has passed at all, and we're right back in the world of milkmaids and the like. Only now— importantly—Dante is "supposed to be there" that day. He's not the hired help...he's the boss. He has *chosen* to work at the Quick Stop and embraced responsibility in a way that doesn't feel like a sellout.

Clerks II charts the same territory: Smith returns to his humble beginnings, but on his own remarkable, affecting, irreverent terms. On the surface, *Clerks II* might look like a strategic retreat after a box office drubbing, but it is a stealth movie and something else altogether. Kevin Smith again has something intensely personal to say.

Donkey show and all.

10

Zack and Miri Make a Porno (2008)

SOMETIMES, WE JUST NEED SOMEONE TO SHOW US SOMETHING WE CAN'T SEE FOR OURSELVES

Seth Rogen and Elizabeth Banks made a movie so titillating that we can only show you this drawing.

CAST AND CREW

BLUE ASKEW, THE WEINSTEIN COMPANY, AND VIEW ASKEW PRESENT *ZACK AND MIRI MAKE A PORNO*

Written and directed by: Kevin Smith
Produced by: Scott Mosier
Co-Producer: Laura Greenlee
Executive Producers: Bob and Harvey Weinstein, Carla Gardini
Cinematography: David Klein
Edited by: Kevin Smith
Music: James L. Venable
Production Designer: Robert Holtzman
Costume Designer: Salvador Perez
Casting: Nancy Mosser
M.P.A.A. Rating: R
Running time: 101 minutes

Starring

Elizabeth Banks | *Miri*
Seth Rogen | *Zack*
Craig Robinson | *Delaney*
Brandon Routh | *Bobby Long*
Justin Long | *Brandon*
Jennifer Schwalbach | *Betsy*
Tom Savini | *Jenkins*
Jeff Anderson | *Deacon*
Jason Mewes | *Lester*
Katie Morgan | *Stacey*
Ricky Mabe | *Barry*
Traci Lords | *Bubbles*
Tyler Labine | *Drunk Customer*
Tisha Campbell-Martin | *Delaney's Wife*
Zak Knutson | *Todd Spilotti*

THE STORY SO FAR...

BEST FRIENDS SINCE HIGH SCHOOL, misfits and roommates Zack and Miri are out of money. The power and water (and also the heat...) in the apartment they share are turned off during the holidays, leaving them with precious few options. On the night of their fifteen-year high school reunion, Zack comes up with the idea of making a porno movie they can market to their former classmates.

After some initial hesitation, Miri agrees to the plan, and the couple begins planning an elaborate production entitled *Star Whores*. But even with all the costumes created and parts cast, disaster strikes the duo again. Their studio space is destroyed by a wrecking crew, leaving Zack to devise a compromise. Working after hours, he and Miri film a new porno in the strip-mall coffee shop where they work.

All seems to be going well, until it is time for Zack and Miri to film their sex scene together. Suddenly, what seemed like such a good idea now threatens to destroy the foundation of their friendship.

THE STORY BEHIND THE MOVIE

After a successful return to familiar but funny ground with the sequel *Clerks II*, Kevin Smith commenced work on his next cinematic project. It was to be another "slacker" comedy—but one set firmly outside the boundaries of the familiar View Askewniverse. In selecting his material, Smith returned to an idea he'd first proposed a decade earlier, circa 1996:

> [At] the end of Chasing Amy *we wanted to make this movie called* Name *that dealt with the porn industry . . . as one of the main characters has kind of gone off to work in porn and then returned home years later. And I wanted to do it with Joey [Lauren Adams], Jason [Lee] and Ben [Affleck]. Then, after* Chasing Amy, *me and Joey broke up . . . and then also we got the opportunity to move forward on* Dogma.[1]

In particular, Smith sought to make a movie about "people who find love in a weird set of circumstances," set on "the outskirts of porn."[2] Recalling the *Magnolia*/Paul Thomas Anderson kerfuffle, Smith was also quick to report that he intended to steer clear of any material that might seem too reminiscent of that director's undisputed 1997 porn-themed masterpiece, *Boogie Nights*.

When journalists asked how he prepped to create a film even tangentially about the world of porn, Smith noted, in more than one venue, that he had "been researching *Zack and Miri*" since he was eleven, sometimes "three times a day, depending on who was in the house."[3]

Legendarily, Harvey Weinstein, now at the Weinstein Company, green-lit Smith's new script instantaneously upon hearing the title for the first time. As Smith reported:

> I told (producer) Harvey Weinstein the title and he said, "Done." And I said, "Don't you want to know what it's about?" And he said, "Is it really about anything more than that title?" And I said, "God I hope so, when all's said and done."[4]

Zack and Miri Make a Porno was budgeted at $24 million—nearly five times *Clerks II*'s cost—and this considerable sum of money meant Smith could afford actors who had previously been unavailable for lower-budget works. First and foremost among these was Seth Rogen, the portly star of such high-grossing comedies as *The 40 Year Old Virgin* (2005) and *Knocked Up* (2007). Both blockbuster productions had been directed and produced by Judd Apatow, an up-and-comer in Hollywood films and a talent who, according to Rogen, had found inspiration in Smith's work, particularly *Clerks*. Rogen shared Apatow's esteem for Smith, and considered himself a fan too.

"He was really influential on me as a writer, and he just really laid the groundwork for the type of movies we make now, and it was always something I would have hoped to do was work with him," Rogen declared. "It's like one of those things. It's amazing to me that I get to work with the people who directly influenced me."[5]

After Rogen took on the role of Zack in Smith's film, he noted that "it only feels right. In a lot of ways, our comedy comes from Kevin. I have often, and Judd has also, talked about how *Clerks* was one of the first movies showing guys talking how we talk. It seems very simple, but it was a revelation in many ways for guys who wanted to write comedy."[6]

Cast opposite Rogen was Elizabeth Banks, who during the same year as *Zack and Miri* portrayed America's former first lady, Laura Bush, in Oliver Stone's biopic *W.* She came highly recommended to Smith by Rogen during casting, according to Smith:

> So Seth comes over and before I could even finish, he's just like, "Elizabeth Banks. She was awesome. I worked with her in The 40 Year Old Virgin, but she also got really far in the Knocked Up auditions. She was almost the female lead." He was like, "She's funny, she can do your dialogue, she can lift it, she's good-looking, and she's got this charm to her, man."[7]

With Rogen—Smith's so-called "Affleck 2.0"—and Banks ensconced in the leading roles, Smith also brought in two View Askew regulars, Jeff Anderson and Jason Mewes, to play the supporting roles of Deacon the cinematographer and Lester, a wannabe porn star, respectively. From the world of porn itself, the film also featured sultry Traci Lords (as Bubbles) and Katie Morgan. Rounding out the cast was another Apatow veteran, Craig Robinson, as would-be producer Delaney.

Although the original intent had been to shoot *Zack and Miri Make a Porno* in Minnesota (like *Mallrats*), the team eventually settled on another location: Pennsylvania. In particular, the crew would spend the forty-day shoot in and around Pittsburgh and Monroeville.

For horror fans, Monroeville represents a kind of modern, pop culture mecca. East of Pittsburgh, the city and its famous Monroeville Mall famously hosted horror director George A. Romero for his cult smash *Dawn of the Dead* (1978). Although that shoot at the mall took place way back in 1977, horror fans the world around remember the location and frequently make pilgrimages there. At one point, *Zack and Miri Makes a Porno* even returns to the world-famous mall for a scene, and features a cameo by *Dawn of the Dead* actor and special effects guru Tom Savini.

Besides this connection to moviemaking history, Pittsburgh in winter offered a great visual for Smith and his returning cinematographer, David Klein: "The main reason Kevin chose Pittsburgh in winter was that he wanted a cold, urban environment as the background of a warm love story. Pittsburgh in winter is one of the last places where you would envision people making a pornographic movie, but that is part of the charm that makes it believable. Zack and Miri come across as likeable...naive, ordinary people in a believable setting. The architecture also gives you a sense of place."[8]

In terms of the picture's look, Klein and Smith emphasized the romantic nature of the material with a 1.85:1 aspect ratio. As Smith noted:

> *As a romantic relationship evolves between Zack and Miri, there is an intimacy that plays on their faces that is very moving. When that happens, the rest of the world disappears for them. That's a testimony to the talent Seth and Elizabeth brought to the film. You can feel the heat in the love they have for each other. It's a very powerful and emotional drama in the midst of a bawdy comedy.*[9]

According to reports, the shooting of *Zack and Miri Make a Porno* went along quite swimmingly. It wasn't until after Smith edited the film, in fact, that trouble reared its head. In particular, a film envisioned as a "hard R" by Smith was instead slapped with the commercial kiss of death by the M.P.A.A.: the NC-17. Smith reedited and submitted the film three times to win the coveted R rating,[10] and in the process trimmed two sex scenes from the film's final cut.[11]

Still, *Zack and Miri*'s problems were far from resolved. More than a dozen newspapers rejected the advertisements for the movie because they were deemed too sexually explicit[12], and a prominent megaplex chain in conservative Utah also refused to show the film, on the basis of family values. The issue that was so galvanizing was the word "porno" in the film's title—ironically, the same title that had gotten the film instantly green-lit.

The original ads for the film were subbed out, with ads featuring stick figures of Seth Rogen and Elizabeth Banks, but some media outlets were still uncomfortable with the film and refused to promote it.

Despite these problems, expectations were high that *Zack and Miri Make a Porno* would open big when released. Exhibitor Relations analyst Jeff Bock told *USA Today* that the film had one of the best titles of the year and that Smith's fans would follow him anywhere.[13] Indeed, this seemed precisely the case in the era of R-rated Judd Apatow comedies, all of which had reached blockbuster status. The *Los Angeles Times* even called *Zack and Miri Make a Porno* the "most commercially viable"[14] project in Kevin Smith's film career. As Smith himself noted:

> I thank God for Judd [Apatow] because he shattered what I assumed was a thirty million ceiling.[15]

Unfortunately, though it opened in more than 2,700 theaters, *Zack and Miri Make a Porno* actually did only..."Kevin Smith–level" business.

On its opening weekend, the film placed a strong second, beating out franchise, Halloween-themed films such as *Saw V*, and Clint Eastwood's latest film, *Changeling*. Still, when all the receipts had been counted, *Zack and Miri*'s opening weekend brought in only a little over $10 million. It was a huge disappointment to Smith, and a turning point in his film career.

"This was going to validate my comedy," Smith reported. "In my head I had everything riding on it. My mind just snapped. I thought, 'I guess I'm just no damn good at this.'"[16]

Despite the lackluster box office performance of the film, which went on to gross over $42 million worldwide, many critics were overwhelmingly appreciative of *Zack and Miri Make a Porno*.

Richard Corliss at *Time* opined that at age thirty-eight, "the grand old man of raunch talk has figured out how to make a movie that's sweet, funny, and (a little) sexy."[17] *Rolling Stone*'s review proved equally positive. "For those who wonder what happened to the Smith of the first *Clerks* and *Chasing Amy*, here's your answer," the magazine reported.[18]

Variety's Todd McCarthy agreed with such sentiments, calling *Zack and Miri Make a Porno* a "cheerfully vulgar love story or a sweet-hearted sex farce, however you want to look at it. Very much of a piece with Kevin Smith's previous down-and-dirty working-stiff comedies."[19]

Smith wasn't the only one receiving plaudits, either. In *Esquire*, critic Peter Martin took special note of Jason Mewes in his non-Jay mode. He reported that Mewes brought an "unexpected element to the offensive charm he displayed as the more loquacious half of the pothead duo Jay and Silent Bob: acting. As a dim-witted porn star, he shows a comic sensibility that rivals costar Seth Rogen's."[20]

Many other reviews, however, labeled *Zack and Miri Makes a Porno* an imitation (or downright "theft") of Judd Apatow's films, an insult to go with the box office injury.

Seth Rogen himself was able to clarify, quite well, the different approaches Smith and Apatow boasted of when it came to their work. "Well, the movies are similar in how they mix raunch with sweetness, but their styles on set are very different," Rogen said. "It's as simple as Judd not knowing what he wants, but he knows what he wants the scenes to be about. How the information comes out, what the jokes are—he discovers that while we're shooting. And Kevin is very specific. He knows what the shots are, he literally edits the movie. So that's the fundamental difference."[21]

In the end, such distinctions probably didn't matter to Kevin Smith. A well-reviewed film that should have been a mega-hit failed to live up to expectations, and his entire world fell into chaos. It was at this juncture that Smith's methods for creating art came up for debate in the mass media. For, on set, Seth Rogen had introduced Smith to the idea that he could be a productive, creative director…all while smoking weed.

For Smith, this was a huge change in approaching his work. His wife, Jennifer Schwalbach, told me in 2002 that "He lives very quietly. He doesn't drink. He doesn't do drugs. He doesn't even like to take NyQuil. He looks at life very straight, and his eyes are wide open."

Clearly, something had changed dramatically, according to Smith himself.

I became a stoner because of Seth Rogen. He was the first person I'd ever met who was a weed smoker who comes to work on time, never has a problem, has brilliant ideas and is constantly writing.[22]

It was a lifestyle Smith sought to emulate, smoking and working creatively—but some in the industry viewed it as a problem or concern, while others believed it was Smith's way of hiding or shielding himself from the negative aspects of his career, from *Zack and Miri*'s failure to perform as expected at the box office.

OKAY! LET'S MAKE A PORNO

Zack and Miri Make a Porno finds writer-director Smith at his bawdiest and indeed, his most clever. I'll be more specific even than that: This comedy is likely Smith's finest cinematic outing since *Chasing Amy* and perhaps the funniest since *Clerks*. I usually mock critics who declare that movies are laugh-out-loud funny, but—*hell*—I laughed out loud at *Zack and Miri*.

A lot.

Only Smith, an unrepentant Generation Xer, could so daringly marry the contemporary, syrupy rom-com formula with the bracing, ridiculous nature of X-rated adult films and emerge with a movie that is not simply sweet, not merely compassionate, but actually life-affirming and uplifting.

And surely, only the imaginative Smith could pepper his genre-bending comedy with so many off-the-wall-references to arcane pop culture history. For instance, he gives the two-season memory *Buck Rogers in the 25th Century* (1979–1981) a shout-out with a reference to Twiki and Dr. Theopolis...but in an unexpectedly sexual context. And then Smith proceeds to give 1980s action-television a nod with an allusion to one character being something akin to a "filthy MacGyver."

Smith doesn't stop there. He sets his entire movie in Monroeville, the very burb where George A. Romero shot *Dawn of the Dead*. He even takes his cameras to the very same mall (interior and exterior) where most of that movie's horrific action took place...*and it looks exactly the same, thirty years later*.

Given that fact, there's some ironic subtext here about Zack and Miri being distinctly un-zombie-like in a town and world that seem to encourage conformity, consumption, and, well, zombie-ism. Trying to pay our bills, meet the responsibilities of our low-paying jobs, and just keep going, we all feel like zombies sometimes. *Zack and Miri Make a Porno* is about two thirty-somethings who, instead of joining the ranks of the living dead, figure out how to really live.

And surely, only Kevin Smith could get away with Zack and Miri's first effort at a porno film. It's a film titled *Star Whores*, and it features characters including Darth Vibrator, Hung Solo, Luke Skybanger, and R2-T-Bag.

And did I mention the phallus-shaped Dia-Noga?

Clearly, the porn-centric, pun-filled world of adult movies has given Kevin Smith free rein to express his off-the-wall, creative side, and the film is all the better for it.

In terms of story, *Zack and Miri Make a Porno* is the tale of two lovable losers who have been best friends since high school and now share an apartment together. Still, they've put up force fields in their personal life, careful never to stray into the dangers of a romantic (or sexual) relationship. Like so many of us in 2008, Zack and Miri are scraping to get by, and trying to figure out how to get ahead in an economy that is leaking jobs like a sieve.

At their fifteen-year high school reunion, Zack comes up with a brilliant money-making scheme after an encounter with two gay porn stars (Justin Long and Brandon Routh). He decides he and Miri should make a porno film. He wants to be a moviemaker and entrepreneur in the age of YouTube and social media.

So, with an entourage of crazy characters in tow—from money man Delaney (Craig Robinson) and videographer Deacon (Jeff Anderson), to a porno wannabe named Lester (Jason Mewes) and an industry veteran named Bubbles (Traci Lords)—Miri and Zack are set to emerge as porn stars for the Internet Age. Much of the film's tension (and comedy) arises from the fact that Miri and Zack—always "just friends"—will finally have sex together... *but on camera.* The film's final act deals with the repercussions of their decision to do just that.

Given this setup, the first half of the film is a raunchy extravaganza, and the last half is something a bit more touching. Often, a good director knows how to get out of the way of his story and characters... *and just let things unfold in front of the camera.* That's what a trusting, confident, and mellow Smith does with dynamic effect in the third act here.

As Zack and Miri prepare to take center stage and film their sex scene together, all the outrageous comedy bells and whistles drop away. The audience is left with a painfully earnest, clumsy, raw, *honest* sequence that acknowledges the deep friendship between this "couple," and the gentleness, irritation, and love with which they treat each other. In typical Smith fashion, the awkward scene unfolds and Zack and Miri never stop talking, never stop bickering, never stop being... *in love.*

I often decry the state of American film comedy in the twenty-first century. I dislike how disposable studio comedies pretend to be brutal, but serve only to reinforce the status quo in their third acts. I'm reminded, for example, of the abominable and inexplicably popular *Wedding Crashers*. That movie introduced two great scoundrels in Owen Wilson and Vince Vaughn's characters, gave them some truly wicked comedic business to vet—but then spent the entire, overlong film reforming them both and proving that wedding crashing is, *you know*, bad.

The 40 Year Old Virgin is very much the same story. It starts out wicked and wonderful, but ends up all smug happiness—hugs and puppies. It doesn't live up to the brutality of its title, and a comedy without brutality isn't worth a pot of spit.

What I enjoyed so much about *Zack and Miri Make a Porno* is that neither the characters nor Smith himself back away from the premise, or ever stand in judgment of it. Zack and Miri *do have sex on camera*, in a porno, in this very movie, and they don't torture or punish themselves over that fact.

Even better, the movie doesn't ask us to judge them or their illicit activities as immoral, bad, or worthy of condemnation. Good comedy is observation, not judgment. Where movies like *Wedding Crashers* or *The 40 Year Old Virgin* forget or ignore that important fact, *Zack and Miri* remembers it. We don't go see a comedy to laugh a little, and then get a sermon about how we should behave. We see a comedy to laugh, and if we're lucky, connect with a unique worldview or experience.

Also, Smith doesn't trade in stereotypes. His characters are sometimes slightly exaggerated (or larger than life, perhaps), but they're also—*miracu-lously*—very true to life. As with Holden and Alyssa in *Chasing Amy*, you'll detect something of yourself and your mate, spouse, or significant other in the tribulations, victories and even pettiness of Zack and Miri. You'll recognize their fears, insecurities, and dreams . . . and become invested in them and their success.

That Smith can forge so strong a sense of identification with Zack and Miri amidst ridiculous humor (including a bubble gag with Traci Lords, and the best constipation joke in years . . .) is a testament to his talent for observation. At listening, understanding, and then successfully transmitting the sweet, silly nuances of human behavior. This is exactly the kind of "digging" his wife spoke of in the introduction to this book.

Kevin Smith's movies are simultaneously blunt and guileless . . . and he's made a lot of enemies on all sides of the political spectrum by simply telling the truth, by revealing things as they are. From the right, Catholics went to war with Smith (one of their own) over *Dogma*, and Smith had to contend with bomb threats against his family on a daily basis. From the left, Smith was bombarded by the Gestapo-like tactics of GLAAD for his use of the word "gay" as a playground pejorative in *Jay and Silent Bob Strike Back*. Like that never happened before Kevin Smith...

And, true to form, *Zack and Miri Make a Porno* also proved highly controversial to moral watchdogs simply because of the word *porno* in the title. A result of such controversy is that the movie didn't make nearly as much money as it should have. That's a shame, because it's a great comedy, and a perfect example of Smith's unique filmmaking voice.

In the tradition of *Clerks* and *Chasing Amy*, *Zack and Miri Make a Porno* is also a highly personal film, at least if gazed upon in a certain way. The film very much involves the idea of characters looking outside their experience—to cinema—as a means of escaping drudgery and career servitude. Once introduced to the world of film, those characters very much fall in love with the process of filmmaking—with the incipient challenges, with the triumphs, and with the esprit de corps that emerges when people collaborate to create something magical. That's the essence of the filmmaking experience, or at least the first filmmaking experience.

In case you couldn't tell, that's also very much the story of Kevin Smith and his career—the story of how he made *Clerks* back in the early 1990s. As much as *Zack and Miri Make a Porno* is a love story between Zack and Miri, it's also love story about Kevin Smith and the movies. It's true, Zack and Miri's porno movie looks painfully and humorously inept, and porn is hardly a respectable business. But encoded in this situation is Smith's conviction that the individual can step outside dreary routine and responsibility (embodied in the film by the wintry atmosphere of Monroeville) and create something special and meaningful in art.

As always, Smith is the first to dismiss the artistry of his own films, but *Zack and Miri Make a Porno* impresses not just with its satirical flights of fancy, and not merely in its human characters, but also in relaying a message that embodied 1990s independent filmmaking: Go for broke. Go for the gusto. *Do something*. Make a movie.

It'll change your life. Just like it changed Kevin Smith's.

11

COP OUT (2010)
IT JUST WENT SOUTH, RIGHT AWAY

Rock out with your glock out.

Cast and Crew

Directed by: Kevin Smith
Written by: Robb and Mark Cullen
Produced by: Polly Cohen Johnsen, Marc Platt, Michael Tadross
Executive Producers: Mark and Robb Cullen, Adam Siegel
Cinematography: David Klein
Edited by: Kevin Smith
Music: Harold Faltermeyer
Production Designer: Michael Shaw
Costume Designer: Juliet Polcsa
Casting: Jennifer Euston
M.P.A.A. rating: R
Running time: 107 minutes

Starring

Bruce Willis | *Jimmy Monroe*
Tracy Morgan | *Paul Hodges*
Seann William Scott | *Dave*
Kevin Pollak | *Hunsaker*
Adam Brody | *Barry Mangold*
Guillermo Diaz | *Poh Boy*

Michelle Trachtenberg | *Ava*
Jason Lee | *Roy*
Francie Swift | *Pam*
Rashida Jones | *Debbie*
Keith Joe Dick | *Big Al*
Jim Norton | *George*

THE STORY SO FAR...

CELEBRATING NINE YEARS OF WORKING TOGETHER IN THE NYPD, partners Jimmy Monroe and Paul Hodges nonetheless face some tough times on the job and off. On the former front, they have just screwed up an established, important criminal investigation by coworkers Hunsaker and Mangold. And on the latter, Paul fears his beautiful wife is cheating on him.

The taciturn Jimmy, meanwhile, faces a financial problem. His daughter Ava is getting married, and she needs $48,000 to pay for the event, a sum her new stepfather can easily afford, but which Jimmy cannot.

Hoping to do right by his daughter, Jimmy decides to sell a valuable baseball trading card, a collectible from 1952 worth tens of thousands. Unfortunately, the card is stolen by a wisecracking *parkour* expert and thief named Dave, and soon falls into the hands of a violent career criminal named Poh Boy.

To get the card back and pay for the wedding, Jimmy and Paul must put aside domestic strife and bring Poh Boy to justice. They enlist Dave to the cause, but face an uphill battle...

THE STORY BEHIND THE MOVIE

When *Zack and Miri Make a Porno* failed to perform at the box office as many had hoped for, Kevin Smith had some deep soul-searching to do about his next film project, and the direction of his career itself.

Although Smith widely professed to love *Zack and Miri* with all his heart, even he had to acknowledge the painful reality that the film didn't do more than what he termed "Kevin Smith business"—meaning it earned approximately $30 million.

Smith reportedly withdrew from his blog and the Internet itself for six months to reevaluate his priorities and his careers. He noted in an interview:

"Okay, I'm done. I give up. I can't stand it anymore. I just keep beating my head against the wall making movies."[1]

However, in 2009, Smith was contacted via email by executive Jeff Robinov at Warner Bros. regarding a movie project called *A Couple of Dicks*, written by Robb and Mark Cullen, writers with whom Smith had worked on the premiere cable pilot *Manchild* back in 2005. Their script had famously been included on Hollywood's Black List—a tallying of the best unproduced scripts in Tinsel Town—and Smith was suddenly in the position of being offered an assignment he had rejected on numerous occasions throughout his career: directing a film based on another author's screenplay.

Believing that as director but not writer of *A Couple of Dicks*, he couldn't be held responsible if things went wrong at the box office, Smith signed on to direct the big-budget cop buddy picture, a frantic, farcical throwback to 1980s cinematic efforts such as *48 Hours, Beverly Hills Cop, Running Scared*, and *Lethal Weapon*. Bruce Willis and Tracy Morgan were signed to star in the project, and before long, Smith was shooting the film in New York City with his favorite DP, David Klein. For the first time in his career, however, Smith would be working without his regular producer, Scott Mosier, and without the participation of View Askew Productions. On his new film, he was truly a hired gun.

Working on the cop film, Tracy Morgan noted that his inspiration came from "people like Eddie Murphy, Martin Lawrence, and Will Smith,"[2] and from movies including *Bad Boys* and *Rush Hour*. In terms of practice, however, Morgan brought his trademark improvisational skills to the set every day, frequently going off script and developing the humor from his admittedly wild personal aesthetic.

"It was all collaboration," Morgan stressed. "We made it our business to do it the way it was written, and then we would all get together with Kevin and the writers; the writers were there every day. And if I did something funny, they came up with something even more funny, and then it just evolved into what it is."[3]

Bruce Willis indicated he was on board with that approach and noted that "at a certain point we drew the line, just said, 'You know what? We're going to make this funny'... we went balls out for comedy."[4]

However, that doesn't mean Willis didn't have some adjusting to do in terms of his expectations: "Our first day of shooting was interesting. Within five minutes of the first scene in the diner, our timing, our overlapping dialogue and pauses and stuff, it all fell into place."[5]

In fact, Kevin Smith suggested while promoting the film that Willis served as the film's comedy barometer—that the goal of Morgan and the filmmakers was to make the A-list movie star laugh, and allow him to judge, essentially, what was funny.

"It never hurts to always unleash, because you can always rein it in in the editing room," Smith noted. "So while we were on set, I think for the first week, Bruce was like, 'Why aren't we cutting yet?' because we would just keep rolling. The scene proper would be done, but I'd still be rolling, because I knew Tracy would be like, 'Okay, now the scene's about to begin.' It took awhile for everybody to catch on that we're just going to go and see what happens . . . Having Bruce absolutely helped, because Bruce would be truly a governor, where he would be like, 'This is not funny. Why are we talking about this?'"[6]

Smith also found directing the established star a whole new ballgame in terms of his communication skills: "I was going at it like, 'Bruce, do it like this.' I was directing Bruce the way I direct everybody else. And Bruce was like, 'I've been acting like Bruce Willis for twenty-five years. Do you really think there's anything you're going to tell me that I don't know?' So he was very much the author of his own performance."[7]

After shooting on A Couple of Dicks was completed, a new problem reared its head: the title. Like Zack and Miri Make a Porno immediately before it, the movie would see its title deemed commercial suicide by the powers that be. ABC, in particular, wouldn't allow Warner Bros. to advertise a movie with that name.[8]

Having been through a similar experience all too recently, Smith didn't object to a title switch. "Seeing the effect that title had on the movie, I was like Chief Brody in Jaws II when (Warner Bros.) told me they wanted to make the switch. I was like, 'I've seen a shark close up, and I don't want to go through that hell again.' I said, 'Go ahead, call it something else. Anything that gets people in seats.'"[9]

The underwhelming A Couple of Cops was bandied about, but Smith's suggestion—Cop Out—was ultimately selected as the new title. And to Smith's delight, he was given, largely, a free hand to edit the picture himself:

> [Warner Bros.] were really nice about actually letting me edit the film, which I think most of the studios were kind of leery about . . . In my world, with Miramax and Weinstein Company, those guys were kind of 'Yeah,

*do what you want.' They were very like free parents—the parents that
send you to the Montessori school… Over at Warner Bros., they're much
more like, 'You can go to parochial school for eight years, you can wear a
skirt and shit like that, or a jumper,' but you know they've got very strict
rules.*[11]

When *Cop Out* was released on February 26, 2010, in more than three thousand theaters across America, the new Kevin Smith racked up solid business. The film stayed in theaters a healthy twelve weeks, and on its first weekend grossed a more-than-respectable $18 million. By the end of its theatrical run, the film grossed over $55 million, making it Smith's biggest moneymaker to date. And impressively, the film did such business in the face of hyperbolic, over-the-top negative reviews that singled out Smith for derision.

Variety noted that "[g]iven the absence" of Smith's "garrulous dialogue and sweetly obscene sensibilities, the shortcomings of his craft are made all the more apparent."[12]

And that dig was just the tip of the iceberg.

Esteemed critic Roger Ebert actually reviewed the film as if Smith had written it himself, calling the movie lame. He noted that "many of the gags possibly looked good on paper, but watching Willis and Morgan struggle with them is like watching third graders do Noel Coward, if Noel Coward had been rewritten by Kevin Smith."[13]

Some reviews were even nastier. One headline read, "Kevin Smith should be arrested."[14]

Not all reviews were scathing, of course. *People* noted that *Cop Out* was stuffed "with raunchy gags and about every obscenity imaginable (both are specialties of director Kevin Smith)," and that the film "benefits from the contrast between Morgan's manic energy and Willis's seen-it-all cool."[15]

At *Film Journal International*, Ethan Alter noted that if "Smith's primary goal in making *Cop Out* was to show that he could helm a polished studio picture, then it's fair to say that he succeeded. While it's long been standard-operating procedure to knock his behind-the-camera skills (a tradition that he's encouraged in his typically self-deprecating way), the truth is that he's been an entirely competent commercial director for some time…"[16]

Still, these sympathetic reviews were not the norm, by any means. Contrarily, it looked very much like it was open season on Kevin Smith, and in part that fact had to do with a widely publicized incident that occurred shortly before the film's release.

On February 13, 2010, Southwest Airlines ejected Kevin Smith prior to a flight over concerns about his weight. Namely, the company asserted that the director's girth made Smith a "safety concern."

On his Twitter account, Smith immediately took Southwest to task for its impolite decision, but then the mainstream media latched onto the story and ran with it...excessively. Very shortly, Smith's weight became joke fodder for every late-night comedian, including Bill Maher on HBO's *Real Time*. This obsession with Smith's weight showcased the entertainment industry at its absolute worst and most personally destructive. Smith was reportedly horrified that his weight had become a national punch line, and faced some very difficult personal moments.

The out-of-proportion critical response to *Cop Out* suggests that many film critics indeed smelled fresh blood in the water and glommed on, tearing down the onetime indie darling with a ferocity and savagery that can only be termed gleeful. Never one to absorb criticism quietly, Smith counterattacked the contemporary profession of film criticism on his Twitter account and further alienated the same batch of reviewers.

This was war, and even some of Smith's most ardent admirers complained he was being too thin-skinned, or that his attack on film critics was unnecessary and the result of not an inflated girth, but an inflated sense of self and ego.

Still, amid the specifics of this battle were some important very points to consider. While many Internet critics asked if Kevin Smith was losing his mind,[17] relatively few were asking if his arguments about the profession of film criticism in the Age of the Internet had some validity.

And of course, they do.

Very often today, film criticism on the net is a dedicated race to the bottom: personal attacks and "opinions" disguised as a critique of a filmmaker or a film. The name of the game in much Internet film criticism is to write something so absurd, so over-the-top, so incendiary and inappropriate that it draws many eyes to your site, and more attention to your work. The writer can always apologize for his ill-considered words later, after all, but the important thing is getting the clicks in the first place.

Inevitably, this shaky business model gets the audiences it deserves. And yet the dynamic endures, based upon shaky pillars of invective, attack, and cruelty. Rarely are intellectual arguments made about the films widely reviewed. Actually, films often aren't discussed in terms of influences or merit. Instead, the personality of the performers or the director is the subject matter.

It hasn't always been this way, of course. But increasingly so, this is the rule on the Internet. In part, this approach results from the fact that anyone can claim to be a movie critic and start publishing reviews on the Web almost instantaneously. It's essentially the Wild West, and there's no standard of conduct or behavior to police the realm. Smith himself covered this terrain rather ably in *Jay and Silent Bob Strike Back*, uncovering some so-called critics as angry twelve-year-old boys.

Suffice it to say, this is only a slight exaggeration.

Considering this dynamic, part of the reason Smith's work invariably draws such negative reviews is his own biography. It's not about the work, for many critics, but about *him* and what he accomplished instead. Many of the most questionable Internet film critics today are frustrated writers.

In Kevin Smith's career and success, these critics invariably see what they have not, personally or professionally, achieved. He did what they expressly couldn't: He broke into the industry, succeeded, and has subsequently had a fifteen-plus-year career. Love him or hate him, Kevin Smith is a star in his own right, and he's endured the ups and downs of his films with a large following intact. The critics who despise him with such gusto judge him harshly because they look in the mirror and must face themselves and acknowledge that he has succeeded where they did not. In cutting him down, they are affirming that he is unworthy of his career and that somehow, they are *really* the worthy ones. It's kind of sickening: a form of self-loathing imprinted on an artist who doesn't deserve the venom, and who has almost never struck a self-righteous note.

None of this means that a critic can't write a negative review of *Cop Out* and provide support for his or her low opinion of the film. Kevin Smith has faced bad reviews before (regarding *Mallrats*, early in his career) and handled them with grace and dignity. The difference this time was the poisonous tone of the negative reviews. Some critics clearly want him to fail, and so when Smith states that critics should have a filmmaker's best interests at heart in their reviews, he's responding directly to that tone, which indicates, frankly, they'd rather see him in jail or a loony bin than judge his films on their actual merits.

Film critics have a very real responsibility and obligation to put personal feelings about Smith aside, or to put aside stories like the Southwest Airlines debacle, and simply review a film as a text. Behind-the-scenes stories are interesting, certainly. Real-life incidents make for great gossip. But they should not factor in to how one receives and reacts to a particular movie. That line has been crossed in regard to Smith again and again. What Smith seems to be responding to so vehemently is this very fact—that the line gets crossed again and again, and he's expected to take it all prone, without a response.

The sad part of this dynamic is, of course, that Smith himself has grown embittered about the film world. He has apparently let these haters get to him on a deep level and affect his own feelings of self-worth when, clearly, he's the target of a lot of sour-grapes commentary. Also, if Smith bears any responsibility in this caustic dynamic it is that he has, on so many occasions, willfully downplayed his skills as a director. He has given the critics ample ammo with which to target him, again and again. Self-deprecation is one thing; assisted suicide is something else entirely.

A low point of the *Cop Out* era was probably the back-and-forth between Smith's and Willis's representatives in the press. Smith publicly stated that directing Willis was akin to a soul-deadening experience, while Willis's representatives argued that Smith smoked too much weed and hadn't actively taken the role of director on set.

No one emerged from this public relations debacle unscathed, and the fallout around *Cop Out* remains an absolute low point in Smith's career. No wonder he began telling audiences that podcasting was a preferable assignment to filmmaking:

"No bosses saying, 'You can't do that or this is going to cost too much money. No dealing *with difficult stars. That'll kill your fucking soul.*"18

What this diatribe sounds very much like, no doubt, is an artist fed up with the system and bitter about his experiences in that system. He has good reasons to feel wronged, but again, Smith must honestly assess—in the mirror—what his role has been in dealing with the critics.

Fortunately, his next film, *Red State*, would offer the filmmaker a more profound and positive way to express his pent-up feelings about the industry, and once more land Kevin Smith at the vanguard of truly independent film.

YOU JUST STEAL ALL THE BULLSHIT LINES YOU HEAR ON TV AND THE MOVIES THAT YOU LIKE

Once upon a time in Hollywood, back in the Reagan 1980s, the cop buddy movie was a surefire hit at the box office. It's easy to determine why the genre satisfied so many audiences. Usually, such movies were headlined by a team of big stars you previously wouldn't have imagined together onscreen. And more to the point, the films, though not always deftly, blended comedy with action, thus satisfying more than one demographic. Films such as *48 Hours* (1982), *Running Scared* (1986), *Stakeout* (1987), *Lethal Weapon* (1987), and *The Last Boy Scout* (1991) all played with this form and succeeded at the box office.

It's important to remember, however, that cop buddy movies almost never succeeded with film critics, who felt, largely, that they relied on old cop movie clichés and skated by on the personalities and charisma of actors and comedians such as Eddie Murphy, Nick Nolte, Billy Crystal, Richard Dreyfuss, Mel Gibson, Danny Glover, Bruce Willis, and Damon Wayans.

So while the genre was undeniably popular with moviegoing audiences, it was never really well liked by reviewers. Recalling that fact helps establish, at least a little bit, what Smith was up against with *Cop Out*.

Right down to the score by Harold Faltermeyer of *Beverly Hills Cop* (1984) fame, Kevin Smith's *Cop Out* is a paean to the great buddy cop movies of the 1980s. The Cullen brothers' story blends comedy and action, and thrives on the yin and yang between two diverse men, here played by cool-as-ice Willis and whirling dervish Morgan. Smith has always been a big fan of the cop buddy movies, and the script announces almost from its first scene the intention that the film be viewed as homage to what came before. Few reviewers sought to understand *Cop Out* on the grounds of this self-stated mission, and instead tended to comment on the film's gross-out humor.

Yet on the grounds of homage, *Cop Out* succeeds. It brings up all the old conventions of the form, including the troubles on the home front, the quirky informant or perp (here portrayed by the brilliant Seann Scott Williams), and even the wrongheaded police superior. Some of the movie-quoting dialogue (referencing *Heat*, *Star Wars*, *Die Hard*, *Scarface*, *RoboCop*, *Dirty Dancing*, etc.) is right on the mark and generates knowing laughs.

These moments, in particular, feel very much in tune with Smith's history as a reflexive filmmaker. Most importantly, *Cop Out* is genuinely funny at points, especially when Williams and Morgan share scenes. The film also keeps on surprising too, namely during the scene in which a parkour stunt goes unexpectedly, horribly wrong.

Where *Cop Out* fails most egregiously is at the same juncture that most cop buddies hit the skids: the last act. After two-thirds of a film about charismatic, bickering partners, an action scene doesn't seem like adequate and true resolution. That's the case here, as it is in virtually every other cop buddy movie ever made. The problem is not the staging of the action (which is adroit), just the fact that humor and humanity must, in the end, give way to good guy–versus–bad guy gunfire. Let's face it: Gunshots are intrinsically less interesting than verbal flights of fancy, at least where Kevin Smith is concerned. Though Smith stages the action splendidly, *Cop Out*'s last act simply feels overly mechanical, like the script has slipped into an automatic groove. Again, however, that's the terrain of the genre. You can't blame the director for it.

In terms of Kevin Smith's career obsessions, it's easy to see why *Cop Out* proved an appealing option for his first "gun for hire" situation. There's plenty of raunchy talk about sex and relationships here, and the movie's success—as critic John Brodeur described it—"comes down to the dudes doing the talking."[19] Whether or not there were problems on set, or in the specific director/actor relationship, Bruce Willis is pretty good here playing straight man to Tracy Morgan's loose cannon. Similarly, the film's central conceit—a missing pop culture collectible—seems abundantly Smithian in concept.

Cop Out is not a favorite Smith film by a long shot, but it's difficult to see how this slick, thoroughly professional, self-stated homage to a mostly moribund genre raised the ire of so many critics to such an alarming and poisonous degree. Part of the problem may simply be that many young critics today don't have a history of reviewing cop buddy pictures. Except for the works of Michael Bay, these films have been out of vogue for almost a generation.

Critics without a historical, contextual framework for *Cop Out* would not likely understand what vibe Smith was reaching for. Indeed, reading the majority of the negative reviews, it's unclear exactly what Smith did wrong in *Cop Out*. In essence, he has been pilloried for making a scatological film, but even the very best (and award-winning) films in his oeuvre feature scatological humor, and they were never treated with such casual cruelty.

It's not enough to claim that the gags in *Cop Out* are "lame" or that the cop buddy milieu is "exhausted." Why doesn't *this* film work? That's the argument generally missing from the reviews, a sense—beyond personal bias—of what makes the film fail to tick. If the visuals are poor, provide an example. If the acting is subpar, produce an instance of it. This is what sometimes makes Internet criticism so poor: It's all unsupported opinions, with no sense of film as an art form with a distinctive grammar and purpose. No wonder Smith gets frustrated.

Though not in the top-tier of Smith films (*Chasing Amy*, *Clerks*, *Dogma*, *Red State*, and *Zack and Miri*), *Cop Out* is still a good, harmless time at the movies, and in no way deserving of the caustic response it received. As Karina Longworth observed in *LA Weekly*: "It's a movie that shamelessly traffics in the clichés of other cop movies, while also engaging both characters and audience in the spectator sport of catching references to those very movies. *Cop Out* only works as well as it does—and it works exponentially better than it should—because the movie-trivia game is played smirk-free, with palpable joy from everyone involved."[20]

Finally, as Kevin Smith has said on more than one occasion, the box office success of *Cop Out* led directly to the production of *Red State*. Indeed, that's often how the business works: a personal project alternating with a more commercial one. Kevin Smith invested enough of himself in this project to make *Cop Out* entertaining and very funny, but the critics are the ones who really transformed this film into a personal work, going out of their way to bash the artist for "selling out," when nothing could have been further from the truth.

12

RED STATE (2011)

PEOPLE JUST DO THE STRANGEST THINGS WHEN THEY BELIEVE THEY'RE ENTITLED. BUT THEY DO EVEN STRANGER THINGS WHEN THEY JUST PLAIN BELIEVE.

Love Thy Neighbor.
Fear God.

CAST AND CREW

Written and directed by: Kevin Smith
Produced by: Jonathan Gordon
Executive Producers: Shea Kammer, Victor Choy, Jason Clark, Harvey Cohen, Philip Elway, Nhalean McMillan, Elyse Seiden
Edited by: Kevin Smith
Cinematography: David Klein
Production Designer: Cabot McMullen
Costume Design: Beth Pasternak
Casting: Deborah Aquila, Tricia Wood
M.P.A.A. rating: R
Running time: 97 minutes

STARRING

Michael Parks | *Abin Cooper*
John Goodman | *Joseph Keenan*
Kevin Pollak | *Brooks*
Melissa Leo | *Sara*
Kyle Gallner | *Jarod*
Molly Livingston | *Fiona May*
James Parks | *Mordechai*
Michael Angarano | *Travis*
Deborah Aquila | *Mrs. Vasquez*
Nicholas Braun | *Billy-Ray*
Ronnie Connell | *Randy*
Kaylee DeFer | *Dana*
Anna Gunn | *Travis's Mother*
Jennifer Schwalbach | *Esther*
Matt Jones | *Deputy Pete*
John Lacy | *Travis's Father*
Catherine McCord | *New Reporter*
Alexa Nikolas | *Jesse*
Stephen Root | *Sheriff Wynan*
Betty Aberlin | *Abigail*

THE STORY SO FAR...

THREE HORNY TEENAGE BOYS IN MIDDLE AMERICA answer the wrong Internet come-on for group sex and end up in the grasp of Abin Cooper, a fire-and-brimstone preacher who doesn't just hate sinners... he murders them.

After the boys go missing, the local police investigate, and a bloody gunfight ensues. Soon, federal authorities arrive on the scene and the situation grows exponentially worse. Locked up in his compound, Cooper is ready to die for his draconian beliefs, and to take his followers with him. And outside the compound, ATF Agent Joseph Keenan is ready to kill to protect his reputation and the reputation of his agency.

The situation couldn't be more explosive... until Gabriel's Horn is heard on the horizon. Has Judgment Day come?

THE STORY BEHIND THE MOVIE

Kevin Smith's lowest-budgeted movie since *Chasing Amy* in 1997, *Red State* succeeds on the basis of its razor-sharp storytelling and also, importantly, on the authentic nature of its remarkable villain, Abin Cooper. In real life, Smith apparently became aware of ex-lawyer and preacher Fred Phelps after seeing snippets of an interview with the minister in Malcolm Ingram's film *Small Town Gay Bar*.

For those who don't know of Phelps, he's an unrepentant voice of hatred and intolerance in modern American, a pastor at the notorious Westboro Baptist Church in Kansas. Under Phelps's direction, his "flock" pickets funerals for gay soldiers with signs that read "God hates fags." Westboro Baptist Church is considered a "hate group" by the Anti-Defamation League and the Southern Poverty Law Center, among other organizations.

Over the years, Phelps has verbally upbraided such high-profile Americans as Fred Rogers, Bill O'Reilly, Stephen Colbert, Billy Graham, and President Barack Obama, the last of whom he calls "the Antichrist." Frequently warning of God's "anger," Phelps has claimed that the September 11 terrorist attacks were God's punishment for a morally loose America, and he has even protested the U.S. Holocaust Memorial Museum in Washington, D.C. In all, it is estimated that Phelps has been involved in more than ten thousand protests in more than six hundred cities.

Although Phelps has never been firmly tied to violent acts such as murder, his rhetoric is nonetheless incredibly hateful and divisive. And although Kevin Smith went to great lengths, even in the text of the movie itself, not to associate his preacher Abin Cooper directly with Phelps, it is nonetheless clear that Phelps's extreme belief system (predicated on God's hatred and anger) is the inspiration for *Red State*. As Smith reports:

> *He looks like a grandfather or your favorite uncle, and he speaks with "Aw, shucks" home-spun-isms, but the content of what he's talking about is pure fuckin' Hitler.*[1]

Cast in this horror film as the hateful spiritual leader Cooper is actor Michael Parks, who is also very careful to distance himself from the widely held notion that Abin is actually Phelps: "The first thing I said is, 'This is not Fred Phelps.' And if it was Fred Phelps perfectly, then I don't think I want to do him, because he bores me to tears, the person himself. If I did him, I'd certainly be

capable, but I think it would just bore the hell of the audience. He's boring…
and I saw an opportunity to do more of a charismatic [character]."[2]

Frequent cinematographer David Klein returned to shoot *Red State*, and
he and Smith decided "early on" to shoot the "whole movie handheld."[3] This
approach would grant the horror film a new level of immediacy, and allow
the filmmakers to "wing it" and "see what the actors are going to do."[4]

For Smith, *Red State* represents a personal statement about religion in
modern America (and the likes of "religious" men such as Phelps), as well as
an opportunity to deliver on his widely held potential as a filmmaker. As he
reported:

> I kind of made Red State *as a spiritual sequel to* Clerks. *You look at
> that movie, it showed a lot of promise across the board… Even the critics
> back then [said]* "This movie shows a sh*t-ton of promise. Oh, he could
> be good one day. He could do some cool sh*t. That's what* Red State *is.
> To me, it's the answer to that promise. It's me delivering on that
> promise.*[5]

The most talked-about aspect of Smith's 2011 film, however, was not the
controversial subject matter, but his decision to return to his independent
roots and devise a new strategy to get his film widely seen. In particular, after
an early screening of the film at Sundance in early 2011, Smith bought the
rights to distribute the film… for $20. This brash and innovative move
deeply angered many traditionalists in the movie industry, but was also met
with cheers from many of those who had followed the trajectory of Smith's
career with interest.

For Smith, self-distributing *Red State* seemed like a no-brainer, given the
size of his following (represented mathematically by his Twitter numbers):

> "I didn't want to see [Red State] go the way that every film I've done
> has gone, which is, I make it for as cheaply as I can and somebody spends
> way too much money marketing it. I always wanted to see if I could sell
> a movie to the public without doing any marketing, because my philoso-
> phy was like, hey man, I'm reaching my audience every day. I'm twit-
> tering with them… there's no need in spending money to get to the
> audience.[6]

Smith thus conceived what many industry insiders viewed as a step toward
creative independence in his brash, before-a-live-audience move at Sundance.

He took the reins not just of making his art, but of distributing it. Supporters termed his speech an "inspired screw-the-system rant in which Smith demonstrated an abiding passion for independent filmmaking."[7]

Others weren't so impressed with the move. HitFix's Drew McWeeny claimed audiences were "basically lured into the theater so that Kevin Smith could read us a press release instead of doing what he claimed he would do."[8]

But what does the daring move to self-distribute *Red State* really tell us about Kevin Smith and his state of mind in 2011? Well, quite simply, it reveals he's fed up with the system and not going to take it anymore. Instead of seeing film after film of his fail at the box office because of ridiculously expensive marketing campaigns, Smith—*as he did in 1993 and 1994*—took his future into his own hands. One definition of insanity is to repeat the same behavior over and over again and expect different results, and Smith, by broaching this experiment in self-distribution, at the very least presents an opportunity to really achieve different results. As Smith reported in his now notorious speech:

> *I never wanted to know jack shit about the business. Ladies and gentlemen, I'm a fat, masturbating stoner... If somebody told me all the stupid, horseshit, soul-killing, uncreative, backwards-ass bullshit business that I now have in my head... It's too much fucking horsehit.*[9]

This indeed sounds a lot like a *Network* (1978)-style rant, and yet there is a strong economic basis for Smith's actions: to market *Red State* to the folks who actually stand a chance of going to see it, not to folks in ... ahem, red states, who will never go see a Kevin Smith movie, no matter how friendly and comfortable expensive commercials make the film look.

The Smith business plan vis-à-vis *Red State* was to self-distribute the horror movie after a twelve-city road show starting in March 2011 at Radio City Musical Hall. Although tickets were more expensive than for a typical movie, the *Red State* tour also included live question-and-answer sessions with Smith as an added incentive.

As of this writing, *Red State* has already more than earned back the initial $4 million investment in the film, and it stands every chance of making much more money as it is released to DVD or Blu-ray, especially based on the strong reviews it has received. As he did in 1993, Smith has put himself at the vanguard of independent film, and a new generation watches with intrigue.

Unfortunately, the establishment response to Smith regarding his strategy for monetary success reveals precisely why Smith says he plans to leave the movie business after a two-part hockey movie hurrah in 2012 and 2013. In particular, many critics have once again taken to reviewing Smith rather than *Red State*.

One reviewer who actually loved the film nonetheless likened Smith to a "suicide bomber" who was imploding. Yet another interviewer attempted to insinuate that Smith has become erratic because of smoking too much weed. My answer to that attack is that if he keeps making films as good as *Red State*, Smith should smoke whatever the hell he wants.

But seriously, one must wonder if Kevin Smith would have ever entered the film business (with his own money, no less) had he been attacked by so many "alarmist ninnies," as he frequently calls them. And the very thing they are so upset about is that Kevin Smith had the audacity to question the "system"—the system that requires huge marketing budgets; the system that requires kickbacks to film critics in exchange for a good review; the system that never has and never will understand his work.

At the very least, critics should admire Smith for trying something new and different. Unless, of course, there's a vested interest in seeing this experiment fail. Makes you wonder, doesn't it?

But given how so many reviewers of *Red State* have taken to reviewing Smith's gambit instead of the movie, it's no wonder the director sees imminent retirement as a much-needed escape hatch. As Smith observes:

> *I'm not a filmmaker It's difficult for me. This is not my first language.*[10]

It's finally come to that. The self-deprecating Smith is now making the point for the haters. He's claiming he's not good at moviemaking. That represents a surrender of sorts, and it's very sad to see it.

FEAR GOD

Red State represents a return to greatness for Kevin Smith, and simultaneously a return to greatness for the modern horror genre itself. I've written about this in the past, but the idea applies here in spades. If the 1990s had not witnessed the surprise advent of the indie film movement, it is highly likely that talents such as Kevin Smith would have initially gotten into filmmaking through the avenue of the horror picture.

Indeed, this is how it has been done for several decades, with young filmmakers making their names in a genre that allows them to transcend expectations in a way that reveals a sense of individual style and guarantees a sizable audience. So Kevin Smith creating a horror film in 2011 not only feels like a career rebirth but, in some respects, a fulfillment of destiny itself. If things had been slightly different in the early 1990s, *Red State* might have been the first picture the talent made.

And like Wes Craven, George Romero, and other great horror directors of ages past, Smith understands well the odd alchemy of the great genre film: that a terrific horror movie must simultaneously be incredibly scary and violent and yet also comment meaningfully on violence. That social good is, in a very real sense, what *Red State* achieves so magnificently. The film gazes objectively at the violence and hatred roiling modern America, especially since the election of Barack Obama. Notably, this is violence encouraged by the "eliminationist" rhetoric on the far-right fringe of the political spectrum. This form of rhetoric insists that those who believe differently from God's self-named "chosen" aren't merely wrong, but actually deserve to die for their beliefs. Smith doesn't back away from exposing this facet of modern religious life, but he is careful not to tarnish any political group in the mainstream, which means *Red State* is a political film, but not a partisan one.

In the tradition of great, unsettling horror efforts such as *Night of the Living Dead* (1968) or *The Last House on the Left* (1972), Kevin Smith begins *Red State* with the mundane, with life seeming to unfolding normally, the characters' intersection with cruel and random fate not yet evident. In particular, a suburban mother drives her teenage son to school in the family car, and the chatter is such that we all recognize it from our everyday family lives. Then, unexpectedly, the car passes a funeral—a funeral being picketed by religious zealots—and only then do we detect the danger simmering under the placid surface of American middle-class life.

Then, in the esteemed tradition of Carpenter's *Halloween* (1978) and Wes Craven's *A Nightmare on Elm Street* (1984), Smith marshals the conceit of a didactic high school classroom lesson to set out the thematic terrain of the film. In *Halloween*, Laurie Strode (Jamie Lee Curtis) discussed "fate" in an English lit class, and the discussion led to the film's main idea: of one girl's inescapable fate in connection with the bogeyman himself. In *A Nightmare on Elm Street*, Heather Langenkamp's heroine Nancy Thompson discussed the concept of "digging" for the truth in a high school English class debating Shakespeare's *Hamlet*. Throughout that film, Nancy had to similarly dig beneath the surface of suburbia to excavate the truth about Freddy Krueger and his life and death.

In *Red State*, Kevin Smith sends his three irreverent, youthful protagonists to a high school social studies or history class where the topic is, importantly, the First Amendment. The discussion thus revolves around a very contemporary and powerful notion: *How far does freedom of speech extend?* What about hate speech? Does hate speech do harm and incite people to violence against citizens who don't share the same point of view?

These are the movie's central concepts, set up beautifully and effectively in a tradition that speaks knowingly to the genre's history.

Smith reveals his strong horror chops in another fashion, too. He plants and generates uncertainty in the audience by constantly shifting our central point of identification and sympathy. To a high degree, this is a technique Hitchcock utilized brilliantly in *Psycho* (1960) to keep viewers off base and discomforted. Hitchcock made Janet Leigh's Marion Crane the focal point of audience identification and then, after her surprising death, that same audience felt vulnerable and willing to shift its allegiance to any likely protagonist...even to Norman Bates.

In *Red State*, Smith starts off with the raunchy but ultimately harmless triumvirate of sex-starved teens as our point of identification. But then, when they become trapped/incarcerated/killed, Smith moves on to John Goodman's world-weary ATF agent. When it becomes plain that Agent Keenan is not exactly a true-blue guy, audience identification shifts again to one of Abin Cooper's daughters, who seeks to escape the compound with several innocent children in tow. The net effect of this bouncing around is that the audience feels uncertain, and vulnerable to shock and surprise.

Red State is filled with a kind of mean, lean vitality, with a handheld immediacy that absolutely rivets one's attention. Smith not only frequently shifts perspectives to keep audiences off-balance, but stages at least three horrifying "jolt" moments to punctuate the proceedings. These moments linger in the memory, and genuinely disturb. In the first such moment, there's a flyby fender bender (caused by a gay sheriff's assignation) that rivets focus. In the second, Kevin Pollak's ATF agent gets offed unexpectedly and violently, curtailing what appears to be a major role. And the third "jolt" involves two innocent teenagers and the ATF agents.

At St. Michael's Church in Pittsburgh, the renegade angel Bartleby (Ben Affleck) unfurls the full glory of Vincent Guastini-designed wings from *Dogma* (1999). (photo: Vincent Guastini)

Right: With bloodied knife in hand, Bartleby moves in to kill Loki. Ben Affleck, on location for the finale of *Dogma*. (photo: Vincent Guastini)

Left: A special effects "bust" of Ben Affleck, created for the explosive finale of *Dogma*, designed and built by Vincent Guastini Productions. (photo: Vincent Guastini)

A look at Kevin Smith's excremental shit demon, the Golgothan, both snarling (left) and with angry mouth wide open (right). Animatronic head designed and built by Vincent Guastini Productions. (photo: Vincent Guastini)

Smith (right) mugs it up with stuntman Golgothan, minus his animatronic head, behind the scenes on *Dogma*. (photo: Vincent Guastini)

That's a wrap: Kevin Smith and Jason Mewes review a take behind the scenes on *Jay and Silent Bob Strike Back* (2001).

Cut and print! Chaka (Chris Rock) shoots the stirring finale of *Bluntman and Chronic: the Movie.*

Cat women of the world unite! Left to right: Eliza Dushku, Ali Larter, Shannon Elizabeth, and Jennifer Schwalbach (that's Kevin Smith's wife to you!) strike seductive poses.

Snootchie bootchies! Jason Mewes "macks" on co-star Shannon Elizabeth on the Mooby set.

Something tells me they're not in Jersey anymore. Stoners Jay and Silent Bob turn the Miramax lot upside down.

A bunch of savages in this town! Randal (voiced by Jeff Anderson) peruses a nudie magazine while Jay (voiced by Jason Mewes) causes trouble in *Clerks: The Animated Series*.

Men in black seize Randal for a top-secret assignment while Dante plans to coach a pathetic little league team in episode #5.

Randal and Dante discover reality isn't what it used to be when the series' artist magically re-draws them in a gay bar in the final episode.

Parenthood in the 'burbs. Left to right: Ollie Trinkle (Ben Affleck) and daughter Gertie (Raquel Castro) share some quality time in *Jersey Girl* (2004).

"Would you like fries with that?" Left to right: Randal (Jeff Anderson) and Dante (Brian O'Halloran) join the glamorous world of fast food at Mooby's in *Clerks 2* (2006).

Left to right: Zack (Seth Rogen) and Miri (Elizabeth Banks) find entrepreneurial inspiration in the sex trade, in *Zack and Miri Make a Porno* (2008).

Crime never pays . . . unless you happen to know Parkour. Left to right: Jimmy Munroe (Bruce Willis), Dave (Seann William Scott), and Paul Hodges (Tracy Morgan) scope-out a break-in during *Cop-Out* (2010).

In his mouth, the Word of God is the Word of Hate. Abin Cooper (Michael Parks) preaches fire and brimstone in *Red State* (2011).

These moments are like the gasoline that keeps *Red State* barreling forward and prevents it from ever slowing down or losing the audience's interest. The film's final jolt becomes, in a way only Kevin Smith could orchestrate it, a wicked joke involving the Trumpet of Gabriel. This plot twist is so audacious, so wild, so unexpected that it makes a viewer question all of his or her assumptions about the film and the nature of the narrative. Smith has been abundantly creative before, but he has never been so effectively manipulative as a director, so ahead of his audience. His work here is nothing short of virtuoso.

Once again, *Red State* reveals Kevin Smith's strong moral leanings. As I wrote above, that's an important element in great horror. Here, Smith's point involves the "tribal" aspect of religion and humanity. We see Abin's people heartlessly murder "sinners" without batting an eye. But then, they turn around and deeply mourn the loss of their own flock members. To these folks, some people are clearly more "human" than others, and more deserving of love and empathy. *Only those who believe what Abin believes will be saved. The rest deserve death... even though they too have families, and hopes and aspirations.* What *Red State* meaningfully concerns is the inability of many people on the religious right to empathize with those who don't happen to agree with their extreme points of view. It's easier to kill the infidel and remove the "threat" than to try to live side by side with those they disagree with.

This religious, exclusionary judgment about who deserves to live and die (based on a literal reading of certain scriptural passages) is intentionally mirrored in the ATF's brutal behavior. These government agents indiscriminately commit murder not because of belief or religion, but because of fear of bad PR or the sanctioning from superiors. Although in no way is Abin "better" than the government people, at least he genuinely believes in what he preaches. He's a monster, but at least he's not a hypocrite about it. The ATF agents, contrarily, possess no set of firm beliefs, except saving their own skin. The film thus proves a critique of both secular and religious forces who seek to destroy threats rather than deal with people as simply different from them.

Red State certainly could not have premiered at a better time. The film arrived in late 2011, just as the race for president was heating up in America. In three short weeks during August and September of that year, Americans saw three GOP debates where live audiences cheered at the pain and suffering of other human beings. These audiences cheered the death penalty and 234 executions in Texas, the death of a hypothetical thirty-year-old man without health insurance, and then booed a gay soldier who had been defending

America's freedom in Iraq. What these debates exposed was a truth very much at the heart of *Red State*. When we break down into tribes and mobs, it's easier for us to hate others than to love them. And of course, that's a message that goes deeply against Christ's teachings, isn't it? We are supposed to love one another unconditionally, or love the sinner and hate the sin. Here, as in *Red State*, we see Americans hating the sinner . . . and actually lusting for the sinner's death.

Timely, tightly structured, and incredibly provocative, there's a strong case to be made that *Red State* is the best film Kevin Smith has yet made. It pulls no punches, seeks no easy answers, and is not concerned at all with pleasing or mollifying a mainstream audience. Like the finest and most beloved of Smith's films, it is didactic, irreverent, and original—the grim, existentialist yin to *Chasing Amy's* life-affirming yang.

13

Kevin Smith Around the Galaxy

KEVIN SMITH REMAINS . . .

. . . A REALLY BUSY FELLOW. During the interview period for the first edition of this book, for instance, Smith filmed a cameo appearance for the Ben Affleck superhero film, *Daredevil* (on April 2, 2002) and directed two commercials in Toronto. He went on the lecture circuit, filmed several "Roadside Attractions" for Jay Leno's *Tonight Show*, and completed the first draft of his next View Askew feature, *Jersey Girl*.

A quick perusal of video releases reveals Smith appearances virtually everywhere. He appeared in *Starwoids*, a documentary about fans awaiting the premiere of *Star Wars Episode I: The Phantom Menace*, and a similar documentary about the *Spider-Man* movie with *Mallrats* buddy Stan Lee. The latter is a Columbia Tri-Star Home Entertainment Release entitled *Stan Lee's Mutants, Monsters & Marvels*, and it's a one-on-one interview between the ultimate fan, Kevin Smith, and the revered creator of the best comic books the world has ever seen.

Smith also had a substantial supporting role as a computer hacker named Warlock in *Live Free or Die Hard* (2007), the fourth entry in Bruce Willis's popular action franchise. But dedicated fans could also find Smith making appearances on the late, lamented TV detective series *Veronica Mars* (2005–2007), or contributing his voice talents to *Superman/Doomsday* (2007) and even to the children's hit *Phineas and Ferb* (2010). Smith also cameoed in the *Star Wars*-themed *Fanboys* (2008) and found time to visit *Degrassi: The Next Generation* (2005–2009) with his friend and colleague Jason Mewes.

Beyond appearances in front of cameras, Smith has also penned several comic books. For example, he resurrected the slumping *Daredevil* and *Green Arrow* titles with exciting new story lines in the early 2000s, and even brought four-color life to *Bluntman & Chronic* (for Oni Press), his crazy *Clerks*, and Jay and Silent Bob.

In the matter of *Daredevil*, sales of the book skyrocketed nearly fifty percent after Smith began writing. *Green Arrow*, Walt Flanagan's favorite title, proved similarly successful under Smith's guidance. For his comic book work, Smith has received an Eagle Award, a Harvey Award, and a Wizard Fan Award.

For Smith, these comic assignments, toiling in the realms of heroes like Peter Parker, Daredevil, and Green Arrow, represents more than a dream come true:

> *Before I became a filmmaker, I wanted to write comics, but was told it was too tough a market to crack, so I went into films, which oddly enough proved more accessible.*[1]

Kevin Smith hasn't always been so lucky, of course. He was paid a substantial salary to write *Superman Lives* for producer Jon Peters and Warner Brothers, a screenplay that would have substantially and creatively reimagined the Man of Steel's movie franchise for the 1990s. But Smith's efforts were "shitcanned" when *Batman* director Tim Burton joined the team and went in a different direction.[2]

SHORTS: THE FLYING CAR

In the View Askewniverse continuity, Smith has filmed *The Flying Car*, a *Clerks* short for Jay Leno and *The Tonight Show*. Starring Brian O'Halloran and Jeff Anderson, the ten-minute film was shot in New Jersey after *Jay and Silent Bob Strike Back*'s release in November 2001. It aired in late February of 2002.

"When Kevin first approached me to do it, the script was written for a Ford Company corporate meeting," O'Halloran reveals. "Then it got canceled because the budget wasn't right or something. But Kevin had ownership of the script. Then, when Kevin was promoting *Jay and Silent Bob Strike Back* on Leno, *The Tonight Show* approached him to do a short film. It was such a funny little piece, and Kevin had had it for two years, so he brought it out. Shooting it was hysterical. We were back to the original style of dialogue we had in *Clerks*."

Jeff Anderson describes the premise: "In the *Tonight Show* piece, Dante and Randal get stuck in traffic because they're heading to a strip bar. The script was about nine pages, and the eighth page was a long monologue."

For Randal.

"At the time we shot *Clerks*, I would never have been able to do it," Anderson says of the speech. "When Kevin faxed the script over, I wondered what he was trying to do to me. Randal was getting more and more wordy. I read the short three or four times, and then had a friend read it with me. Probably on my fourth reading, I nearly got the whole thing out."

"I have to hand it to Jeff," adds O'Halloran. "He has a great grasp of dialogue. Especially in *The Flying Car*, where he has so much dialogue and long, long diatribes. But it was weird how easy it was for us to fall back into our characters. It's very rare to have that chemistry as an actor, to work with someone who you can just pick it up with."

Shooting *The Flying Car* was so much fun for all the people involved because, for one thing, it offered Smith, Anderson, and O'Halloran the opportunity to reminisce about the short-lived *Clerks* cartoon while shooting it.

"Randal in the movie was this pain-in-the-ass, serious guy and not very animated," Anderson considers. "I even said to Kevin once, watch me get into Randal's character: all I do is put a piece of gum in my mouth, I chew the gum, and then just scowl like the gum tastes bad. Then I push my eyebrows together. It's all in the eyes and a forever furrowed brow."

But the cartoon had changed that forever, and Randal had developed into a more lively personality.

"So when we shot the short, the first take we did on the whole thing was a single shot on me. We went through the whole nine pages, and I did it all how the movie Randal would have.

"Then we changed the setup and did the two-shot, and I did it the same way," Anderson says. "Then it was time to shoot Brian. During that setup, Brian and I were joking about the cartoon and our favorite moments. Then when we came to Brian's close-up, I started reading my lines as Cartoon Randal."

"I remember looking over at Kevin's face and he was laughing. That's when I knew he was going to come back to me. When we got done with Brian, he made me do my part again, this time as Cartoon Randal. So that's what's on the Leno show. My eyes are a little bulgy, my pitch is a little higher, and my hands are flying around. I became Cartoon Randal for real."

MR. EXECUTIVE PRODUCER

Everybody remembers how Kevin Smith helped out his pal and leading man Ben Affleck in 1997. *Good Will Hunting* co-authors Affleck and Matt Damon were having trouble with the powers that be and shepherding their project to the screen, and Smith stepped in, led the actors to Miramax, and rescued the project. Executive produced by Smith and Scott Mosier, *Good Will Hunting* eventually grossed over $100 million and earned Affleck and Damon a golden Oscar trophy for their screenplay.

What many people may not know about Kevin Smith is that this kind of help is simply a matter of course for him. He does it all the time. Perhaps cognizant of his own good fortune in the industry, Smith has made it a point in his career (as has über-producer Mosier) to help those who helped him. In the process, he has provided a creative outlet for several new and important filmmakers.

Walt Flanagan, who runs Smith's comic book store in Red Bank, New Jersey (Jay and Silent Bob's Secret Stash), has seen Smith's generosity up close and remains wowed by it.

"Here's a guy who has absolutely showered his friends with the ability to be a part of his success," Flanagan says. "He's given other people a chance to make films, what with Bryan [Johnson], Malcolm [Ingram], and Matt [Gissing], and Vinnie [Pereira]. He never misses an opportunity to share his success. I would like to say if it were me, I'd do it too, but I'm not sure I would. He gives so much back to his circle of friends."

"It's very bizarre, and kind of shocking," Jennifer Schwalbach says of her husband's priority to help others. "He doesn't have an ego that interferes with his generosity. He wants to see his friends do as well as he has, or better. There isn't anybody who is excluded from his success. He's very self-deprecating, where he feels like if he did it, anybody can. And he wants to lend a hand in any way he can without expecting anything in return."

To wit: *Drawing Flies*, *A Better Place*, and *Vulgar*—three View Askew films executive produced and partially financed by Kevin Smith and Scott Mosier. These small-budget films, not unlike *Clerks*, reveal burgeoning talent in suburban New Jersey, and the creative talents of new artists with distinct visions.

Of the three pictures, *Drawing Flies*—written, edited, produced, and directed by Matt Gissing and Malcolm Ingram—is perhaps the most evocative of *Clerks* in terms of its look and theme. It's another black-and-white, perfectly pitched, self-aware encapsulation of the Generation X experience, as a group of directionless twentysomethings, including Jason Lee, Renee Humphreys, Jason Mewes, Carmen Lee, and Martin Brooks, leave behind a meaningless "party" life in Vancouver for a seemingly endless camping trip.

Unbeknownst to the group at large, their leader, Donner (as in "Donner party"), has become obsessed with the idea of finding Big Foot, or rather, Sasquatch. Where did he get such a peculiar notion? Why—in perfect Generation X fashion, of course—from watching a marathon of *The Six Million Dollar Man* reruns.

At times absurd, at times unnerving, *Drawing Flies* follows the degeneration of its lead character (portrayed ably by Lee) as he goes progressively "native," *Apocalypse Now*-style, going so far as to ingest Sasquatch shit.

Shot immediately after *Mallrats* in 1995, the Gissing/Ingram film was finally released on DVD in 2002, and the seventy-six-minute, black-and-white features cameos by Ethan Suplee, Kevin Smith, and Joey Lauren Adams.

Ambitiously shot, replete with great natural locales (including a really scary-looking suspension bridge), *Drawing Flies* is a quirky, amusing movie that speaks to some of the same ennui captured so memorably by *Clerks*, only with a different group of characters and a different comedic sensibility behind the camera.

Vincent Pereira's film, *A Better Place*, was also shot in New Jersey, after *Mallrats* and before *Chasing Amy*. It marks the writing and directorial debut of this talented View Askew historian. It's the story of a teenage loner, Ryan, and his friendship with the new kid in school, Barret. At first, they share the status of "outsider," but before long, Barret has made new friends, and starts to grow fearful of Ryan, who evinces a negative, and very violent, worldview.

"Kevin was always the writer, and I wanted to be the filmmaker," Pereira remembers of the project's genesis. "I sort of said to myself that I wanted to make a film myself at the same age Kevin was when he directed *Clerks*. So I set the summer of 1995 as the time I wanted to make a movie. I think it was around the end of 1993 when I saw a *Nightline* about the Bolger case in Britain."

The story had made news around the world. On February 12, 1993, a two-and-a-half-year-old boy, Jamie Bolger, had been abducted from a shopping mall in Liverpool by two ten-year-old boys. They brutalized and eventually killed the smaller child. It was a stunning and horrible story.

"That case sparked something in my mind, and I thought I should make a movie about teenage violence," Pereira explains. "*A Better Place* wasn't based on the case, but it got me thinking. I was kind of a hothead at that age. In high school, I was pretty angry and antisocial, and I thought it would be interesting to put those feelings into a movie.

"So I wrote this script about a fucked-up kid who makes his first friend in many, many years, and you think maybe he'll be all right, but things spiral out of control."

Participating in the View Askew films, it turned out, helped prepare Pereira to shoot his own movie. "I've learned a lot just from being on a film set. The best thing I learned from working with Kevin Smith was being on the set and seeing how it was all done. I think we have very different styles of directing. He writes such great dialogue, and my biggest stumbling block is dialogue. But he has a specific idea of how lines should be said and generally doesn't allow improvisation. I'm not nearly as confident a writer of dialogue as he is."

A Better Place went through two years of post-production and hit the festival circuit in the fall/winter of 1997. It received glowing reviews, but, alas, didn't go into theatrical release. "It was right around the time all those school shootings started," Pereira reports. "I guess it had been on the festival circuit for about a year and a half."

Unlike *Clerks* or *Drawing Flies*, *A Better Place* is a distinctly dark vision of suburban life. Like some of the early, almost visceral work of director Wes Craven in the 1970s, the film constantly surprises with its unexpected descents into bloody terror. Two deaths, in particular, are shot with such straight-faced bluntness that the audience is left feeling uneasy, almost sick.

And, there is an audacious edit during the film's final confrontation that bears mention. This "cut" heralds the unexpected appearance (or replace-ment) of one character for another, one tormenter for another, and is so courageous, so perfectly executed that one wants to stand up and applaud the film's brutal honesty. That scene and several others of equal intensity reveal a confident director exploring a theme that mainstream films are very reluctant to embrace.

A Better Place also benefits from a terrific sound mix. Pereira remembers how that came about. "*Dogma* was mixed at Skywalker Sound, and Kevin and Scott became good friends with the people there, and after some discussion found out that Skywalker occasionally does pro bono work for independent films. Scott suggested they could do a remix of *A Better Place* for its DVD release, and the guys at Skywalker really loved it. So Skywalker mixed it for free."

There was just one drawback. "It took us about two years to work on the DVD, because the remix had to be scheduled around Skywalker's schedule, but everything got finished in August [of 2001] and the film got some great reviews."

A Better Place is not only genuinely harrowing, it features some fine performances, especially from Robert DiPatri, as Barret, and Eion Bailey of *Fight Club* as the disturbed but ultimately sympathetic Ryan. Scott Mosier, Carmen Lee, Ethan Suplee, and Jason Lee all appear in small, effective roles, but in this case, it is the two leads that focus audience attention.

And then there's Bryan Johnson's *Vulgar*, another View Askew film executive produced by Smith and Mosier, and another twist down a strange, dark alley.

"It's kind of a mix of a psychological thriller and dark comedy, and it walks a weird line," says Johnson of his debut feature. "The way it came about was that Kevin, Walter, and I were hanging out at the Quick Stop. This was when Kevin was trying to maintain a job there even though he was a filmmaker, and Walter and I used to play basketball at night and we'd go down to the store afterwards to see him. And one night we talked to him about the clown [the View Askew Productions logo; first imagined and sketched by Walt Flanagan], and what his story might be. Kevin thought that it was an interesting idea, and that we should write a movie about the clown. I told him I wanted to take a shot at it and he said, 'Fine, but don't make it jokey and stupid.'

"So I went and wrote a few pages of the script and didn't think too much about it. Then, my girlfriend failed chemistry and needed to retake it in the summer. She was studying every night, and I had nothing else to do, so I sat down and wrote the script. It took about twenty-eight days, I showed it to Kevin, and he loved it and said, 'We have to make this movie.'"

Smith also helped Johnson shape the material. "When I gave it to Kevin, he gave me a lot of good notes. He told me what he thought should be cut from the script, and then wrote a note on the cover saying that the notes didn't reflect quality, but rather quantity. 'A tighter movie means more showings at the Angelika,' he wrote, and at the time I was thinking, 'Yeah, right. By the Angelika, he means my parents' living room...'"

Originally, *Vulgar* was to be shot before *Chasing Amy*, but then that film went to production—and Johnson, for one, was glad to have some time for prep. "I had no idea how films were made, and we lifted a lot of the *Chasing Amy* cast and crew. I was glad we waited until [Kevin and Scott] could guide me through the process. At the time, Kevin had deal with Miramax where they'd put up the money for smaller movies, so Miramax kicked in about $40,000 and Kevin kicked in about $40,000."

Vulgar stars Brian O'Halloran as a man who makes a living as a clown named Flappy. One day, he comes up with the idea to make more money (to pay for his mother's stay at a nursing home), and becomes this sort of erotic, specialty clown who wears lingerie, named Vulgar. But when he gets a gig as Vulgar, he's attacked and raped by a really messed-up father (Jerry Lewkowitz) and his twisted two sons (Ethan Suplee and Matthew Maher).

O'Halloran's character survives the terrifying experience, but that's not the end of the story.

"After he gets assaulted, my character saves a child and then becomes famous, but his past comes back to haunt him," O'Halloran reveals. "There are a lot of twists in it that I really enjoyed. It's a very, very dark, twisted movie, so it isn't like a Kevin Smith laugh-a-minute film. It really sucks you in and then disturbs you."

"I love O'Halloran," Johnson says of his lead. "He's very good. He's an actor who pays attention to details."

"It definitely shatters the Dante image," O'Halloran notes of his roles in *Vulgar*. "It is really a complete departure from any of the other characters I play in View Askew films. It's a role that as an actor is extremely challenging. When I read it for the first time, it was so disturbing I had to put it down. I wondered why I ever wanted to do it. Then, in the same breath, I was like, 'Wow, how can I ever turn this down?'"

Vincent Guastini's first job for View Askew Productions was *Vulgar*. "I thought it would be a good calling card. I would get used to them [View Askew] and they would get used to me until the *Dogma* shoot came along," Guastini remembers. "So I did this very violent death scene for Ethan [who gets shot in the face], and it was very effective in the movie; highly detailed and very realistic. I thought Bryan did a really great job for it being his first film and basically for very little money."

At the time of writing, *Vulgar* had gone into limited release at the Angelika theater on April 26, 2002, thereby promising to launch the career of another View Askew director. A good review in *The New York Post* praised the film, noting O'Halloran's "extraordinarily brave and moving performance"[3] and comparing *Vulgar* favorably to the bigger-budgeted *Death to Smoochy*.

Outside of View Askew Productions, Jeff Anderson was also bitten by the directing bug. He helmed and shot *Now You Know*, an independently produced romantic comedy he also wrote. Featured in the film are none other than Kevin Smith and his wife, Jennifer Schwalbach. "I think they have a great cameo piece," Anderson laughs. "She's playing a hooker, and let's just say that Kevin is interacting with her."

"I play a hooker, because I'm Kevin's wife," Jennifer clarifies. "I love Jeff Anderson and wanted to be in his movie. I don't want to be an actress, contrary to what many people think who don't like me, and who say I only married Kevin to become an actress. However, if one of my friends is making a movie, I'm probably going to be in it. Jeff asked me which role I wanted to play, and I said I wanted to be the hooker. He asked if I was sure, because I'd be wearing a little nightie, and I'm Kevin's wife, and he didn't want it to seem too seedy, throwing me out there in some scandalous getup. But I wanted to do it, because I wanted to be in a scene with Kevin.

"And," she confides, "I didn't want him [Kevin] to make out with anybody else. I was there the day he kissed Linda Fiorentino in *Dogma*—it didn't make the final cut—and I didn't want to see that again.

"I just saw *Now You Know*, and it was really funny," Schwalbach reports. "I'm taller than Kevin anyway, and I'm wearing spiked heels in the movie, so I'm literally a foot taller than him. And he's having to step on his tippy-toes to kiss me."

Kevin Smith not only appeared in Anderson's first film, he also offered the first-time director moral support.

"As we got closer to doing the film, I sent Kevin the script," Anderson relates. "He read it and called me back, and I think he was pretty surprised by it. He was great. He told me if I had any questions, I could bounce things off of him."

But Anderson didn't really have any questions, and production of the film went so well that he actually overslept the first morning of shooting. It wasn't until post-production, in fact, that Anderson got worried.

"The editing room was a bit of a nightmare. That's where we first got into trouble," Anderson remembers. "The first time I saw the film at the raw stage with no background sound and music, I panicked. The producers hired a post-production supervisor, yet I never met her. I didn't know much about post-production, but good Lord, I do now. She was basically hired because she's well known around town and they used her name to get good deals, but she never physically came in and did post-production, so I did it. There were some dark days there. It wasn't until I started looking at the dailies tapes and pulling things together that I saw it was going to be all right. I'm very happy with how it all turned out."

Released on DVD in 2006, *Now You Know* had its world premiere at a Vulgarthon, a View Askew/Kevin Smith convention. "It was a beta copy that wasn't quite ready to be shown, but the crowd really responded to it. It's nerve-racking to show your own film, and the first time Kevin saw it, I wanted it to look its best and be its best," Anderson notes. "It's like showing it to your dad. But [Kevin] never got the chance to see it, because he was doing something else in one of the other auditoriums."

Drawing Flies, A Better Place, Vulgar, and *Now You Know* are four independent films that have emerged, either directly or indirectly, from the cinematic experiences of Kevin Smith and View Askew Productions.

But Kevin Smith has proven himself a good friend to people outside View Askew too, giving selflessly of his time and his money. He recently served as a guest auctioneer for a nonprofit charity organization called ACTOR (A Commitment To Our Roots) that supports comic book writers who have seen their fortunes fall with changes in the economy.

After the tragic terrorist attacks on September 11, 2001, Smith added his poetic voice to Alan Moore's and Todd McFarlane's by contributing words and thoughts to *Heroes*, a Marvel comic book benefit special. The proceeds went to victims of the tragedy, and the book has already raised several hundred thousand dollars.

And Smith has also assisted *Chasing Amy* executive producer John Pierson in making one of his personal dreams become a reality.

"There's nobody I'd rather help out, and/or help to be the moral conscience of, than Kevin Smith, and I hope he does the same for me," Pierson notes. "And I feel like we've been intimately involved since *Clerks*, and I don't think anyone went to the mat to defend him more on *Dogma*, especially with the Miramax bullshit, than me. I exposed myself in ways that could have been trouble for me, so I feel good about that."

But Pierson has been looking for new horizons, new direction. "Kevin knows I'm moving away from the old me, the producer's repping, financing John Pierson."

He's been moving toward something else: specifically, the island of Taveuni in the Republic of Fiji, and a movie theater called the 180 Meridian Cinema.

"The Fiji idea came up in the last season of the TV show [*Split Screen*]," Pierson explains. "We were looking for the world's most remote movie theater, to which we could bring some American independent films. 'How far could these movies travel? Could they go to the rain forest on a little island on the international dateline in the South Pacific, in the Republic of Fiji?' That was the gig, and we had a fantastic trip in February 2000, and something happened on that trip."

Pierson elaborates: "They put on a Three Stooges short, which had been screened there for fifty years, three generations of filmgoers, and it's the only one set in the South Pacific. And basically, three hundred people lost their minds laughing at this movie. It was the most extremely moving experience you could have. Ever since that moment, I knew I wanted to go back there and write about what it's like where there's no other entertainment, to find out what movies mean at the edge of the world.

"When I went back last summer to see how far I could take that idea, I learned that the man who owned the theater was getting ready to emigrate," Pierson says. "So I bought the theater. But once I bought it, I had issues of where the money was coming from. I'm in the process of writing a book derived from all this, and there's probably going to be an HBO documentary, but these things are still shaping up.

"In the meantime, I went to the filmmakers I feel closest to, and I feel maybe I helped the most: Spike, Kevin, the *Blair Witch* guys, and Matt Stone from *South Park*. And they've all come through in just fantastic ways. But Kevin came forward first and foremost when I needed support—seed money, I guess you'd call it—to get this going. He was supportive, both financially and emotionally, in ways that make you tear up a little bit."

Of course, that doesn't mean people should expect to see Smith frequenting the 180 Meridian Theater any time soon. "Kevin says things like, 'There's too much dirt in the jungle.' You will not be seeing Kevin on an island where he can't be on the Internet twenty-four hours a day."

TV DIRECTOR

For the 2007–2008 TV season, Kevin Smith served as a consultant on the science fiction/horror/comedy series *Reaper* and also directed the pilot episode. Rewardingly, the series is very much a piece with his film canon. Specifically, *Reaper* concerns the idea of growing up and learning to balance life's responsibilities.

In *Reaper*, a young man named Sam Oliver (Bret Harrison) learns that his parents have "arranged" (meaning: made a Faustian bargain) for him to become the Devil's highly unlikely bounty hunter. Meanwhile, Sam works at a Home Depot–type store called the Work Bench and has an insufferable boss named Ted, and a buddy named Sock (Tyler Labine) whom he has to constantly keep in line, lest they lose their jobs. The series is very much *Clerks* meets *Supernatural*.

Yet what could have been half-assed and utterly ludicrous is instead ingenious and incredibly funny. The Devil's dialogue, as delivered by actor Ray Wise, is delightful and clever. This material is really sharp, especially since it overturns the preachy, ridiculous, self-righteous "God is my co-pilot" approach of such canceled shows of the same era as *Joan of Arcadia* and *The Book of Daniel* (2007).

So *Reaper* is about a twentysomething kid attempting to balance friends with a rotten, low-paying job, while he tries to figure out who he is. Then one day, he finds out this burden is even greater: He's got two rotten jobs, and his boss is Satan himself. Like Smith's film, the premise feels universal. After all, haven't we all worked for someone we are certain was a demon put on earth to make our lives miserable?

Reaper ran for two seasons on the CW, and a total of thirty-one episodes before it was canceled, and Kevin Smith was the guy who launched the program.

TALK STAR

As Kevin Smith's movie career has proven more and more vexing for the talent, he has turned, in large part to the art of "talking." In the press, Smith has declared he is "sick of movies" and that all he wants to do is "talk, talk, talk."[4] To that end, Smith partners with Scott Mosier for the popular SModcast, keeps in touch with his nearly two million fans on Twitter, and frequently delivers lectures at universities and conventions. Smith equates his new career with a dream come true: "When somebody is paying you to talk about yourself, you've won."[5]

As of 2011 and the deadline for the second edition of this book, Smith was also preparing a new reality series for AMC. The series has been described as a "one-hour series that captures the world of the local comic book store."[6]

14

A Tribute to Jay and Silent Bob

THE WASHINGTON POST has dubbed them a sophomoric Greek Chorus and a Gen X Cheech and Chong. *Time* has called them Vladimir and Estragon, characters from Beckett's *Waiting for Godot*.

In chat rooms across America, Jay and Silent Bob have been compared to every comedy duo dating back to the beginning of the medium: Laurel and Hardy; Abbott and Costello; Bill and Ted; Wayne and Garth; even those lovable droids from *Star Wars*, R2-D2 and C3PO. But the fact remains, no matter who these guys remind us of, Jay and Silent Bob have become an important part of our contemporary pop culture tapestry.

So far, they've appeared in seven films (if one includes their cameo in *Scream 3*), a cartoon TV series, comic books, music videos, and TV commercials. They've done their "stoner schtick" everywhere, making it, in fact "Stoner Chic." And people—especially those of Kevin Smith's generation—love them. The question remains, why? What is it about this comedy team that is so appealing? The answers below come straight from the book's interviewees, and, as you'll see, run the gamut. There is some psychobabble, historical references, philosophy, and even discussion of the magical.

Jason Mewes, the actor who has made the vocal portion of the comedy team so memorable. Just for safe measure, some participants in this discussion had more than one answer...

THEORY ONE

Jay represents the id; Silent Bob, the ego.
(Proposed by Vincent Pereira)

"Jay is everybody uncensored," says Pereira. "If you took everything that is built into a person by society, growing up: that you can't say certain things;

that you can't tell people this or that, and then remove all that, what you've got left is Jay. He is the id. What you see is what you get.

"Bob is the silent conscience. Even though he hangs out with Jay, he has a little more wisdom. If Jay were alone, he'd have no one to talk to. He'd be ranting and raving to space and looking like a lunatic. So Bob is his built-in audience, and the one who holds him back."

THEORY TWO

Jay and Silent Bob represent wish-fulfillment.
They do what others only wish they could.
(Proposed by Walt Flanagan)

"Jay can pull off saying just about the crudest, nastiest dialogue, and yet not come across as threatening," notes Flanagan. "Instead, he comes across as almost cartoonish and likable. No matter what he's saying, even if he's calling Randal and Dante some derogatory name, he's no threat."

Flanagan has an additional thought: "I also gotta chalk it [their popularity] up to Jay's never-ending energy to get pussy or stoned. That just appeals to everyone."

Dwight Ewell subscribes to this theory as well. "I think for the most part, people are slackers. In essence, none of us want to work. We all want the good times and the great experiences, just like them."

THEORY THREE

Historical precedents.
(Proposed by Scott Mosier, Jennifer Schwalbach, and
Brian O'Halloran)

"I think every generation has a duo like them," reports Scott Mosier. "Even Bob Hope and Bing Crosby to some extent. Bob Hope was always a little dumber, Bing Crosby a little more suave."

"The general consensus," Schwalbach notes, "is that they're Laurel and Hardy for Gen X."

"Everybody enjoys buddy movies," O'Halloran explains. "Jay is the stoner friend who goes back to the days of Shaggy on *Scooby Doo*, and I guess that makes Bob his silent buddy, Scooby. It's R2-D2 and C3PO. It's

Laurel and Hardy. It's just that buddy dynamic that so many people seem to enjoy."

THEORY FOUR

Jay and Silent Bob almost seem real.
(Proposed by Bryan Johnson, Ethan Suplee, and Dwight Ewell)

"You know, these guys probably could exist," Bryan Johnson weighs in. "At their advanced age now, I'm not so sure, but those wacky hijinks are, for the most part, almost believable."

"They're like your cousins," adds Ethan Suplee. "You'd like to hang out with them maybe once a year. They're such the yin and yang, the silent genius and the crazy, outspoken lunatic."

"I don't know if it's because we worked together or something, but he [Jay] feels like my cousin," echoes Dwight Ewell. "He's like a relative."

THEORY FIVE

Jay and Silent Bob are actually very wise, yet also incredibly stupid.
(Proposed by Jeff Anderson)

"The thing that always gets me," says Anderson, "is that Jay and Silent Bob can come into a scene and be completely clueless, but then in the next minute become all-knowing. My favorite scene with them was in *Chasing Amy*. That was Jay and Silent Bob at their best. From scene to scene they can be dumb, and yet they still have all the answers to life's questions."

THEORY SIX

They are the thread that stitches together the fabric of the (Askew)niverse
(Proposed by Jennifer Schwalbach)

"I think people enjoy the consistency from movie to movie; getting to know these two characters; getting to know their relationship. It's fun seeing them go from *Clerks*, a black-and-white independent film, and evolving—if you can use that word in regards to Jay and Silent Bob—into something fascinating enough to make basically, a blockbuster movie where they're the stars."

THEORY SEVEN

It is the comedic genius known as Jason Mewes.
(Proposed by John Pierson, Dwight Ewell,
and Brian O'Halloran)

"Jay Mewes in that role is such a loveable character," O'Halloran notes.

"Jason and I hung out a lot on *Dogma*. Jason is beautiful. Period," Ewell states emphatically. "He's not like what you think at all. He's a beautiful person, and you just want to take care of him."

"It's great how Kevin found him and decided he had the screen charisma the world is demanding," muses John Pierson. "Or, whatever it was *People* magazine said: 'Whatever rock this guy crawled out from under, let's hope there's nobody else under there.' I don't even if know if there's a character like Jay on a one-off basis in a movie, let alone a continuing character in a series of them. What's been interesting, of course, is that over time, you've seen the sweetness that goes along with this raunchy character."

Finally, in this discussion of Jay and Silent Bob we'll leave the last words to the fellow who always gets the last words in these movies: Jason Mewes.

"Everybody tells me that Jay says stuff that people want to, but can't. But I also hear a lot of times that people have friends who act just like Jay," Mewes notes. "I think Jay is just a kid people relate to. He smokes weed and a lot of the people who like the films smoke weed. And I also think [they are popular] because Jay and Silent Bob are into *Star Wars*, wreaking havoc, and just trying to get pussy."

For the record, this author's theory is that everybody in the world has either a Jay or a Silent Bob within; that the characters represent two basic, core human personality types. Keeping that in mind, the interviewees for this book were questioned about whether he/she had more in common with Jay or Silent Bob.

"I don't think you'll find many people who admit they're Jay," warned Vincent Pereira. "He's got no inhibitions."

For the most part, he was right. Jeff Anderson, Bryan Johnson, Scott Mosier, Brian O'Halloran, Walt Flanagan, Vincent Pereira, and Ethan Suplee all felt they had more in common with Silent Bob.

But, courageous Dwight Ewell and Jennifer Schwalbach bucked the trend by identifying themselves as being "closer" in real life to Jay.

That may be something the fans will be pleased to know; that the world's real Silent Bob (Kevin Smith) has ended up marrying a woman who identifies herself as being close to his alter-ego's hetero-life mate, Jay.

Epilogue
YOU'RE CLOSED!

THE ADVENTURES OF KEVIN SMITH began with a humble origin story. A bright and creative kid from the Jersey suburbs fell in love with the movies. By the time he was a young adult, surrounded by a group of colorful friends, Smith was already keen observer of the human condition, inspired by the low-budget ingenuity and intelligent presentation of Richard Linklater's *Slacker*.

Now, nearly two decades later, this situation has come full circle. To paraphrase Darth Vader in *Star Wars*, the learner has become the master, and it is the triumphs and works of Kevin Smith that have served to awaken the creative urges of a new set of filmmakers, including Seth Rogen and Judd Apatow.

"I've always said in terms of the whole independent movie boom, from 1995 to 2000, the second half of the 90s, the two most influential films—one for good and one for bad—are *Clerks* and *The Brothers McMullen*," John Pierson reports. "These two films are very influential. The bad part is that the accessibility factor is really high. People look at those films and think, 'I can do that.' My opinion on the [Edward] Burns front is that it's so crappy, you *can* do that. But on the *Clerks* front, it's hard to be that funny."

So often in the moviemaking business, imitation is the name of the game, and few films have inspired as many low-budget wannabes as *Clerks*. "People would always say, 'I made the Canadian *Clerks*. I did *Clerks* in a graveyard,'" Pierson notes of the proliferating knockoffs.

But the good news is that just as *Slacker* inspired *Clerks*, so has *Clerks* no doubt inspired another masterpiece, the powerful debut of another interesting voice. "Out of those 995 people who maybe shouldn't have been inspired by *Clerks*, there's maybe five who take the right lesson away from it," Pierson says.

And in the end, that means five good films.

How else have Kevin Smith's films been influential? The names Ben Affleck and Jason Lee pop immediately to mind. These charismatic, gifted actors still have many great performances to give the world, and it is the cinema of Kevin Smith that nursed them to stardom in the mid-1990s.

Similarly, Jeff Anderson, Brian O'Halloran, Bryan Johnson, Malcom Ingram, and Vincent Pereira are just a few other talents who transformed their association with Kevin Smith, Scott Mosier, and *Clerks* into new and exciting film visions.

On other fronts, Kevin Smith's films have been remarkably successful themselves. *Chasing Amy* is one of those movies that stands the test of time, and has already become a perennial rerun on cable television. Rising from the ashes of its commercial failure, *Mallrats* is indisputably a cult favorite. *Red State* looks poised to take the world by storm, a great horror film.

Kevin Smith, the ultimate fanboy himself, has brilliantly tapped the culture that loves *Star Wars*, comic books, and raunchy humor. In return, on his best days and in his best films, he has accomplished something more than making us laugh: He's made us think about ourselves, primarily about our everyday relationships. Relationships with God, significant others, best friends, and also with our children.

And I truly believe it's for that emotional honesty and self-examination—not merely the fart and dick jokes—that the generations to come will return to the films of Kevin Smith.

The Quick Stop may be closed for now (and perhaps permanently, upon Smith's impending retirement after 2013), but movie fans will be talking about that place for years to come.

NOTES

INTRODUCTION: AN ASKEW VIEW 2012

1. David Ansen, "The Laugh Factory," *Newsweek*, November 10, 2008, p. 57.
2. Teresa Wiltz, "Silent Bob's Last Words; Director Kevin Smith Takes the Scenic Route for His Final Jersey Chronicle," *The Washington Post*, August 23, 2001, p. C01.
3. Frank N. Magill (Ed.), *Magill's Cinema Annual 1995: A Survey of the Films of 1994* (14th Edition), "Clerks" (Farmington Hills, MI: Gale Group, 1995), p. 117.
4. Andy Seiler, "Kevin Smith is seldom 'Silent,'" *USA Today*, August 24, 2001, p. 1, http://www.usatoday.com/life/enter/movies/2001-08-24-kevin-smith.html.
5. Owen Gleiberman, *Entertainment Weekly*. March 5, 2010, p. 74.
6. Peter Travers, "Jay and Silent Bob Strike Back," *Rolling Stone*, September 13, 2001, p. 115.
7. Devin Gordon, "A Phatty Boom Batty Flick," *Newsweek*, August 27, 2001, p. 55.
8. Tanya D. Marsh, "*Dogma*: Episode I—The Catholic Menace," *The Buzz*, October 1999, p. 2. http://www.the-buzz.com/dogma1.html.
9. Ethan Alter, "Zack and Miri Make a Porno," *Film Journal International*, December 2008, p. 75-76.
10. David Denby, "Dirty Secrets," *The New Yorker*, November 10, 2008, p. 92–93.

CHAPTER 1: COMING OF AGE IN NEW JERSEY

1. Claudia Ansorge, "Kevin Smith—Star Wars: This Generation," *The Two River Times*, http://www.viewaskew.com/press.trt.html
2. Chris Smith, "Register Dogs," *New York*, October 24, 1994, p. 50.
3. Stephen Lowenstein (Ed.), *My First Movie: Twenty Celebrated Directors Talk About Their First Film* (New York: Pantheon Books, 2000), p. 73.
4. "The Monster That Ate Hollywood: Interviews: Kevin Smith," *Frontline*, p. 1, http://www.pbs.org/wgbh/pages/frontline/shows/hollywood/interviews/smith.html.
5. Rick Lyman, "Watching Movies with Kevin Smith: The Thrill Is Just Talk." *The New York Times*, July 20, 2001, p. 13.
6. Fred Topel, "Kevin Smith's Final Strike," *Entertainment Today Feature Story*, August 24, 2001, p. 4, http://www.ent-today.com/8-24/smith-feature.html.

7. Steve Ryfle, "On Fart Jokes, *Planet of the Apes* and the Making of *Jay and Silent Bob*," *IFilm: the Internet Movie Guide*, August 22, 2001, http://www.ifilm.com/news_and_features/feature/0,3536,608,00.html

8. Kenneth M. Chanko, "A Lot Happens at a Convenience Store," *The New York Times*, October 16, 1994, Section 4, p. 20.

CHAPTER 2: CLERKS

1. John Pierson, *Spike, Mike, Slackers & Dykes: A Guided Tour Across a Decade of American Independent Cinema* (New York: Hyperion and Miramax Books, 1995), p. 80.

2. Owen Gleiberman, "Smooth Mewes, As half of the dopey duo in *Jay and Silent Bob Strike Back*, Jason Mewes plays a rebel without a pause," *Entertainment Weekly*, September 7, 2001, p. 134.

3. Linda Lee, "A Night Out with Kevin Smith: Not the Dogmatic Type," *The New York Times*, November 14, 1999, Section 4, p. 3.

4. Stephen Lowenstein (Ed.), *My First Movie: Twenty Celebrated Directors Talk About Their First Film* (New York: Pantheon Books, 2000), p. 89.

5. Eileen N. Moon, "A Store Clerk's First Film Earns a Festival Showing," *The New York Times*, January 30, 1994, New Jersey Section, pp. 1, 9.

6. Chris Smith, "Register Dogs," *New York*, October 24, 1994, p. 53.

7. Pierson, p. 287.

8. Peter Travers, "Clerks—Dangerous Talk," *Rolling Stone*, November 3, 1994, p. 104.

9. Carrie Rickey, "*Clerks*," *Knight-Ridder/Tribune News Service*, November 2, 1994, p. 110.

10. David Ansen, "Dante's Day in Jersey Hell, Convenience Store Blues," *Newsweek*, October 31, 1994, p. 67.

11. Janet Maslin, "At a Convenience Store, Coolness to Go," *The New York Times*, March 25, 1994, p. C10.

12. Jeff Gordinier, "The Directors," *Entertainment Weekly*, November-December 1997, p. 65.

13. Beth Pinkser, "Filmmakers in the Fast Lane," *Entertainment Weekly*, June 23, 1995, p. 26.

14. Robert Strauss, "Jersey Boy Makes Good and Comes Back Home," *The New York Times*, December 5, 1999, New Jersey Section "On the Town," p. 2.

15. "Waiting for Godot," *World Book Online Americas Edition*, March 14, 2002, http://www.aolsvc.worldbook.aold.com/wbol/wbPage/na/ar/co/748633.

16. Margot Hornblower, "Great Xpectations," *Time*, June 1997, p. 68.

17. "Kevin Smith: breaks the silence," *Verbosity*, Issue no. 3, 1996, http://www//verbosity wiw.org/issue3/ksmith.html.

CHAPTER 3: MALLRATS

1. Cindy Pearlman, "Rat Patrol," *Entertainment Weekly*, November 11, 1994, p. 16.
2. "Star Brenda," *Entertainment Weekly*, June 9, 1995, p. 12.
3. Christopher Allan Smith, "Smith talks to Stan Lee," *Cinescape Online: DVD News*, April 15, 2002, p. 1, www.cinescape.com
4. Kenneth Turan, "*Mallrats*, No Match for Ultra-Low-Budget *Clerks*," *The Los Angeles Times*, October 20, 1995.
5. Michael Medved, *The New York Post*, October 20, 1995.
6. Richard Corliss, *Time*, "*Mallrats*," November 6, 1995, p. 78.
7. Janet Maslin, "Whiling Away the Day at the Shopping Center," *The New York Times*, November, 1995, p. C8.
8. Graham Fuller, "Mr. Smith Goes to Emotion," *Interview*, April 1997, p. 42.
9. Monica Roman, "Indie's Prodigal Son (independent film producer Kevin Smith)," *Variety*, January 26, 1998, v369, n11, p. 3.
10. Graham Fuller, "*Mallrats*," *Interview*, November 1995, p. 48.
11. *The Riverside Shakespeare* (Boston, MA: Houghton Mifflin Company, 1974), p. 217.
12. Ibid.
13. "Interview with Kevin Smith," *Independent Film Channel*, June 1998, http://www .newsaskew.com/ifc.-Kevin/.

CHAPTER 4: CHASING AMY

1. Allison Gaines, "Chasing Down the Rumors: Did Kevin Smith Date a Lesbian?" *Entertainment Weekly*, November 28, 1997, p. 87.
2. Kevin Smith, *Chasing Amy Liner Notes*, September 20, 1997, http://www.godamong directors.com/smith/amystory/shtml.
3. David Hochman and Jessica Shaw, "Clip'n'save (profiles of actress Renee Zellweger, Joey Lauren Adams, and Jewel)," *Entertainment Weekly*, June 13, 1997, n383, p. 12.
4. Deanna Kizis, "Joey Lauren Adams," *Cosmopolitan*, July 1999, v227, p. 156.
5. Gregg Kilday, "Straight Outta Jersey," *The Advocate*, July 4, 2000, p. 62.
6. Andrew Sarris, "The Next Scorsese: Kevin Smith," *Esquire*, March, 2000, p. 218.
7. Chris Willman, "Biting Criticism: *Dogma* Director Kevin Smith disses *Magnolia*," *Entertainment Weekly*, January 27, 2000, p. 1, http://www.ew.com/ew/report/0, 6115,84950~1~~00.html
8. Terry Teachout, "Moving from Carnal Bliss to Something Truly Divine," *The New York Times*, May 25, 1997, pp. 9, 12.
9. Stephan Talty. "The Clerk, the Girl and the Corduroy Hand Job," *Playboy*, Volume 45, no. 12, December 1998, p. 1, http://www.newsaskew.com/playboy.

CHAPTER 5: DOGMA

1. Michael Atkinson, "Kevin Smith Stirs It Up," *Interview*, October 1999, p. 180.
2. Dave Kehr, "Deflator of the Faith? Director Begs to Differ," *The New York Times*, August 1, 1999, pp. 7, 12.
3. Jessica Shaw, "A Hollywood Dogfight," *Entertainment Weekly*, April 23, 1999, p. 9.
4. Bernard Weinraub, "Disney and Miramax Collide Over Church Issues in New Film," *The New York Times*, April 8, 1999, p. C4.
5. "*Touched by an Angel* objects to *Dogma's* ad Campaign," *CBC Radio Arts, Iculture*, November 18, 1999, p. 1. http://www.infoculture.cbc.ca.archives.filmtv/filmtv/11171999_angelsbattle.phtml.
6. John Brodie, *Gentleman's Quarterly*, November 1999, p. 208.
7. Richard A. Blake, "Fallen Angels," *America*, December 4, 1999, p. 20.
8. Douglas Le Blanc, "Dogmatically Anti-dogma," *Christianity Today*, January 10, 2000, p. 80.
9. Jeff Giles, "Knocking on Heaven's Door," *Newsweek*, November 15, 1999, p. 88.
10. Karl Stevens, "Old Dogma," *Christian Century*, December 15, 1999. v116, p. 1235.
11. Bruce Frett, "Unholy Mess," *Entertainment Weekly*, December 1, 1999, p. 1.
12. Oliver Jones, "Dogma duo re-ups 3 years at Miramax (continuation of Miramax contracts for producer and director Scott Mosier and Kevin Smith)," *Variety*, November 22, 1999, v377, p. 17.
13. Albert Wertheim, "Morality Play," *World Book Online, Americas Edition*, March 1, 2002, http://www.aolsvce.worldbook.aol.com/wbol/wPage/na/ar/co/37070.
14. "Kevin Smith: Stirring Up *Dogma*." *CBC Radio Arts, Iculture*, November 19, 1999, p. 1, http://www.infoculture.cbc.ca/archives/filmtv/filmtv_11181999_kevinsmith.phtm.
15. Cliff Stephenson, "Chasing Kevin: An Interview with Kevin Smith," *DVDFile.com*, May 1, 2000, http://www.dvdfile.com/new/special_report/interviews.

CHAPTER 6: JAY AND SILENT BOB STRIKE BACK

1. "Is it Theft Or Is It Freedom? Seven Views of the Web's Impact on Culture Clashes," *The New York Times*, September 20, 2000, p. 42.
2. "Kevin Smith is Moving On," *CNN.com, ShowbizToday*, August 21, 2001, http://www.cnn.com/CNN/Programs/showbiz.today/featured.story/0108/21/html.
3. Andy Seiler, "Kevin Smith is seldom 'Silent,'" *USA Today*, August 24, 2001, p. 1, http://www.usatoday.com/life/enter/movies/2001-08-24-kevin-smith.html.
4. William Keck, "On Nuns, Star Wars & Evil Designers," *Esquire*, August 2001, p. 30.
5. Stacie Hougland, "Kevin Smith Breaks the Silence," *Hollywood.com*, http://www.hollywood.com/celebs/features/feature770297/page 2.

6. Eugene Hernandez, "Kevin Smith Strikes Back," *Indie Wire*, August 30, 2001, p. 2, http://www.indiewire.com/film/interviews/int_Smith_Kevin_010830.html.

7. Rebecca Asher-Walsh, "Reel World: News From Hollywood," *Entertainment Weekly*, August 10, 2001, p. 46.

8. Scott Seomin, "Scott Seomin's Letter to Kevin Smith, Writer/Director of *Jay and Silent Bob Strike Back*," *G.L.A.A.D. Documents*, July 26, 2001, p. 1, http://www.glaad .org/org/publications/documenta/index.html?record=2814.

9. Teresa Wiltz, "Silent Bob's Last Words; Director Kevin Smith Takes the Scenic Route for His Final 'Jersey Chronicle,'" *The Washington Post*, August 23, 2001, p. C01.

10. Seomin, p. 1.

11. Rob Blackwelder, "Silent Bob Speaks Out: Writer-director Kevin Smith kisses his famous cameo character goodbye in new Hollywood farce," *SPLICEDwire*, August 2, 2001, http://www.splicedonline.com/01features/ksmith.html.

CHAPTER 7: CLERKS

1. Rick Lyman, "At the Movies: A Risque Kiss? So Very Quaint," *The New York Times*, September 17, 1999, p. E14.

2. John Dempsey, "Miramax rings Clerks in DVD key." *Variety*, August 14, 2000, p. 37.

3. Terry Kelleher, "Picks and Pans," *People Weekly*, June 5, 2000, p. 27.

4. Jeff Jensen, "'Night, *Clerks*," *Entertainment Weekly*, June 7, 2000, p. 1, http://www .ew.com/ew/report/0,6115.85266~3~~,00.html.

CHAPTER 8: JERSEY GIRL

1. Jeff Jensen: "Mr. Smith Goes to Hollywood: The Voice Behind Silent Bob Weighs In on His Return to 'Mallrats' Culture," *Entertainment Weekly*, August 24, 2001, p. 104.

2. Antony Teofilo: "Through the Wringer: An interview with Ben Affleck, from the set of *Jersey Girl*." http://jerseygirl-movie.com/interviews/30.html.

3. Steve Head: "An interview with Liv Tyler: Bringing it home for *Jersey Girl*," *IGN*, April 2, 2004. http://movies.ign.com/articles/504/504007p1.html.

4. Alysse Minkoff: "10 Burning Questions with George Carlin." *ESPN.com*, March 29, 2004. http://sports.espn.go.com/espn/page3/story?page=10bqs/carlin.

5. Nancy Griffin: "When Love Hurts," *The New York Times*, April 27, 2003, p. 1.

6. Rebecca Winters Keegan: "Q&A: Kevin Smith," *Time International*, July 24, 2006, p. 47.

7. Fred Topel, Rebecca Murray: "Interview with *Jersey Girl* Producer Scott Mosier The Man Behind the Scenes at *View Askew*," About.com, March 17, 2004. http:// movies.about/com/cs/jerseygirl/a/jrsysm031704.htm.

8. Jancee Dunn: "A Hollywood Ending," *Rolling Stone*, April 1, 2004, p. 50–56.
9. David Ansen, "Chasing Kevin," *Newsweek*, March 29, 2004, p. 50–51.
10. Dimitri Ehrlich. *Interview*, April 2004, p. 70.
11. Joey Leydon, "Jersey Girl," *Variety*, March 22, 2004, p. 40–41.
12. Mike Clark: "Jersey Girl; Feel-good fatherhood," *USA Today*, March 26, 2004, Life, p. 3D.
13. Elaine Loring: "Kevin Smith directed Bennifer in *Jersey Girl*." Teen Tribute, Spring 2004, p. 31.

CHAPTER 9: CLERKS II

1. Jeff Jensen: "What's the Story with … *Clerks II*," *Entertainment Weekly*, September 24, 2004, p. 82.
2. Kevin Cahillane: "For the Stars of *Clerks*, It's Take Two," *The New York Times*, July 16, 2006, p. 10.
3. Jeffrey M. Anderson: "Interview with Jeff Anderson and Brian O'Halloran: Jeff Anderson meets Jeff Anderson," *Combustible Celluloid*, June 15, 2006. http://www .combustiblecelluloid.com/interviews/clerksint.shtml.
4. Anthony Breznican: "*Clerks II*: Growth and gross-outs," *USA Today*, February 6, 2006, p. 9D.
5. Jonah Weiland: "The *Clerks II*: Interviews: Brian O'Halloran and Jeff Anderson," *Comic Book Resources*, July 16, 2006. http://www.comicbookresources.com/?page= article&id=7579.
6. Peter Hartlaub: "Who says aging slackers can't be funny?" *The San Francisco Chronicle*, July 21, 2006. http://www.sfgate.com/cgi-bin/article.cgi?f=/c/a/2006/07/21/ DDGA8K22F71.DTL#ixzz1ZGBpUrSH.
7. Stephanie Zacharek: "*Clerks II*," *Salon.com*, July 21, 2006. http://www.salon .com/entertainment/movies/review/2006/07/21/clerks_2/index.html?CP=IMD& DN=110.
8. Scott Weinberg: "Kevin Smith Absolutely Flips Out on Joel Siegel," *Cinematical*, July 12, 2006. http://blog.moviefone.com/2006/07/19/kevin-smith-absolutely- flips-out-on-joel-siegel/.
9. *Reelz Channel, YouTube*: "Kevin Smith's Comments on Joel Siegel's Death. http:// www.youtube.com/watch?v=tOKNrQuX9ac.

CHAPTER 10: ZACK AND MIRI MAKE A PORNO

1. Erik Davis, "Kevin Smith on the Origins and Original Cast of Zack and Miri," *Cinematical*, October 29, 2008. http://blog.moviefone.com/2008/10/29/kevin- smith-on-the-origins-and-original-cast-of-zack-and-miri/.

2. *Access Hollywood*: "Kevin Smith Talks *Zack and Miri Makes a Porno.*"http://www.access hollywood.com/kevin-smith-talks-zack-and-miri-make-a-porno_video_774641.

3. *Newsweek*: "Kevin Smith Plays Dirty," October 27, 2008, p. 71.

4. Mark Rahner, "Kevin Smith, director of *Zack and Miri Make a Porno*," *The Seattle Times*, October 28, 2008. http://seattletimes.nwsource.com/html/movies/2008 318894_kevinsmithqampa28.html.

5. Steve "Frosty" Weintraub, "Seth Rogen Interview *Zack and Miri Make a Porno*," Collider.com., October 28, 2008. http://collider.com/entertainment/article.asp/ aid/9657/cid/13/tcid/1.

6. Anthony Breznican, "Porno legitimizes Kevin Smith's career," *USA Today*, October 30, 2008, p. 6D.

7. Anthony Breznican, "Banks swings into stardom," *USA Today*, October 27, 2008, Life, p. 1.

8. *Kodak OnFilm*: "David Klein and Kevin Smith." http://motion.kodak.com/ motion/Publications/On_Film_Interviews/smithKlein.htm#ixzz1X7n6HwU2.

9. Bob Fisher, "A Conversation with *Zack and Miri Make a Porno* director Kevin Smith and cinematographer David Klein," Moviemaker.com, October 30, 2008. http:// www.moviemaker.com/cinematography/page2/kevin_smith_david_klein_zack_and _miri_make_a_porno_20081014/.

10. Steven McElroy, "More Sneak Peeks at Comic-Con," *The New York Times*, July 28, 2008, p. 2.

11. Julie Bloom, "Movie wins R Rating," *The New York Times*, August 7, 2008, p. 2.

12. Anne Thompson, "Media picky about 'Porno,'" *Variety*, October 27, 2008, p. 5.

13. Anthony Breznican, "If the Title Says Porno," *USA Today*, March 5, 2008, Life, p. 2D.

14. Chris Lee, "Dude, High Five," *Los Angeles Times*, October 20, 2008. http://articles .latimes.com/2008/oct/30/entertainment/et-smith30.

15. Dave Itzkoff, "They're not Judd Apatow. Really," *The New York Times*, October 26, 2008, p. 17.

16. Jason Guerrasio, "Kevin Smith: The Fat Man Tweets," *LA Weekly*, February 26, 2010. http://www.laweekly.com/2010-02-26/film-tv/kevin-smith-the-fat-man-tweets/.

17. Richard Corliss, "Sex , Pals and Videotape," *Time*, November 10, 2008, p. 125.

18. *Rolling Stone*, November 13, 2008, p. 98.

19. Todd McCarthy, "Snappy, sweet 'Porno,'" *Variety*, September 15, 2008, p. 18.

20. Peter Martin, "The Hall of Cultural Significance," *Esquire*, November 2008, p. 26.

21. Artie, "Interview Seth Rogen for Zach [sic] and Miri Make a Porno," *Screencrave*, October 22, 2008. http://screencrave.com/2008-10-22/interview-seth-rogen-for-zach-and-miri-make-a-porno/.

22. Josh Wigler, "Happy 4/20: Kevin Smith reveals his Seth Rogen-Inspired Stoner Philosophy," *MTV Movies Blog*, April 20, 2011. http://moviesblog.mtv.com/2011/ 04/20/happy-420-kevin-smith-reveals-his-seth-rogen-inspired-stoner-philosophy/.

CHAPTER 11: COP OUT

1. Carla Hay: "Kevin Smith makes no apologies for his foul-mouthed filmmaking," *The Examiner*, February 26, 2010. http://www.examiner.com/celebrity-q-a-in-national/ kevin-smith-makes-no-apologies-for-his-foul-mouthed-filmmaking#ixzz1XYNnb JPl.
2. Kam Williams: "Tracy Morgan *Cop Out* Interview with Kam Williams," *News Blaze*, February 22, 2010. http://newsblaze.com/story/20100222141525kamw.nb/topstory .html.
3. *Culture.com*: "*Cop Out*: Bruce Willis and Tracy Morgan Interview." http://www.culture .com/articles/7016/cop-out-bruce-willis-and-tracy-morgan-interview.phtml.
4. Robert Levin: "Interview: Bruce Willis and Tracy Morgan Talk *Cop Out*," *Film School Rejects*, February 26, 2010. http://www.filmschoolrejects.com/features/ interview-bruce-willis-and-tracy-morgan-talk-cop-out.php.
5. Lisa Rose: "Kevin Smith, Bruce Willis, Tracy Morgan and the cast discuss 'Cop Out,'" *The Star-Ledger*, February 26, 2010. http://www.nj.com/entertainment/ index/ssf/2010/02/kevin_smith_bruce_willis_tracy.
6. Edward Douglas: "Kevin Smith Rocks Out with His *Cop Out*," *Coming Soon.net*, February 24, 2010. http://www.comingsoon.net/news/movienews.php?id=63449 #ixzz1XYLR8tqz.
7. BrentJS: "Kevin Smith Discusses Working with Bruce Willis on *A Couple Of Dicks*," Reelz.com, November 21, 2009. http://www.reelz.com/movie-news/4839/kevin-smith-discusses-working-with-bruce-willis-on-a-couple-of-dicks/.
8. Doug Liman, *30Ninjas.com*, February 24, 2010. http://30ninjas.com/blog/doug-liman-blog-busted-by-bruce-willis-and-mark-and-robb-cullen-for-bumming-dinner-at-cop-out-premiere-party.
9. Morfo Addie: "Gotham Perp Walk," *Variety*, March 1, 2010, Vol. 418, Issue 3, p. 31.
10. Katie Hasty: "Why Kevin Smith directed *Cop Out*," *HitFix*, February 24, 2010. http://www.hitfix.com/articles/why-did-kevin-smith-direct-cop-out.
11. Andrew Barker: "*Cop Out*," *Variety*, March 1, 2010, Vol. 415, Issue 3, p. 19.
12. Roger Ebert: "*Cop Out*," Roger Ebert.com, February 24, 2010. http://rogerebert .suntimes.com/apps/pbcs.dll/article?AID=/20100224/REVIEWS/100229988.
13. David Wildman: "Kevin Smith should be arrested," *Worcester Mag*, June 3, 2010. http://www.worcestermag.com/night-and-day/film/95575419.html.
14. Sara Vilkomerson: "*Cop Out*," *People*, March 8, 2010, p. 34.
15. Ethan Alter, *Film Journal International*, April 2010, p. 133–134.
16. Maryann Johanson: "Question of the day: What filmmakers seem to have lost their minds?" *The Flick Filosopher*, February 3, 2011. http://www.flickfilosopher .com/blog/2011/02/question_of_the_day_what_filmm.html.

17. Ari Karpel: "Silent Bob Strikes Back," *Fast Company*, December 2010/January 2011, Issue 51, p. 46–47.

18. John Brodeur: "Buddies in Blue," *New York Amsterdam News*. February 25, 2010, p. 19.

19. Karina Longworth: "Kevin Smith's *Cop Out* So Cliché-Filled It Just Might Work!" *LA Weekly*, February 23, 2010. http://www.villagevoice.com/2010-02-23/film/kevin-smith-s-cop-out-so-clich-eacute-filled-it-just-might-work/.

CHAPTER 12: RED STATE

1. Alex Godfrey: "Kevin Smith hits out at Harvey Weinstein, critics, and rightwing bigots." *The Guardian*, September 23, 2011. http://www.guardian.co.uk/film/2011/sep/24/kevin-smith-red-state.

2. Joey Cole: "Actor Michael Parks discusses the mystery surrounding *Red State*," *Daily Blam.com*, January 23, 2011. http://www.dailyblam.com/news/2011/01/23/Michael-Parks-interview-of-red-state.

3. "Cinematographer David Klein, ASC, *Red State*," DV.com, February 2, 2011. http://www.dv.com/article/102638.

4. Ibid.

5. Robert Fischer: "The GQ Q&A: Kevin Smith," *GQ*, August 13, 2011. http://www.gq.com/entertainment/movies-and-tv/201108/kevin-smith-interview-red-state#ixzz1XURckKtw.

6. "Profoundly cringey interview with Kevin Smith about 'Red State' and why he dislikes the press," *On No They Didn't*. August 31, 2011. http://ohnotheydidnt.livejournal.com/62380119.html#ixzz1XUSZJ3zt1.

7. Justin Chang: "*Red State*," *Variety*, January 31, 2011, p. 27.

8. Rachel Abrams. "Smith goes it alone. Helmer spurns biz with distrib plan," *Variety*, January 25, 2011, p. 4.

9. Kim Masters: "'Alarmist Ninnies' Misinterpreted Sundance Outburst," *Hollywood Reporter*, February 3, 2011. http://www.hollywoodreporter.com/news/kevin-smith-alarmist-ninnies-misinterpreted-95811.

10. Karina Longworth: "Kevin Smith: I Am So, Like, Sick of Movies and Shit," *LA Weekly*, Film and TV, April 7, 2011. http://www.laweekly.com/2011-04-07/film-tv/kevin-smith-i-am-so-like-sick-of-movies-and-shit/.

CHAPTER 13: KEVIN SMITH AROUND THE GALAXY

1. Jeff Jensen, "Chasing Glory: Filmmaker Tries Hands at Comics," *Advertising Age*, October 19, 1998, p. 24.

2. Tricia Laine, Dan Snierson, and Shirley Fung, "Flashes (brief reports on filmmaker Kevin Smith's comic books)," *Entertainment Weekly*, February 20, 1998, n8, p. 12.

3. Lou Lumenick, "Send in the Clown—If You Can Take It," *The New York Post*, April 26, 2002, p. 1, http://www.nypost.com/movies/41936.htm.

4. Karina Longworth: "I am so, like, sick of movies and shit." *LA Weekly*, April 7, 2001. http://www.laweekly.com/2011-04-07/film-tv/kevin-smith-i-am-so-like-sick-of-movies-and-shit/.

5. Tammy La Groce: "A New Jersey Native Returns, Anything But Silent," *The New York Times*, April 17, 2011, p. 8.

6. *Ain't It Cool*: "Cost-cutting AMC Greenlights Two Reality Shows, Including Kevin Smith's *Secret Stash*. Plus *Walking Dead* Premiere Expands to 90 minutes." September 1, 2011. http://aintitcool.com/node/51049.

APPENDIX

F@&%-ING BABY TALK: THE KEVIN SMITH LEXICON

KEVIN SMITH'S FIRST FILM, *Clerks*, features a number of "section breaks," or inter-titles between sequences, a technique sometimes used by Woody Allen. These breaks are marked by the display of very impressive vocabulary words (like "vagary") that nicely mirror the events, themes, and moods during that particular portion of the film. Included below is a listing of those words, and the way in which *Clerks* reflects their meaning.

Now if somebody will just step forward and reveal the derivation of snootchie bootchies, snootch to the nootch, or snoogans.

DANTE: Okay, everybody knows that Dante is the name of Brian O'Halloran's long-suffering Quick Stop character. But, it also happens to be the name of someone else, the author of *The Inferno*, an epic poem that looked at the various levels of Hell. Allegedly, an early version of *Clerks* would have featured very different inter-titles—not these tongue-twisters—but the nine levels of Hell; all equated with Dante and his job at the Quick Stop.

VILIFICATION: The act of speaking evil of someone. Of course, this title refers to a Chewlie's Gum rep's efforts to paint Dante (or 'vilify' him) as a "death merchant," to equate him with the Nazis because he sells cigarettes.

JAY AND SILENT BOB: I have no idea what this refers to. Seriously, this section of the film introduces our heroes as they take up their familiar position outside the Quick Stop. There, Jay makes the immortal remark, "I'll fuck anything that moves."

RANDAL: Ditto. The introduction of Jeff Anderson into the film, as Dante's best friend.

SYNTAX: is the way words are assembled into bigger constructions, like sentences. And, it is in this section that Dante attempts to re-define his relationship with Caitlin. Yes, she cheated on him eight-and-a-half times, but Dante re-structures the cheating in his mind so it isn't that bad. Also, Randal assembles a long batch of words (porno movie titles), to construct a totally offensive "whole."

VAGARY: A vagary is a whim, and it defines Randal's unplanned response to a customer in the video store who attempts to pull an unexpected "ruse" on him. He bans her from the store.

PURGATION: This word means "the act of ridding of sin," but oddly, the term pointedly contrasts with the action in the film. Here, Randal sins most egregiously: selling cigarettes to a four year-old girl.

MALAISE: A vague feeling of depression settles on Dante as he realizes he is "ever backing down" and that his boss has gone to Vermont. Ostensibly, his hockey game with Sanford and friends should lighten Dante's malaise, but has the opposite effect.

HARBINGER: A harbinger is a forerunner or signal of things to come. In this section of *Clerks*, an old man goes into the bathroom with a porno mag, not to be heard from again, at least for a while. But, inevitably, he will return, with catastrophic results for Dante and Caitlin. This section of the film signals what is to come during *Clerks'* climax.

PERSPICACITY: explains to Dante how title does not dictate behavior, but actions do. To prove his point, Randal spits water on a customer. Dante immediately gets the point.

PARADIGM: A paradigm is an example or model, and during this section in *Clerks*, Rick Derris, the town stud, shows up to remind Dante how out-of-shape he is. Derris is clearly a physical paradigm. On the other hand, this is also the section in which Dante is fined for selling cigarettes to a minor, and so his (or rather, Randal's) behavior is a paradigm of bad behavior.

WHIMSY: A whimsy is a quaint or fanciful idea. There is nothing quaint about what happens in this part of *Clerks*: Caitlin screws the dead guy in the bathroom.

QUANDARY: Caitlin's activities in the bathroom leave Dante in something of a quandary. His dilemma: who was really back in that room with her? Also, the coroner has a quandary to contend with: what kind of a convenience store do these guys run, anyway?

LAMENTATION: A lamentation is an expression of sorrow, and in this section, we bear witness to Dante's self-pity party, wherein he stews about his life and inability to improve his station.

JUXTAPOSITION: By comparing the loyal, supportive Veronica (who brought Dante lasagna for lunch) and the fickle Caitlin (who cheated on him 8 and a half times, got engaged to an Asian design major named Sang, and screwed a dead guy), Dante is juxtaposing his girlfriends. Jay and Silent Bob are especially helpful in this regard.

CATHARSIS: A catharsis is a release, a cleansing of emotions, and in this case, Randal and Dante get into a food fight. And though the FDS stings, at least according to Dante, the food fight leads the two best friends to an epiphany about their lives, a point of confrontation and cleansing.

DENOUEMENT: A more verbose way of saying, "You're closed!"

BIBLIOGRAPHY

BOOKS

Brennan, Shawn (Ed.). *Magill's Cinema Annual 1996: A Survey of the Films of 1995* (Farmington Hills, MI: Gale Group, 1996).

Brooks, Tim and Earle Marsh. *The Complete Directory to Prime Time Network TV Shows 1946–Present* (Third Edition) (New York: Ballantine Books, 1985).

Ebert, Robert. *Roger Ebert's Movie Yearbook 2000* (Kansas City, MO: Andrews McMeel Publishing, 2000).

Katz, Ephraim. *The Film Encyclopedia* (New York: Harper and Row, 1979).

Lowenstein, Stephen. *My First Movie: Twenty Celebrated Directors Talk About Their First Film* (New York: Pantheon Books, 2000).

Magill, Frank N. (Ed.). *Magill's Cinema Annual 1995: A Survey of the Films of 1994* (14th Edition) (Farmington Hills, MI: Gale Group, 1995).

Pierson, John. *Spike, Mike, Slackers & Dykes: A Guided tour Across a Decade of American Independent Cinema* (New York: Hyperion and Miramax Books, 1995).

The Riverside Shakespeare (Boston, MA: Houghton Mifflin Company, 1974).

PERIODICALS

Abele, Robert. "Home is Where the Art Is: Whether making electronic music or hanging paintings in his fancifully furnished apartment-cum-gallery, indie-film ace Jason Lee is a man of many muses," *In Style*, September 1, 2000, v7, p. 511.

Ansen, David. "Dante's Day in Jersey Hell, Convenience Store Blues," *Newsweek*, October 31, 1994, p. 67.

Ascher-Walsh, Rebecca. "Reel World: News from Hollywood (portrayal of gays in 'Jay and Silent Bob Strike Back')," *Entertainment Weekly*, August 10, 2001, p. 46.

Atkinson, Michael. "Kevin Smith Stirs It Up," *Interview*, October, 1999, v29, p. 180.

Blake, Richard A. "Fallen Angels," *America*, December 4, 1999, v181, p. 20.

Brodie, John. "Mr. Smith Goes to Hell," November 1999, *Gentleman's Quarterly*, pp. 205–208.

Chanko, Kenneth M. "A Lot Happens at a Convenience Store," *The New York Times*, October 16, 1994, Section 2, p. 20.

Dempsey, John, "Miramax rings 'Clerks' on DVD key," *Variety*, August 14, 2001, v379, p. 37.

Driver, Minnie. "Joey Lauren Adams," *Interview*, June 2000, v30, p. 52.

Entertainment Weekly. "Star Brenda," June 9, 1995, n278 p. 12.

Etter, Jonathan. "Richard Anderson—How Gary Cooper Got Him Into the Movies," *Filmfax*, pp. 58-65, 90-92.

Fitzpatrick, Kevin. "Kevin Smith's Jedi Mind Trick: The indie filmmaker on Boba Fett and loving *The Empire Strikes Back*," *Star Wars Galaxy Magazine*, April 3, 1995, pp. 1, 2, http://www.fitzbrothers.com/writing/writing012/html.

Fuller, Graham. "Mallrats," *Interview*, November 1995, v25, n11, p. 48.

Fuller, Graham. "Mr. Smith goes to emotion," *Interview*, April 1997, v27, n4, p. 42.

Gaines, Allison. "Chasing Down the Rumors: Did Kevin Smith Date a Lesbian?" *Entertainment Weekly*, November 28, 1997, p. 87.

Giles, Jeff. "Knocking on Heaven's Door," *Newsweek*, November 15, 1999, p. 88.

Gleiberman, Owen. "Smooth Mewes: As half of the dopey duo in *Jay and Silent Bob Strike Back*, Jason Mewes plays a rebel without a pause," *Entertainment Weekly*, September 7, 2001, p. 134.

Gordinier, Jeff. "The directors (filmmakers Richard Linklater, Errol Morris and Kevin Smith are three top independent directors in the business)," *Entertainment Weekly*, November–December 1997, p. 65.

Gordon, Devin. "A Phatty Boom Batty Flick: With his new movie, director Kevin Smith says thanks to family, friends, and yes, those nutty fans on the Web," *Newsweek*, August 27, 2001, p. 55.

Hochman, David and Jessica Shaw. "Clip'n'save (profiles of actress Renee Zellweger, Joey Lauren Adams, and Jewel)," *Entertainment Weekly*, June 13, 1997, n383, p. 12.

Hornblower, Margot. "Great Xpectations," *Time*, June 1997, p. 68.

Jensen, Jeff. "Chasing glory: Filmmaker tries hand at comics," *Advertising Age*, October 19, 1998, p. 24.

Jensen, Jeff. "Mr. Smith Goes to Hollywood: The Voice Behind Silent Bob Weighs in On His Return to 'Mallrats' Culture," *Entertainment Weekly*, August 24, 2001, p. 104.

Jones, Oliver. "*Dogma* duo re-ups 3 years at Miramax (continuation of Miramax contracts for producer and director Scott Mosier and Kevin Smith)," *Variety*, November 22, 1999, v377, p. 17.

Keck, William. "On Nuns, *Star Wars* & Evil Designers," *Esquire*, August 2001, p. 30.

Kelleher, Terry. "Picks and Pans," *People Weekly*, June 5, 2000, v53, p. 27-28.

Kempley, Rita. "Silent Bob's Inside Joke; Kevin Smith Takes a Starring Role but No Chances in a Moronic Riff on Hollywood," *The Washington Post*, August 24, 2001, p. C01.

Kilday, Greg. "Straight outta Jersey," *The Advocate*, July 4, 2000, p. 62.

Kizis, Deanna. "Joey Lauren Adams," *Cosmopolitan*, July 1999, v227, p. 156.

Laine, Tricia, Dan Snierson, and Shirley Fung. "Flashes (brief reports on filmmaker Kevin Smith's comic books)," *Entertainment Weekly*, February 20, 1998, n8, p. 12.

Le Blanc, Douglas. "Dogmatically Anti-Dogma," *Christianity Today*, January 10, 2000, v44, p. 80.

Lee, Linda. "A Night Out with Kevin Smith: Not the dogmatic type," *The New York Times*, November 14, 1999, Section 4, p. 3.

Lopate, Phillip. "Snoochie Boochies, The Gospel According to Kevin Smith," *Film Comment*, November–December 1999, pp. 60–65.

Lyman, Rick. "A Risque Kiss? So Very Quaint," *The New York Times*, September 17, 1999, p. E14.

Lyman, Rick. "Watching Movies with Kevin Smith: The Thrill is Just Talk," *The New York Times*, July 20, 2001, pp. 1, 13.

Maslin, Janet. "At a Convenience Store, Coolness to Go," *The New York Times*, March 25, 1994, p. C10.

Maslin, Janet. "At Cannes, New Faith, Simplicity and Dignity," *The New York Times*, May 22, 1999, p. B5.

Men's Health, "A Few Words from Captain Clerk," June 2001, p. 112.

Moon, Eileen N. "A Store Clerk's First Film Earns a Festival Showing," *The New York Times*, January 30, 1994, Section XIII, p. 1, 9.

The New York Times, "Is it Theft Or Is It Freedom? Seven Views of the Web's Impact on Culture Clashes," September 20, 2000, p. 42.

Pearlman, Cindy. "Rat Patrol," *Entertainment Weekly*, November 11, 1994, n248, p. 16.

People Weekly, "Shelf Employed: Ex-store Clerk Kevin Smith turns a bad job into a hit movie, but still slacks off at his convenience," December 12, 1994, p. 156.

Pinkser, Beth. "Filmmakers in the Fast Lane (Erich Schaeffer, Rusty Cundieff, Robert Rodriguez and Kevin Smith)," *Entertainment Weekly*, June 23, 1995, n280, pp. 26–29.

Richter, Erin. "The view askew-niverse (www.viewaskew.com addresses works by filmmaker Kevin Smith.)," *Entertainment Weekly*, April 25, 1997, n376, p. 77.

Rickey, Carrie. "*Clerks*," *Knight-Ridder/Tribune News Service*, November 2, 1994, p. 110.

Roman, Monica. "Indie's Prodigal Son (independent film producer Kevin Smith)," *Variety*, January 26, 1998, v369, n11, p. 3.

Sarris, Andrew. "The Next Scorsese: Kevin Smith," *Esquire*, March 2000, p. 218.

Shaw, Jessica. "A Hollywood Dogfight," *Entertainment Weekly*, April 23, 1999, p. 9.

Silberg, John. "Community Access (how director Kevin Smith has used the Internet)," *Variety*, December 18, 2000, 381 I5, p. S36.

Smith, Chris. "Register Dogs," *New York*, October 24, 1994, pp. 50–54.

Stevens, Karl. "Old Dogma," *The Christian Century*, December 15, 1999, v116, p. 1235.

Strauss, Robert. "On the Towns: Jersey Boy Makes Good And Comes Back Home," *The New York Times*, December 5, 1999, p. 20.

Teachout, Terry. "Moving From Carnal Bliss to Something Truly Divine," *The New York Times*, May 25, 1997, pp. 9, 12.

Travers, Peter. "Clerks—Dangerous Talk," *Rolling Stone*, November 3, 1994, p. 104.

Travers, Peter. "Jay and Silent Bob Strike Back," *Rolling Stone*, September 13, 2001, p. 115.

Weinraub, Bernard. "Disney and Miramax Collide Over Church Issues in New Film," *The New York Times*, April 8, 1999, p. C4.

Wiltz, Teresa. "Silent Bob's Last Words; Director Kevin Smith Takes the Scenic Route for His Final 'Jersey Chronicle,'" *The Washington Post*, August 23, 2001, p. C01.

Zahed, Ramin. "Indie farm team fields future H'wood stars. (independent filmmaker Kevin Smith)," *Variety*, February 23, 1998, v370, p. A14.

INTERNET

Ansorge, Claudia. "Kevin Smith—Star Wars: This Generation," *The Two River Times*, http://www.viewaskew.com/press.trt.html.

CBC Radio Arts, Iculture. "*Touched by an Angel* objects to *Dogma*'s ad Campaign," November 18, 1999, pp. 1, 2, http://www.infoculture.cbc.ca.archives.filmtv/filmtv/11171999_angelsbattle.phtml.

CBC Radio Arts, Iculture. "Kevin Smith: Stirring Up *Dogma*." November 19, 1999, pp. 1–3, http://www.infoculture.cbc.ca/archives/filmtv/filmtv_11181999_kevinsmith .phtml.

CNN.com.ShowbizToday. "Kevin Smith is moving on," August 21, 2001, http:// www.cnn.com/CNN/Programs/showbiz.today/featured.story/0108/21.html.

Frontline. "The Monster that ate Hollywood: interview: Kevin Smith," http://www .pbs.org/wgbh/pages/frontline/shows/hollywood/interviews/smith.html.

GodAmongDirectors.com. "Kevin Smith: *Chasing Amy* Liner Notes," September 20, 1997, www.godamongdirectors.com/smith/amystory/shtml.

Hargrave, John. "Kevin Smith-o-Rama: The Zug Interview," *Zug*, http://www.zug.com/ scrawl/ksmith/intview.html.

Hernandez, Eugene. "Interview: Kevin Smith Strikes Back," *IndieWIRE*, August 30, 2001, http://www.indiewire.com/film/interviews/int_Smith_Kevin_010830.html.

Hollywood.com. "Kevin Smith Breaks the Silence," August 21, 2001, http://www.holly wood.com/celebs/features/feature/770296/page/2.

Jensen, Jeff. "'Night, Clerks," *Entertainment Weekly*, June 7, 2000, p. 1, http://www.ew .com/ew/report/0,6115.85266~3~~,00.html.

Lumenick, Lou. "Send in the Clown—If You Can Take It," *The New York Post*, April 26, 2002, pp. 1, 2, http://www.nypost.com/movies/41936.htm.

Marsh, Tanya D. "Dogma: Episode I—The Catholic Menace," *The Buzz*, October 1999, http://www.the-buzz.com/dogma1.html.

Mogil, Michelle. "An Evening—no, a NIGHT—with Kevin Smith," *14850 Today*, March 14, 2001, http://www.14850.com/today/kevinsmithmm.html.

Phipps, Keith. "Kevin Smith," *The Onion A.V. Club*: http://www.theavclub.com/avclub 3115/avfeature3115.html.

Project Greenlight. "Kevin Smith Answers Back," http://www.projectgreenlight.liveplanet .com/community/kevin_smith.jsp.

Ryfle, Steve. "On fart jokes, *Planet of the Apes* and the making of *Jay and Silent Bob*," *IFilm: the Internet Movie Guide*, August 22, 2001, www.ifilm.com/news_and_features/ feature/0,3536,608,00.html.

Schmitz, Greg Dean. "Jersey Girl," *Upcoming Movies.com*, http://www.upcomingmovies .com/kevinsmith20002.html.

Seiler, Andy. "Kevin Smith is seldom 'Silent,'" *U.S.A. Today*, August 24, 2001, http://www.usatoday.com/life/enter/movies/2001-08/24-kevin-smith.html.

Scott Seomin. "Scott Seomin's Letter to Kevin Smith, Writer/Director of *Jay and Silent Bob Strike Back*," *G.L.A.A.D. Documents*, July 26, 2001, p. 1, http://www.glaad.org/ org/publications/documenta/index.html?record=2814.

Smith, Christopher Allan. "Smith talks to Stan Lee," *Cinescape Online: DVD News*, April 15, 2002, http://www.cinescape.com.

Smith, Christopher Allan. "Kevin Smith to break ground on TONIGHT SHOW," *Cinescape Online: Comic Book News*, April 17, 2002, http://www.cinescape.com.

Sweeney, Jennifer Foote. "Grandma sees *Dogma*," *Salon.com*, November 9, 1999, http://www.salon.com/mwt/feature/1999/11/09/dogma/index.html.

Topel, Fred. "Kevin Smith's Final Strike," *Entertainment Today Feature Story*, August 24, 2001, pp. 1–4, http://www.ent-today.com/8-24/smith-feature.html.

Willman, Chris. "Biting Criticism: Dogma Director Kevin Smith disses *Magnolia*," *Entertainment Weekly*, January 27, 2000, p. 1, http://www.ew.com/ew/report/0, 6115,84950~1~~00.html.

INDEX

ABOUT THE AUTHOR

JOHN KENNETH MUIR is the author of twenty-five reference books including award-winners *Terror Television* (a 2001 Booklist Editor's Choice), *Horror Films of the 1970s* (A 2002 Booklist Editor's Choice), and *The Encyclopedia of Superheroes on Film and Television*. He is also creator of the web series *The House Between*, and blogs at http://reflectionsonfilmandtelevision.blogspot .com.

New Jersey born and bred, John lives in Charlotte, North Carolina with his wife, Kathryn, his son, Joel, and three cats.